THE ROLE OF THE PRIME MINISTER IN FRANCE, 1981–91

The Role of the Prime Minister in France, 1981–91

Robert Elgie

Lecturer in Politics
Loughborough University

St. Martin's Press

First published in Great Britain 1993 by
THE MACMILLAN PRESS LTD
Houndmills, Basingstoke, Hampshire RG21 2XS
and London
Companies and representatives
throughout the world

A catalogue record for this book is available
from the British Library.

ISBN 0-333-59204-2

Printed in Great Britain by
Antony Rowe Ltd
Chippenham, Wiltshire

First published in the United States of America 1993 by
Scholarly and Reference Division,
ST. MARTIN'S PRESS, INC.,
175 Fifth Avenue,
New York, N.Y. 10010

ISBN 0-312-10194-5

Library of Congress Cataloging-in-Publication Data
Elgie, Robert.
The role of the Prime Minister in France, 1981-91 / Robert Elgie.
p.   cm.
Includes bibliographical references and index.
ISBN 0-312-10194-5
1. Prime ministers—France.   2. France—Politics and
government—1981-   I. Title.
JN2684.E58   1993
354.4403'13—dc20   93-1890
                                                  CIP

To Etain and all my family

Contents

List of Tables

List of Abbreviations

CDS	Centre des Démocrates Sociaux
CFDT	Confédération Française Démocratique du Travail
CGT	Confédération Générale du Travail
CMP	Commission Mixte Paritaire
CNA	Conseil National d'Audiovisuel
CNCL	Conseil National de la Communication et des Libertés
CSA	Conseil Supérieur de l'Audiovisuel
DOM-TOM	Département d'Outre-Mer – Territoire d'Outre-Mer
EMS	European Monetary System
FEN	Fédération de l'Education Nationale
FO	Force Ouvrière
GDP	Gross Domestic Product
GERUF	Groupe d'Etude pour la Rénovation de l'Université Française
GNP	Gross National Product
GSG	General Secretariat of the Government
HLM	Habitation à Loyer Modéré
MRG	Mouvement des Radicaux de Gauche
PCF	Parti Communiste Français
PR	Parti Républicain
PS	Parti Socialiste
RPR	Rassemblement Pour la République
SFP	Société Française de Production
SGCI	Secrétariat Général du Comité Interministériel pour les Affaires Européennes
SGDN	Secrétariat Général de la Défense Nationale
SJTI	Service Juridique et Technique de l'Information
SNT	Société National de Télévision
TDF	Télédiffusion de France
UDC	Union du Centre
UDF	Union pour la Démocratie Française

Acknowledgements

This book is derived from a Ph.D. thesis that I was engaged upon at the London School of Economics and Political Science from 1988 to 1992. As such, I must extend my warmest thanks to my former supervisor there, Dr Howard Machin, for guiding me through the ins and outs of contemporary French politics. I would also like to thank Professor Patrick Dunleavy for his comments on what became Chapter 2 of this book and Dr Moshe Maor, whose own research style was the inspiration behind my merciless pursuit of interviewees whilst in France. Thanks must also go to the secretarial staff in the government department at the LSE who provided me with great support during my time there.

1 The French Prime Minister

The French political system is dominated by the President. Since 1958 and the triumphal return of de Gaulle to the centre of the political stage, the presidency has become the focus of attention for the public, the media and the political élite alike. It is a much coveted institution. Presidential hopefuls prepare their election campaigns years in advance. The election of a new President is usually met with euphoria by the successful candidate's supporters, even if the candidate himself has to keep his *sang-froid*. Following a presidential election, there is the feeling that things will change. There is the belief that problems will be solved. The presidency is the keystone of the system. Presidents no longer simply open flower shows. They take decisions which affect the lives of everyone in the country. Indeed, in recent presidential commitments to defend Germany from invasion, in presidential decisions to send forces to the Gulf and in the President's control over France's nuclear arsenal, presidential decisions affect more than just the lives of the French.

In comparison with the presidency, the institution of the Prime Minister would appear to be of much less importance. When people aspire to hold the premiership, it is usually only because they see it as a way of furthering their presidential ambitions. The Prime Minister's task is a thankless one. While the President rubs shoulders with the leaders of the world's seven richest nations, the Prime Minister is at home trying to resolve the latest wave of industrial unrest. While the President is in charge of 'high' politics, the Prime Minister deals with everything which is decidedly 'low'. The Prime Minister does most of the work and receives little of the glory. When things go well, the President often receives the credit. When things go badly, the Prime Minister usually takes the blame. If things go very badly and the President starts to be criticised, then the Prime Minister is replaced. If things go very well and the Prime Minister starts to be praised, then the Prime Minister is also replaced. Presidents can neither tolerate Prime Ministers who are failures nor Prime Ministers who are a success. Both are a threat to the President's own authority and both have to be dismissed.

This book examines the institution of the Prime Minister in France. More specifically, it examines the extent to which the Prime Minister is able influence the outcome of the public policy-making process in the country. In this respect, it is not a book which is primarily concerned with

1

presidential/prime ministerial relations. Although the extent of the Prime Minister's influence in the policy process is largely determined by the corresponding influence of the President, in the analysis which follows the policy process is examined from the point of view of the Prime Minister. Similarly, although the conclusions which will be drawn at the end of the book may also be applied to the presidency and other governmental organisations, in this case they are applied to the Prime Minister. Therefore, whilst it is hoped that this book will add to the sum of knowledge about French politics in general and also to the understanding of the workings of the French executive as a whole, this study is primarily concerned with advancing the state of prime ministerial studies.

Having emphasised that this book deals primarily with the institution of the French Prime Minister, it is also important to state at the outset that this book will not be arguing that there is prime ministerial government in France. Whilst it will be argued that some of the statements about the extent to which the Fifth Republic has become presidentialised are exaggerated, it will not be argued that the premiership is the most important institution in the political system. Clearly, there has been a form of presidential government throughout much of the history of the Fifth Republic to date. Indeed, the Fifth Republic is designed to encourage presidentialism. This book is not plying a revisionist thesis, claiming that there has not been presidential government during the Fifth Republic. Instead, it concentrates upon the institution of the Prime Minister mainly because few other studies have done so. Certainly, in English there are no full length studies of the French premiership and in French there are very few such studies. In this respect, the book is designed to fill a gap in the academic literature about the Fifth Republic.

It will be argued that the conclusions presented in the final chapter are applicable to the Fifth Republic as a whole. However, this book concentrates on the Prime Minister's influence in the policy process over a ten year period from 1981–91. The period under consideration begins in May 1981 with Mitterrand's victory in the presidential election and ends with Rocard's resignation as Prime Minister in May 1991. This period was chosen for several reasons. Firstly, it is sufficiently long for it to be possible to draw up useful conclusions about the extent of prime ministerial influence. A shorter period of time would simply have provided a snapshot of the political system at a particular moment. A longer period would have rendered it more difficult to compare the experiences of different Prime Ministers. Secondly, the year 1981 and the arrival in power of the left for the first time under the Fifth Republic marked a turning point in the history of the régime to date. As such, it represents a natural starting point for such a study. Thirdly, the political system from 1981–91 operated in various different ways which it is necessary to study. This period saw a socialist/communist majority coalition (1981–84), a socialist majority government (1984–86), a two-year period of *cohabitation* (1986–88) and, finally, a socialist minority government (1988–91). The political system was not static during this time. The Prime Minister's influence under each of these different situations may be compared and a fuller picture of his role may be drawn up.

It must be emphasised that the study to be undertaken does not operate at a purely theoretical level. Wilson has argued that theoretical studies can only reach general conclusions and that they tend to rely on evidence that is impressionistic. Consequently, their findings are weakened.[1] In order to avoid this situation, this study will not posit a hypothesis which will be tested throughout the course of the chapters which follow. Instead, there is a strong empirical emphasis. It is felt that this approach maximises the validity and applicability of the study's findings.

However, there are different types of empirical approaches which might be adopted. Wilson has identified two such approaches which could be used as a method of studying the influence of groups or institutions in the policy process. The first, his favoured method, is to engage upon, 'empirical studies of overall patterns of . . . politics in a country'.[2] If this approach had been adopted here, it would have involved sending out a questionnaire to and conducting interviews with as many Prime Ministers and prime ministerial advisers as was possible. Indeed, it would also have been necessary to contact as many Presidents, Ministers and their advisers as possible. Apart from the logistical difficulties that this approach would have entailed, it would also have meant that the results would have been uneven. There would have been little focus to the study and it would have been difficult, if not impossible, properly to compare the findings.

Instead, a different approach is favoured, namely that of case studies. The problem with this approach lies in the representativeness of the studies to be undertaken. They have to be typical of the policy process and they have to be matching such that comparisons are possible. Cognisant of these problems, eight public policy decisions in the 1981–91 period have been chosen for study. These decisions are: the 1981, 1986 and January 1989 broadcasting acts; the 1985, 1987 and 1990 Finance acts; the crisis surrounding the withdrawal of the Devaquet higher education bill in 1986; and the debate over the third devaluation of the franc in March 1983.

This number is sufficiently large so as to be able to draw up valid conclusions. The chosen studies also permit comparisons to drawn within individual policy sectors and between different sectors over the period in question. They allow for the study of routine policy preparation processes in normal times (the Finance acts); non-routine policy preparation in normal times (the broadcasting acts); and policy preparation during crisis periods (the Devaquet bill and the 1983 devaluation). Thus, the studies which have been chosen are representative and matched and permit valid conclusions to be reached about the Prime Minister's influence in the policy process.

The information about the particular case studies was derived from both primary and secondary sources. Around 60 interviews with Ministers, deputies, members of ministerial, prime ministerial and presidential *cabinets* and representatives from the permanent administration were undertaken (see Appendix). In addition, two former Prime Ministers were interviewed. These interviews were nearly all directly connected with the chosen case studies, although some more general interviews about the overall role of the Prime Minister were also conducted. In addition to these primary sources, secondary information was also used. This information included books and contemporary newspaper accounts of the case studies; biographies and autobiographies of the relevant political actors; and general academic works on the Prime Minister and the French political system as a whole. It is hoped, therefore, as a result of the case study approach and of the collection of primary and secondary information, that valid and detailed conclusions may be drawn up about the nature of prime ministerial influence in France.

It would be wrong, however, to launch straight into the case studies. First, it is necessary to become acquainted with the institution of the French Prime Minister and then to present the competing theories as to the extent of prime ministerial influence in the political system. In this way, the case studies which follow will be placed in context. The rest of this chapter deals with the institution of the Prime Minister, outlining its constitutional, administrative and political powers. The next chapter presents the different models of core executive operations which may be identified from the existing literature on the French political system. In each of these models, the influence of the Prime Minister in the system will be shown to differ. Conclusions as to which of these models, if any, properly accounts for the extent of prime ministerial influence in the policy process will be reached once the case studies have been examined. Firstly, however, it is necessary to make some preliminary remarks about the study of the French Prime Minister to date.

Prime Ministerial Studies to Date

There are innumerable books, journal articles and newspaper stories which have dealt either directly or indirectly with the institutions of the presidency, premiership, ministries and other governmental organisations in France. However, in the main, these studies are to a large extent unrewarding in the sense that they fail to define rigorously the role of these institutions in the political system. What is true of core executive studies in general is true of prime ministerial studies in particular.[3] The role of the Prime Minister remains conceptually underdeveloped. The framework within which the premiership is analysed is poorly defined.

In France, there are two types of prime ministerial studies. Firstly, there are journalistic studies. These studies largely consist of articles appearing in the national daily and weekly press. However, they also include books written by journalists which usually concentrate on the relations between the Prime Minister and the President.[4] This literature is often fascinating, but it also tends to be highly personalised, anecdotal and lacking in analytical rigour. This situation is hardly surprising as the expectations and the constraints within which the press operates are barely conducive to any other sort of study.

Secondly, there are academic studies. These studies are all too often disappointingly incomplete. One type of academic study concentrates upon the Prime Minister's role in terms of constitutional and administrative law. This literature, however, naturally tends to underestimate the political climate within which the Prime Minister has to operate. The other type of academic study considers the Prime Minister in a political context. However, of this type of study, there are only a handful of accounts which focus upon the Prime Minister directly.[5] Whilst these accounts are no doubt useful, they also tend to be out of date and in the main concentrate on the Prime Minister's administrative resources, rather than his influence in the policy process.[6]

There are four main reasons as to why there are so few studies of the French Prime Minister in general and of his influence upon the policy process in particular. Firstly, the political supremacy of the President for much of the Fifth Republic has served to focus attention upon the head of state rather than the head of government. Journalistic and academic attention is naturally directed towards the perceived centre of power in the country. As a result, prime ministerial studies have only been of only secondary importance.

Secondly, since the 1962 constitutional reform which instituted the direct election of the President, French politics has become more personality orientated. This situation has in turn served to personalise both the journalistic and academic literature on French politics. At presidential elections individuals are judged on their capacity to hold the top office and core executive studies too often focus upon the electability of potential *présidentiables*, one of which is more often than not the Prime Minister. The personalisation of the political system has discouraged systematic attempts to determine the influence of the component institutions of the core executive in the policy process.

The third reason for the lack of prime ministerial studies lies in the high level of secrecy which surrounds the workings of the core executive. Secrecy is clearly not a problem confined to France and similar problems have hampered work on the core executive in, for example, the UK.[7] In France, all government documents are classified as secret and do not reach the public domain until years after the event. Moreover, even when minutes of past Council of Ministers, or committee meetings do appear, there is no *procès-verbal* from which to reconstruct a full picture of the governmental debate. Instead, there is only a general résumé of the meeting's conclusions. Such secrecy fosters the impressionistic, anecdotal accounts which characterise journalistic studies of the core executive. These anecdotes are fascinating precisely because of the high level of secrecy and they have the advantage for the author in question in that they are hard to contradict.

The fourth reason is because of the normative element upon which many studies are based. Whilst in the UK this normative element is largely confined to the belief in some quarters that there ought to be cabinet government, in France the doctrinal aspect is much stronger. Mainly because of the institutional shortcomings of the Third and Fourth French Republics, the debate surrounding the organisational structure of the Fifth Republic has been particularly doctrinaire. This debate has typically centred around, on the one hand, the notion supported by the gaullists that there ought to be presidential government and, on the other, the communist (and previously socialist) belief that there ought to be parliamentary government. Much academic and journalistic writing is either consciously, or subconsciously imbued with these normative elements, once again, to the detriment of analytical work on the nature of the core executive.

Therefore, neither the role of the French Prime Minister in the policy process, nor the operation of the French core executive as a whole has been the subject of a great deal of systematic research. The core executive in its entirety remains the 'black box' which translates policy inputs into outputs, but in a mysterious and unidentified way. This book examines one element within the 'black box', the institution of the Prime Minister. To begin, it is

Table 1.1   Presidents and Prime Ministers 1958–91

Year	President	Prime Minister
1958	de Gaulle	Debré
1962	de Gaulle	Pompidou
1968	de Gaulle	Couve de Murville
1969	Pompidou	Chaban-Delmas
1972	Pompidou	Messmer
1974	Giscard d'Estaing	Chirac
1976	Giscard d'Estaing	Barre
1981	Mitterrand	Mauroy
1984	Mitterrand	Fabius
1986	Mitterrand	Chirac
1988	Mitterrand	Rocard

necessary to make some preliminary remarks about the role of the Prime Minister within the political system.

The Prime Minister's Constitutional, Administrative and Political Powers

Since the constitutional amendment of 1962, the Fifth Republic has been classified as a semi-presidential political régime.[8] That is to say, a régime where a directly elected President, with certain constitutional powers, serving for a fixed term in office coexists with a Prime Minister, who also has certain constitutional powers and who is responsible to the legislature. France is one of only a small (if growing) number of such régimes.

In semi-presidential régimes, the key issue centres around the question of whether the President or the Prime Minister is in control of the public policy-making process. From 1958–91, of the ten Prime Ministers who served in office (see Table 1.1), only one, Jacques Chirac from 1986–88, can plausibly be said to have been in control of the policy process. To one extent or another, all the rest were subordinate to the President. In this sense, it has been argued that the Fifth Republic may well be a semi-presidential régime, meaning that the country is organised constitutionally in this way, but that it operates under a presidential system of government, meaning that political power is exercised by the President.[9]

At face value, this situation is surprising, because the three bases of prime ministerial power, the constitutional basis, the administrative basis and the political basis would together suggest that the Prime Minister should be the leading institution in the political system. In theory, there should be a prime ministerial system of government. However, in practice, the President has been able to dominate the policy process. Nevertheless, as an introduction to the institution of the Prime Minister, it is necessary to examine each of the three bases of prime ministerial power in turn.

In constitutional terms, the Prime Minister would seem to be better placed to control the policy process than the presidency or, indeed, any other institution in the political system. The Prime Minister enjoys a considerable set of constitutional powers which would seem to allow him to exercise power continuously. For example, Article 20 states that: 'The Government decides and directs the policies of the nation',[10] whilst Article 21 states that: 'The Prime Minister is in general charge of the work of the Government'. Moreover, the Prime Minister also proposes to the President the names of the people he wishes to become government Ministers (Article 8). In constitutional terms, therefore, the Prime Minister is placed at the head of a team which in theory he has chosen himself and which is responsible for policy making in the country.

What is more, as head of government the Prime Minister is more than simply *primus inter pares*. In addition to Articles 20 and 21, the Prime Minister is also granted certain specific powers by the Constitution which serve to institutionalise his authority over the other members of the government. For example, he has the power to issue decrees in those areas in which the legislature is not competent to legislate (Articles 37 and 21). Article 34 of the Constitution lays down the areas in which Parliament is able to legislate. Outside of these areas, the Prime Minister may issue a decree which has the force of law (*le pouvoir réglementaire*). In this sense, the Prime Minister has come to be a substitute parliamentary chamber. What is more, this power is exercised continuously by the Prime Minister. For example, Ardant has argued that the Prime Minister signs on average 1,500 decrees (*décrets*) and 7–8,000 ministerial orders (*arrêtés*) per year.[11] Although the overwhelming majority of these decrees and orders are prepared by individual Ministers and will be subject simply to the Prime Minister's formal approval and signature, the Prime Minister does have the right to issue his own more general decrees (*le pouvoir réglementaire autonome*).

In addition, the Prime Minister is also constitutionally responsible for national defence (Article 21). To this end, he enjoys the administrative support of a *cabinet militaire* which exists alongside his personal set of advisers (*cabinet civil*). The *cabinet militaire* advises the Prime Minister on defence policy and also undertakes certain routine administrative duties in the field of national defence. In 1989, the *cabinet militaire* was headed by an air force general, Bernard Norlain. He was assisted by five *adjoints*, consisting of three colonels, one captain and one lieutenant colonel drawn from the ranks of all three services. It might be noted that, unlike the members of the Prime Minister's *cabinet civil*, the *chef du cabinet militaire* and his *adjoints* usually remain at their posts even when there is a change of Prime Minister. In this sense, they are in a position more akin to members of the permanent administration than to personal advisers. Also with regard to his responsibility for national defence, the Prime Minister is in charge of the General Secretariat for National Defence (SGDN). Much of the SGDN's work is administrative, liaising between the President, Prime Minister and relevant government departments with a view to organising and chairing meetings of the defence council. However, it also conducts studies and produces reports on specific defence problems. For example, it has a permanent *'cellule de crise'* which examines the world's trouble spots. Whilst the SGDN works as closely with the President as it does with the Prime Minister, nevertheless, it is the latter who is officially responsible for its work.

In addition to these constitutional powers which the Prime Minister may exercise continuously, there are also others which he may employ sporadically. For example, he has the right to make certain military and civilian appointments (Article 21). Undoubtedly, the President's power of appointment is greater than the Prime Minister's. Nevertheless, the Prime Minister may still use his time in office to appoint loyal supporters to key posts in the state structure. For example, Rocard was able to nominate people to the Court of Accounts and the Council of State. Other former rocardian collaborators were appointed to head the Planning Commissariat, Crédit national and Radio-France international.[12]

Another of the Prime Minister's sporadic powers is the ability to call upon the Constitutional Council to determine the constitutionality of a law or treaty (Article 61). This article was originally inserted into the Constitution in 1958, so as to enable the Prime Minister to use the Constitutional Council as a way of striking down anti-governmental legislation that had been passed by a hostile legislature. However, given the docility of Parliament during the Fifth Republic, there has been little need for the Prime Minister to petition (*saisir*) the Constitutional Council in this way. As a result, the Constitutional Council is now normally seized by deputies and senators as a means of publicising the government's abuse of its powers, rather than by the Prime Minister as a way of keeping Parliament in check.

It can be seen, therefore, that the Prime Minister has a whole range of constitutional powers that may be exercised both continuously and sporadically. By contrast, the President has relatively few constitutional

Table 1.2　Nomination of Prime Ministers, 1958–91

Following a presidential election	Following a legislative election	Between elections
1959 Debré	1968 Couve	1962 Pompidou
1969 Chaban-Delmas	1986 Chirac	1972 Messmer
1974 Chirac		1976 Barre
1981 Mauroy		1984 Fabius
1988 Rocard		

powers. In particular, the President has little constitutional authority to intervene in the governmental policy-making process. Only during times of public emergency does the President have the right to assume law-making powers for himself and then only for a limited period of time. These powers are set out in Article 16 of the Constitution. They have been used only once, by de Gaulle in April 1962, following a rebellion in Algiers by generals loyal to Algeria remaining French. In other words, Article 16 grants the President law making powers only in exceptional circumstances.

Otherwise, the President has the constitutional right to intervene continuously in the decision-making process only in the areas of defence and foreign affairs. He is able to intervene in defence policy-making by virtue of being commander-in-chief of the armed forces (Article 15) and because, according to Article 5, he is the protector of the independence of the nation and of the integrity of its territory. That is to say, he has the constitutional obligation to take all necessary steps, so as to ensure that France is not invaded by a hostile force. One consequence of this power is that the President's finger is on the nuclear trigger. The President's constitutional powers to intervene in foreign affairs are derived from Article 52, which states that the President negotiates and ratifies treaties. The President also has the right to accredit ambassadors abroad (Article 14), reinforcing his authority in foreign affairs.

In normal circumstances, outside of these areas, the President's constitutional powers are somewhat limited. The two most important powers that he enjoys are, firstly, the right to appoint the Prime Minister (but not the power to dismiss him) and, secondly, the right to dissolve the National Assembly (but not more than once a year). By allowing the President to appoint the Prime Minister of his choice, the Constitution has largely deprived the National Assembly of either a direct or an indirect say in the formation of the government. Only two Prime Ministers have been appointed following a general election since 1958 and in only one of these cases, Jacques Chirac in 1986, was the appointment of the Prime Minister effectively forced upon the President by the results of the legislative election (see Table 1.2).

Undoubtedly the President's power to appoint the Prime Minister has encouraged the latter to feel a sense of subordination to the former. The President's other main power lies in his ability to dissolve the National Assembly (Article 12). This power has been utilised on four occasions: 1962, 1968, 1981 and 1988. On two of these occasions (1981 and 1988), the dissolution occurred following a presidential election so as to enable the presidential majority to be transformed into a legislative majority as well. Once, in 1962, the National Assembly was dissolved after the government had been defeated on a motion of no-confidence and once, in 1968, the dissolution occurred following a period of social unrest. On all four occasions, the dissolutions served to reinforce the authority of the government with regard to the legislature. In particular, with the possible exception of 1968, they served to reinforce the authority of the President.

The President's other set of constitutional powers remain relatively limited. For example, as was noted above, he is responsible for making certain public appointments (Article 13); he may appoint three people to the Constitutional Council and name its President (Article 56); he chairs the Council of Ministers (Article 9); and, finally, he must endeavour to ensure that the Constitution is respected and he must provide, by his arbitration, for the regular functioning of the public authorities and the continuity of the State (Article 5).

In all, whilst the President's constitutional prerogatives are far from unimportant, in terms of policy making, they are not as great as those of the Prime Minister. Indeed, a careful reading of the Constitution would encourage the conclusion that the system should be operating under a form of prime ministerial government. However, as was noted earlier, the constitutional division of powers has rarely operated in practice. Presidents have been able to assume the position of *de facto* head of government and the Prime Minister has simply become the President's loyal lieutenant. Whilst both the extent of the President's domination and the Prime Minister's subordination has on occasions been exaggerated by various observers (see Chapter 2), nevertheless, the Constitution has not provided a true guide as to where power lies in the political system of the Fifth Republic.

The second basis of prime ministerial power is administrative. Firstly, the Prime Minister has the right to determine the boundaries of departmental competences.[13] For example, he may decide which departments he wishes to have control over personally. For example, in 1986, Chirac was personally responsible for the work of five junior Ministers: two *Ministres délégués* (Public Service and Economic Planning, and Administrative Reforms) and three *Secrétaires d'Etat* (Francophone Communities, Rights of Man and Youth and Sports) In 1988, Rocard was also responsible for five junior ministries. However, on this occasion all of these Ministers held the title of *Secrétaire d'Etat*. Moreover, with the exception of the Economic Planning department, the areas with which Rocard wished to be associated were different to his predecessor (Environment, War Veterans and Humanitarian Action). Rocard also appointed a junior Minister without portfolio, Tony Dreyfus, who acted as an adviser and trouble shooter.

In addition, the Prime Minister may also determine the exact nature of the departments over which his Ministers are to preside. For example, under Raymond Barre there was a Minister for Health and Social Security. However, in 1981 under Mauroy, there was a Minister for Health as well as a *Secrétaire d'Etat* responsible for Social Security who worked under the Minister for National Solidarity. While on occasions such changes may simply be cosmetic, on other occasions they may also be used to reinforce departmental resources in areas which have become governmental priorities. Such was the case in 1981 when the government wished to stress its commitment to social issues.

Secondly, Article 20 states that the Prime Minister has the services of the permanent administration at his disposal. As such, he is formally responsible for a whole range of governmental services (see Table 1.3).[14] According to figures for February 1st 1985, the Prime Minister's administrative staff numbered 5,472 and the total annual budget for the services under his control was over 13 billion francs.[15] The Prime Minister's services include organisations which play a fundamental role in the policy process. Most notably, these services include the General Secretariat of the Government and the Prime Minister's *cabinet*, or set of personal advisers.[16] It is necessary to examine these two institutions more closely as they both play a major role in the decision-making process.

The General Secretariat of the Government (GSG) is the equivalent of the British Cabinet Office. It carries out many of the routine administrative tasks associated with the policy process. As its name suggests, it carries out these tasks for the benefit of the government as a whole, rather than simply the Prime Minister. However, in practice the GSG is responsible to the Prime Minister personally. Indeed, the head of the GSG, the General Secretary, usually occupies an office which adjoins the Prime Minister's office at the Hôtel Matignon. As such, the General Secretary is one of the Prime Minister's closest interlocuters. The General Secretary carries out two main functions. Firstly, he is the Prime Minister's chief legal adviser. For example, he recommends whether legislation is needed for a new reform or whether a decree will suffice. Secondly, he is intimately involved in the preparation of the meetings of the Council of Ministers which

Table 1.3   Prime ministerial services at 20 January 1990

Personal staff
Cabinet
> **Central administrative services**
1. General Secretariat of the Government (GSG)
   Administrative and Financial Services Division
   La Documentation Française
   Le Journal Officiel
2. General Secretariat of National Defence (SGDN)
   Four Divisions and one Task Force
   Interministerial Delegation for the Security of
   Information Systems
   Institute for Higher Defence Studies
   Interministerial Committee for Nuclear Security
3. General Secretariat for the Interministerial Committee on European Economic
   Co-operation (SGCI)
4. Legal and Technical Service on Information (SJTI)
5. Governmental Information Service (SID)

Junior Ministers
1. Secretary of State for Humanitarian Action
2. Secretary of State for the Environment
3. Secretary of State for Economic Planning
4. Secretary of State without portfolio

Common services (examples)
a. Atomic Energy Commissariat
b. Delegation on French Language
c. Financial Controller

---

take place every Wednesday morning. During these meetings he takes the minutes and is responsible for drawing up the official communiqué which is presented to the press afterwards. It should be noted that the GSG is part of the permanent administration and that, with the exception of 1986, the General Secretary does not change with the formation of a new government.

The work of the General Secretary is supported by the other members of the GSG. In all, the organisation totals around 40 people. The main task of the GSG as a whole is to follow the process of policy preparation and to provide administrative services and legal advice to the government. A series of advisers within the GSG (*chargés de mission*) follow the work of the government departments to which they have been assigned. When one of their departments is preparing a reform they organise and chair policy preparation meetings; they circulate the decisions of the meetings; and they report back to the General Secretary about their work. Once a piece of legislation has been passed, they will also ensure that it is implemented and that any necessary *décrets d'application* are issued. It is apparent, therefore, that both the General Secretary and the GSG as a whole play a major role in the decision-making process. They provide essential administrative services and generally help the Prime Minister in his capacity as head of government and in his role as an arbitrator between conflicting government departments (see below).

In addition to the resources of the permanent administration, the Prime Minister also has a personal staff, or *cabinet*, which deals with the more sensitive political aspects of policy making. *Cabinet* members are not part of the permanent administration. Indeed, advisers rarely serve more than one Prime Minister. Instead, each Prime Minister appoints his own set of personal advisers. The appointments are made carefully as it is important for the Prime Minister to have a set of advisers whom he can trust. In general, the number of people serving in the Prime Minister's *cabinet* has increased over the years. However, the figures are subject to certain fluctuations marking an increase or decrease in legislative activity. For example, in 1982 there were 56 people in Mauroy's *cabinet*, reflecting the legislative activity of the new government. However, in 1984 there were only 20 people in Fabius's *cabinet*, corresponding to a period of retrenchment.[17]

The main function of *cabinet* members is to give the Prime Minister advice about public policy. This advice goes beyond the technical and legal advice provided by the GSG and includes political advice, such as whether a reform would be electorally popular, or how best to cope with conflicting ministerial egos. In a similar manner to the GSG, the *cabinet* is organised such that there is at least one adviser (*chargé de mission*) who is following the work of each government department at any one time. In this capacity they attend the various stages of the policy preparation process (see below). In order to co-ordinate the work of the government, these advisers report to certain councillors (*conseillers technique*) who are in charge of the work of a number of related departments. In turn, these councillors report to the head of the *cabinet*, the director (*directeur de cabinet*) who oversees the work of the organisation as a whole (see Table 1.4). The *directeur de cabinet* works very closely with the Prime Minister himself. Indeed, the *directeur* is usually one of the Prime Minister's most long standing and trusted aides. In this way, there is the free flow of information through the *cabinet* with the Prime Minister being the beneficiary of the support and advice of a team of loyal collaborators.

In terms of the policy process, both the GSG and the Prime Minister's *cabinet* play an important role. The fact that both of these organisations

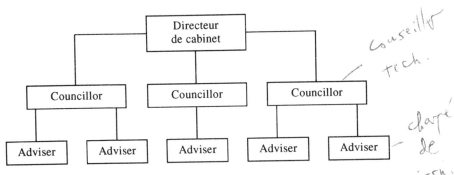

Table 1.4   Typical structure of the Prime Minister's cabinet

report to the head of government suggests that the Prime Minister should be well placed to intervene in this process. However, as will be argued later (see Chapter 8), the importance of the Prime Minister's extensive set of administrative resources flatters to deceive. As has been noted elsewhere:

> The prime minister, however, faces a problem that is not rare in politics: ownership of resources does not coincide with control.[18]

For example, the President has effectively colonised the Prime Minister's administrative resources, such that they carry out the President's wishes, rather than those of the Prime Minister. By virtue of the services under his control, the Prime Minister is undoubtedly at the centre of governmental and administrative co-ordination.[19] However, he has tended to co-ordinate the President's policy programme rather than his own.

The third basis of prime ministerial power is political. There are two aspects to the Prime Minister's political basis of power: firstly, the power to arbitrate between conflicting government Ministers; and, secondly, the responsibility for navigating the passage of government legislation through Parliament. Each of these two aspects of the Prime Minister's political power will be considered in turn.

The Prime Minister's power of arbitration is derived from the strategic position that he holds in the policy-making process. This process consists of a series of meetings which bring together representatives of government departments as well as the Prime Minister, President and/or their advisers. These meetings are the site of interdepartmental conflict as individual Ministers, each defending their own interests, try to ensure that their policy preferences are adopted. These interdepartmental conflicts are resolved by a bargaining process which continues until a compromise has been reached. The Prime Minister's arbitration function consists in

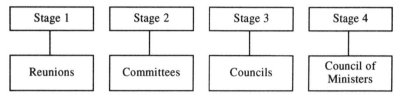

Table 1.5   The stages in the executive part of the policy process

trying to find a compromise which will satisfy the interested parties. If no such compromise is forthcoming, then the Prime Minister may have to impose a solution on the meeting. As Py has noted:

> During the course of the reunion, those present do not intervene on their own behalf, rather they put forward the position of their ministry. If the various positions do not agree, a compromise is sought; if the disagreement continues the Prime Minister has to arbitrate.[20]

At the executive level there are four stages to the policy-making process (see Table 1.5). At two of these stages, reunions and committees, the Prime Minister's arbitration function is clearly exercised.

Interministerial reunions bring together ministerial advisers as well as representatives from Matignon, the Prime Minister's residence, and the Elysée, the presidential palace. At least one member of the GSG also attends in order to carry out routine secretarial functions and, if necessary, to give legal advice on any aspect of the bill. Reunions are usually chaired by a member of the Prime Minister's *cabinet*. These meetings are important because, although only advisers are present, they are the first official stage at which policy decisions are made. Although the decisions taken tend to be of a technical nature, they may have an important impact upon the wording of a bill. One way of gauging their importance is by charting the number of meetings held annually. During the course of the Fifth Republic, the number of reunions has increased greatly (see Table 1.6). In their capacity as chair of the meetings, the Prime Minister's advisers have to wind up debates and identify any unresolved ministerial conflicts. As Bauby has noted: 'The Prime Minister's representative sums up and decides which matters necessitate further arbitration'.[21] All unresolved matters are reserved for the attention of interministerial committees.

It is in committee meetings that the Prime Minister's arbitration function is demonstrated most clearly. Interministerial committees are chaired by the Prime Minister personally. Unlike the situation in reunions where the Prime Minister's arbitration function is carried out on his behalf by his advisers,

Table 1.6   Number of interministerial reunions in selected years,
1961–85[22]

Prime Minister	Year	Number of reunions
Debré	1961	141
Pompidou	1964	395
Chaban	1970	526
Messmer	1973	517
Chirac	1975	792
Barre	1977	738
Mauroy	1982	1,855
Fabius	1985	1,311

at the committee stage the Prime Minister will have to arbitrate personally between the different ministerial viewpoints. Partly because many issues have already been resolved at the reunion stage and partly because of the Prime Minister's other time pressures, only a relatively small number of committee meetings are held annually. In 1961, there were 118; in 170, there were 145; in 1980 there were 59; in 1983, 69 committees were held during the course of the year.[23]

In carrying out his arbitration function the Prime Minister is supposed to be a disinterested figure, arbitrating in a neutral manner between opposing Ministers. However, it must be noted that this version represents a particularly idealised view of the policy process and the chapters which follow will show that the Prime Minister was often more than a disinterested arbiter.

As with reunions, committees are often unable to resolve all of the contentious issues in a bill. These issues have to be examined in the third stage of the policy process, namely, interministerial councils. These meetings are chaired by the President. Councils examine the most fundamental and usually the most controversial aspects of a bill. They are held to look at disputes between Ministers that the Prime Minister has been unable to resolve. They are also held to examine issues where a Minister refuses to accept the Prime Minister's arbitration in the committee. On both occasions the ultimate arbiter in the policy process is the President. His decision is final. In this respect, the President's political basis of power is greater than that of the Prime Minister.

The executive part of the policy process formally ends with the adoption of the bill by the Council of Ministers. These meetings are largely perfunctory and usually play only minor role in policy preparation. It is during the course of the first three stages of the executive policy process that the main policy decisions are taken. Thus, the Council of Ministers

steel { but an exception
to the rules)

serves merely to rubber-stamp decisions which have effectively been taken elsewhere. It must be noted, however, that sometimes the contents of bills are discussed at these meetings. On these occasions, the President will ask for the advice of the Prime Minister and Ministers and a final arbitration is made by the President on the basis of their interventions. However, this situation happens only rarely.

The second component of the Prime Minister's political basis of power can be found in his responsibility for ensuring that government legislation is passed by Parliament. Once again, there are various stages to the parliamentary policy-making process. After a bill has been officially agreed by the Council of Ministers it is immediately placed before one of the two parliamentary chambers. Usually the National Assembly examines the bill before the Senate, but the government has the right to place it before the Senate first if it so wishes. Before the bill is debated on the floor of the chamber, it is first examined in either a special commission created especially for the bill, or in one of the permanent standing commissions. Here, it will be examined clause by clause and a *rapporteur*, appointed from amongst the majority party members of the commission, will draw up a report in which the commission's amendments are detailed. When the bill is debated on the floor of the chamber, the government may accept all or some of these amendments, or it may insist upon its original version.

Once a bill has been passed by one chamber it shuttles to the next where the same process is repeated (*la navette*). If both the National Assembly and the Senate agree upon a common version of the bill, then after three readings in each chamber the bill is considered to be passed. However, if after the second reading there are any textual differences in the bill between the two chambers, then the Prime Minister has the constitutional right (Article 45) to set up a mixed parity commission (*une commission mixte paritaire*) in order to try and iron out the differences and agree upon a common text. If a common wording is found, then the bill is considered once again by both chambers after which time it is definitively passed. If no agreement is forthcoming, then only the National Assembly examines the bill again.

The government has an extensive set of powers over the legislature. It may call upon these powers so as to ensure the passage of its own legislation. The Prime Minister would seem to be the main beneficiary of the government's powers. In certain areas, he is personally given the right to intervene in the parliamentary stage of the policy-making process. For example, he has the power to call an extraordinary session of Parliament (Article 29); he has the right to initiate laws (Article 39); and he may engage the government's responsibility on a particular piece of legislation

(Article 49). In other areas, the Prime Minister may also intervene in the process by virtue of his position as head of government. For example, the government fixes the parliamentary timetable (Article 48); it may declare the passage of a bill to be a matter of urgency (Article 45); it may refuse to accept the discussion of any parliamentary amendments which have not previously been discussed in one of the parliamentary committees (Article 44); it may insist that Parliament votes on a bill as a whole, rather than on its constituent parts (Article 44); and it may ask Parliament to pass an enabling bill, allowing the government to issue ordinances which have the force of law (Article 38).

In constitutional terms, therefore, the Prime Minister is well placed to influence the parliamentary part of the policy-making process. In addition, the Prime Minister also has the administrative resources to intervene effectively in the parliamentary process. In 1989, for example, Rocard's *cabinet* contained no less than three parliamentary advisers. There was also a Minister for Parliamentary Relations, Jean Poperen, whose job it was to liaise with the different party groups in Parliament, so as to facilitate the passage of legislation. Prime Minister also benefited from the help of the legislative division of the GSG. This division ensures that the Prime Minister is kept informed of the parliamentary debates and proposed amendments. What is more, the Prime Minister, in conjunction with relevant Ministers, is responsible for selecting which, if any, of the parliamentary amendments to accept. In this sense, the Prime Minister's arbitration function continues beyond the executive part of the policy process and includes the parliamentary part as well.

Once again, however, the Prime Minister's power has been more theoretical than practical. The Prime Minister's constitutional and administrative powers over Parliament are a necessary but not a sufficient condition for him to have been able to dominate the policy process. There are various reasons for this situation. Firstly, the parliamentary majority has often been loyal to the President. For example, Debré and Pompidou, both of whom came to enjoy a positive relationship with the majority, were still aware that the majority was ultimately loyal to de Gaulle. Similarly, Mauroy, Fabius and Rocard were all obliged to deal with a majority which looked to the President for leadership. The only occasions on which parliamentary loyalty has not generally been assured were during *cohabitation* and under Giscard's presidency.

Secondly, Parliament usually passes what amounts to presidential legislation. At presidential elections, candidates normally campaign on a policy platform which they promise to introduce if elected. Successful candidates, therefore, can claim that they have a mandate to govern. One result of this situation is that Prime Ministers are usually aware that that they are appointed with the express task of ensuring that the President's campaign promises are met. In this sense, the main lines of governmental policy are fixed by the President, as a result of his election, rather than by the Prime Minister or anyone else.

It appears, therefore, as if in terms of his constitutional prerogatives, his administrative resources and his political powers the Prime Minister's capacity to influence the policy-making process in theory is limited in practice. It would appear as if the President, despite enjoying only relatively few constitutional powers and administrative resources, is able to dominate the policy process. As was noted at the beginning of this section, this situation has led observers to categorise France as having a presidential system of government. It may be argued, however, that such a categorisation is misleading. It is a simplification of a more complex reality. In fact, observers of the French system of government do not agree as to what type of system of government the country operates under. In the next chapter, the different classifications of core executive operations in the French political system will be identified. It will be seen that the role of the Prime Minister in the system and the extent of his influence in the policy process differs from one model of core executive operations to the next.

2 Models of Core Executive Operations

The aim of the last chapter was to outline the general constitutional, administrative and political position of the French Prime Minister in the Fifth Republic. It is now necessary to analyse the Prime Minister's role in the policy-making process in more detail. As such, it is important to appreciate that the Prime Minister is only one component of a wider set of institutions, which might collectively be called the core executive.[1] The core executive has been defined as:

> all those organisations and structures which primarily serve to pull together and integrate central government policies, or act as final arbiters within the executive of conflicts between the government machine.[2]

It is clear that in terms of his co-ordination function and his arbitration function the Prime Minister is one of the most integral components of the core executive in France.

As such, as a method of analysing the extent of the Prime Minister's influence in the policy-making process in France, it has been decided to follow the example set by Dunleavy and Rhodes in their work on the nature of the core executive in Britain. In a seminal article which was published in 1990, they examined the existing literature on the long-running debate over whether there is prime ministerial or Cabinet government in Britain. In the course of their work, they identified six variants of the traditional Cabinet/prime ministerial government debate. These variants may be termed models of core executive operations.

In certain respects, a similar debate surrounds the nature of core executive operations in both Britain and France. In Britain, it has long been assumed by many writers that prime ministerial government has superseded Cabinet government. Similarly, in France, for much of the Fifth Republic it has been assumed that there is presidential government. However, as Dunleavy and Rhodes were able to show for Britain, the claim that there is prime ministerial government is based upon certain, perhaps questionable, assumptions. It might also be argued that the claim that, in France, there is a pure form of presidential government is equally questionable. Whilst, as was noted in Chapter 1, it could in no way be argued that there has been prime ministerial government throughout the Fifth Republic, it is at least necessary to examine the claims made about presidential government in order to see whether they stand up to close scrutiny and to identify the assumptions that are made by proponents of this approach.

As a result, in this chapter, Dunleavy and Rhodes's method of approaching core executive studies in Britain will be applied to the French case. As was noted in the first chapter, even if the French Prime Minister has been the primary subject of only a few studies, his role has been discussed tangentially on countless other occasions. From the existing literature it is possible to identify six distinct models of core executive operations for France in each of which the Prime Minister is said to play a particular role. These models vary somewhat from the models which Dunleavy and Rhodes identified in the British case. The models which can be identified in the French case may be classed as: presidential government; segmented decision-making; executive co-operation; prime ministerial government; ministerial government; and the bureaucratic co-ordination model. Each of these different variants will now be examined in turn.

Presidential Government

Presidential government may be defined as 'the exertion of monocratic authority by the President'.[3] That is to say, the situation where the President both initiates government policy and where he decides the content of such policy. These powers exist alongside the ceremonial functions that the President must carry out in his capacity as head of state. For many observers, presidential government began in France in 1958 under de Gaulle. It has since been consolidated and even extended under the Pompidou, Giscard d'Estaing and Mitterrand presidencies.

As was noted in the previous chapter, successive Presidents have exceeded their formal, constitutional powers and have been able to play a major role in both policy initiation and decision making. Presidential control over policy initiation can be demonstrated by virtue of the fact that the government's legislative programme has often been derived derived from the electoral programme presented by candidates at presidential elections, rather than by parties at legislative elections. For example, the '110 Propositions for Government' which Mitterrand presented at the 1981 presidential election were the reference point for the socialist administration which took office after his victory. Similarly, Mitterrand's

Lettre à tous les Français provided Rocard with a ready made legislative programme when he was appointed as Prime Minister in May 1988. Presidential control over day-to-day decision making can be demonstrated by the large number of interministerial councils which take place. As the chair of these meetings, they are the occasion for the President to assert his control over policy making. Moreover, Presidents are not afraid to intervene directly in the decision-making process. As Duhamel has shown:

> The President manages what de Gaulle called 'France's destiny', Pompidou 'the essentials', Giscard 'the long term problems' (*la durée*) and Mitterrand 'the major defining options' (*les grandes orientations*); the Prime Minister is left to deal with 'the action of the moment' (de Gaulle) or, still less grand, 'the problems of daily life' (Mitterrand).[4]

However it may be termed, under the model of presidential government the division of labour between the President and the Prime Minister is clear.

In addition, successive Presidents have used their influence over appointments to ensure that '*fidèles*' have been placed at key positions in the core executive. Aside from the appointment of loyal Prime Ministers and Ministers, the President also has the right to make certain appointments to the permanent administration. For example, Presidents have placed loyal advisers at the head of certain interministerial co-ordinating structures. These structures include both defence and military institutions as well as the committee which co-ordinates EC policy, the SGCI.

So great has been the perceived extent of presidential government that a whole range of convenient epithets have been conjured up to characterise his position in the system. For some, the President resembles a monarch. He is said to exhibit 'regal' characteristics.[5] He is said to be at the head of a country over which he 'reigns and governs at the same time'.[6] It was said during the Giscard d'Estaing presidency that: 'France is governed by an elected sovereign, a republican monarch, almost an enlightened despot'.[7] For others, he is not so much a king as an emperor. As Suleiman has noted:

> If the term 'imperial presidency' can be applied with any degree of validity, one might choose to apply it to the President of France rather than to his counterpart in the United States.[8]

Under Mitterrand the presidency has been apotheosised with the President being addressed as 'God', at least in popular parlance. Whatever the preferred epithet may be, the implication is the same, namely, that the President controls public policy. As Duhamel has noted:

> The French are scarcely aware of the fact, but their President is, by a long way, the most powerful chief executive in the West . . . once elected, his influence becomes literally hegemonic.[9]

If the President has been classified in a number of different ways, then so too has the Prime Minister. He has been variously described as the President's 'chief of staff',[10] an 'executive assistant'[11] and 'the effective head of the President's *cabinet*'.[12]

Under a system of presidential government, the role of the Prime Minister is twofold. In the first place, the Prime Minister is the President's loyal servant. For example, the Prime Minister only remains in office for as long as the President thinks it propitious. The President reserves the utterly unconstitutional right to dismiss the Prime Minister at a moment's notice. For example, Debré's situation applies equally to other Prime Ministers:

> The prime minister knew that his tenure of office depended entirely on his president's pleasure, since he himself could not make any claim to leadership of a parliamentary majority except as de Gaulle's spokesman and assistant.[13]

Subsequent Prime Ministers have reiterated their dual responsibility before both the President and Parliament. Secondly, the Prime Minister has no powers of policy initiation himself and only the slightest powers of decision making. Instead, he faithfully executes decisions which have previously been taken by the President. He has the task of co-ordinating the government's activity, but this activity will be decided by the President.

For many academic commentators, therefore, presidential government was a matter of observable reality. In their study of the Fifth Republic under de Gaulle, Williams and Harrison could only conclude that there was 'no dyarchy at the top'.[14] Moreover, de Gaulle's successors have all been seen to continue with the presidentialist tradition. Even Mitterrand, who was once so opposed to de Gaulle's exercise of power, has been said to be following in his predecessor's footsteps: 'His appetite for power knows no limits. The absolute monarchy is well and truly installed'.[15]

Segmented Decision-Making

By contrast to the previous situation, under the segmented decision-making model, responsibility for policy making and for the control of the services of the central state is not held by a single individual, be it the President or the Prime Minister, rather it is divided sectorally between them. Each institution has its own particular sphere of competence and there is little interaction between the two. Maus has claimed that: 'In practice, there is a careful division of responsibility between the President and the government'.[16] According to some observers, such a division dates back to the early years of de Gaulle's presidency and has been a constant feature of the Republic ever since. The motivation behind this division of responsibility between the President and Prime Minister is twofold. Firstly, the President's staff is relatively small and he does not have enough time to oversee the work of all government departments. Secondly, the President has a constitutional responsibility for certain foreign and defence policy decisions. There are two variants of this model; the traditional domain and the President's extended domain.

i. The traditional domain
The first presentation of the segmented decision-making model was given by Chaban-Delmas to the gaullist party congress at Bordeaux on 17 November 1959. Chaban-Delmas identified a presidential policy-making sector and a governmental one. The governmental sector was comprised of those areas in which the President chose not to intervene. The President's areas conformed to what Williams and Harrison have described as 'noble politics'.[17] Chaban-Delmas stated:

> The presidential sector consists of Algeria, without forgetting the Sahara, the French-African Community, foreign affairs and national defence. Everything else is open. In the first sector the government executes presidential decisions, in the second it decides for itself.[18]

The areas under the President's control were known collectively as his 'reserved domain'. In the areas which Chaban-Delmas identified, the President was wholly and individually responsible for policy making. For example, although Debré was personally opposed to de Gaulle's policy of Algerian independence, he was unable and unwilling to influence policy in this area. This was partly due to Debré's loyalty to de Gaulle, but also due to the fact that the Foreign, Defence and Algerian Ministers were loyal presidential acolytes. If need be, the President could rely on their support in order to push through a policy to which the Prime Minister was opposed. In addition, de Gaulle ensured that he controlled the administrative structures which co-ordinated policy in the areas of the reserved domain. So, for example, he chaired the defence council and in 1962 he streamlined its secretariat, the General Secretariat of National Defence, placing a loyal general at the head of the new organisation.

Outside of these areas, in the sphere of what Williams and Harrison called 'common politics', the Prime Minister was particularly influential. Not only did the initiative for policy making in these other areas lie, by and large, with the Prime Minister, but he was also responsible for decision making as well. Maus described this situation with regard to Debré:

> From 1959 onwards, de Gaulle left it up to Debré to give the necessary orders in all areas which did not impinge upon Algerian, State, or foreign affairs.[19]

In practice, this meant that the Prime Minister was largely responsible for all aspects of domestic policy-making. As Cohen described:

> As for the Prime Minister, he plays a small role in the formulation of foreign and defence policy, whilst he is at the forefront of economic and social policy-making.[20]

The 1961 Education Act, for example, was named after the Prime Minister of the day, Michel Debré. So, the Prime Minister was free of the President's tutelage and he enjoyed considerable freedom of action with regard to his Ministers, who rarely questioned the Prime Minister's authority to decide. In non-presidential areas, the Prime Minister also controlled governmental services, such as the Planning Commissariat and DATAR, the regional planning body.

The reserved domain continued after de Gaulle's departure and it has become an abiding feature of descriptions of core executive operations throughout the Fifth Republic. During the recent Gulf War, for example, relations between the President and the Prime Minister were said to follow this schema. Here, the President was responsible for deciding all substantive policy matters with regard to the crisis:

> All major decisions, be they diplomatic or military, were taken at the Elysée Palace and only at the Elysée Palace.[21]

The Prime Minister, by contrast, was responsible for ensuring the efficient execution of those decisions:

He was responsible for managing the economic and social consequences of the crisis. He was also in charge of interministerial co-ordination and the implementation of decisions . . . Finally, it was up to the Prime Minister, in accordance with the Constitution, to liaise with Parliament.[22]

Once again, therefore, the Mitterrand presidency can be seen to be a continuation of the traditional practices of the régime, rather than a break with the past.

ii. The President's extended domain

Over the years, although the notion of a presidential reserved domain remained plausible, the policy sectors in this domain changed. With the end of the Algerian conflict and the decline in the salience of the French Community, these two areas no longer figured among the President's policy sectors. Instead, Wright has argued that there are now five components to the President's reserved domain. These components are: the traditional domain, less Algerian policy; economic, financial and industrial matters; social and environmental issues; questions which suddenly appeared on the political agenda, because they were politically delicate or explosive (crises); and matters which attracted presidential attention for purely personal reasons.[23]

Economic policy and financial policy has been a part of the President's reserved domain since the end of the Algerian conflict in 1962. Since this time, de Gaulle felt able to intervene more broadly in the affairs of government. Economic independence was seen by him and subsequent Presidents as being as of equal importance as territorial independence. Thus, it became part of the reserved domain. So, for example, de Gaulle took the decision not to devalue the franc in 1968, while Mitterrand decided not to devalue in May 1981. Wright also argues that Giscard was particularly sensitive to social and environmental questions and that Mitterrand has followed his lead. Presidential intervention has also traditionally been seen during times of crisis. Crises are threats to the stability of the state and, as such, the President as constitutional guarantor of state continuity is naturally led towards dealing with such problems when they arise. In addition, all Presidents have had certain areas in which they have personally been interested. For example, Pompidou intervened in broadcasting policy, whilst Mitterrand has been keen to take decisions in the areas of culture and television policy.

This version of the segmented decision-making model has been promoted by various observers. For example, Massot has noted that:

Under Georges Pompidou, it was noted that the head of state's 'reserved domain' went beyond matters of defence and foreign affairs and included industrial development, education reform, urban growth and, above all, the broadcasting system.[24]

Moreover, Gaborit and Mounier have argued that the notion of the traditional reserved domain is outdated and that presidential interventions have occured over a much wider range of areas. They have stated:

> It would be more accurate to say that the president has at his disposal a power of strategic intervention which allows him to take up any governmental matter which seems to him to require a decision at the presidential level.[25]

Thus, as will be argued in Chapter 8, this variant of the segmented decision-making model in France is synonymous with the concept of limited presidential government.

Executive Co-operation

The executive co-operation model is derived from both constitutional theory and practice. According to this account, neither the President nor the Prime Minister is in a position to dominate the policy process, nor is there a clear division of responsibilities between the two institutions. Instead, in all policy areas responsibility for policy making is shared. In this sense, the two institutions co-operate together in the formulation of policy. According to its proponents, the executive co-operation model best sums up the operations of the Fifth Republic to date. One of de Gaulle's closest advisers has argued that during Debré's premiership:

> There was no dyarchy at the head of the state. In other words, there was no division of responsibilities between the President and Prime Minister, each one in charge of his own area, but the common exercise of power.[26]

The model of executive co-operation takes the Constitution as its starting point.

The Constitution was devised so as to force even unwilling Presidents and Prime Ministers to work together. Duhamel has described this situation:

presidential and prime ministerial powers are inextricably intertwined. The Prime Minister must countersign the President's ordinary acts, and those few that are especially exempted never concern, except for Art. 16's emergency powers, matters of public policy decisions.[27]

The Prime Minister proposes the names of future government Ministers to the President. The President chairs meetings of the Council of Ministers and, therefore, he is inescapably associated with the government's policies. The President's countersignature is needed for most prime ministerial decisions of any import, while the reverse is true for presidential actions. Even in the cases where the Prime Minister's approval is not formally necessary, the dissolution of the National Assembly, for example, the President is obliged to consult him.

In addition to these explicitly constitutional requirements, the President and Prime Minister will be obliged to co-operate with each other administratively on many other occasions. For example, the General Secretariat of the Government is obliged to collaborate with the General Secretariat of the Presidency in preparing the agenda for the Council of Ministers. Moreover, the President's advisers and the Prime Minister's advisers will meet along with ministerial representatives in the vast array of policy preparation meetings which are needed to prepare any government bill.

A good example of executive co-operation is defence policy. Whilst the President is commander-in-chief of the armed forces and while he chairs the *conseil de défense*, the Prime Minister is still formally and closely implicated in the elaboration of defence policy. For example, Article 21 of the Constitution states that the Prime Minister is responsible for national defence, whilst he is also officially in charge of the SGDN. In this case, however, prime ministerial involvement goes beyond simply the administrative preparation and execution of presidential decisions. The Prime Minister is present at the meetings of the *conseil de défense*, he intervenes in the debate and his contribution to the formulation of defence policy is considerable. Similarly, the responsibility for appointments is shared between the two institutions. Moreover, the interministerial co-ordinating structures, such as the SGDN and the SGCI, will report to both the President and the Prime Minister.

It appears, therefore, that executive co-operation goes beyond routine administrative consultation between the President and Prime Minister. Indeed, it has been argued that, for the smooth functioning of the system as a whole, the two parts of the executive have to work closely with each other. However, given the rivalry between the two institutions and the political ambitions of the protagonists, it is difficult for the President and Prime Minister to avoid conflict.[28] When the strains between the two protagonists become too great and co-operation is no longer possible, then the Prime Minister resigns, or is dismissed, and a new Prime Minister is appointed who is able to co-operate with the President. This is the escape valve that relieves the political pressure. This situation could account for the replacement of Debré by Pompidou; Pompidou by Couve de Murville; Chaban-Delmas by Messmer; Chirac by Barre; and Mauroy by Fabius. On each occasion, when co-operation was no longer possible, a new face was required, so as to allow normal service to be resumed.[29]

Prime Ministerial Government

In France, the prime ministerial government model was originally to be found only in juridical accounts of core executive behaviour. Such accounts were derived from studies of constitutional and administrative law and, as such, were often divorced from political realities. However, in 1986, the notion of prime ministerial government was extended from juridical accounts alone, so as to include an empirical analysis of the political situation. Following the victory by the right in the 1986 legislative elections, for the first time under the Fifth Republic, the presidential and parliamentary majorities were no longer synchronised. Consequently, Mitterrand had to appoint a Prime Minister, Jacques Chirac, who was acceptable to the National Assembly and who was, therefore, in outright oppostition to the President. Between 1986–88 during the period of *cohabitation*, Chirac was able to rely on the support of a favourable parliamentary majority, so as to be able to exercise political leadership in the country.

In the period immediately preceeding *cohabitation*, there were many good examples of the traditional, juridical approach to prime ministerial government. For example, in the run up to the 1986 legislative elections, there was a debate over the issue of whether or not, in the event of *cohabitation*, the President had the right to refuse the Prime Minister's request to sign a governmental ordinance.[30] A series of articles appeared in which the President's obligation to sign (an example of prime ministerial government), or his right to refuse were debated.[31] Article 13 of the Constitution states that: 'the President of the Republic signs such ordinances and decrees as have been considered by the Council of Ministers'. Much of the debate prior to the 1986 elections centred around the question of whether the term 'signs' (present tense) was tantamount to an imperative, or whether it still left the President with the option not to sign. In fact, the debate was purely academic. Mitterrand's eventual decision to refuse to sign the privatisation ordinance and Chirac's decision not to challenge the President's refusal were both arrived at out of pure political expediency, rather than out of any analysis of the wording of the Constitution.

With the onset of *cohabitation*, prime ministerial government became an observable reality. Prime ministerial leadership could be seen in a number of ways. Firstly, Chirac was able to control governmental appointments. Although the President is constitutionally responsible for certain appointments, such as ambassadors and the military chiefs of staff, the Prime Minister is also responsible for certain others. In the past, however, Prime Ministers tended to appoint people to these posts who were acceptable to the President. In this sense, the President, either directly or indirectly, controlled virtually all governmental posts. Under *cohabitation*, this situation changed. Chirac was able to appoint people whose loyalty was to the Prime Minister and the right-wing government, rather than to the President. For example, immediately on coming to office, Chirac dismissed the head of the GSG, Jacques Fournier, who was close to Mitterrand, and appointed Renaud Denoix de Saint Marc who had previously worked with the gaullist party. It should also be noted that, during this period, the President lost his *de facto* power to dismiss the Prime Minister.

Secondly, Chirac was able to increase the administrative resources available to the Prime Minister and, thus, strengthen his hold over the decision-making process.[32] For example, he created a seven-strong diplomatic cell within his *cabinet*, which informed and advised him about foreign policy matters. He worked more closely with the GSG than any previous Prime Minister. He also ensured that the secret services worked under his orders, rather than those of the President. This situation was seen most clearly with the events in New Caledonia immediately prior to the presidential elections in 1988.[33]

Finally, Chirac was able to assume control of the content of policy making. For example, it was the Prime Minister who decided which parts of the RPR/UDF's election platform should become law. Similarly, it was his decision to restore diplomatic links with Iran and to negotiate with the hostage takers in the Lebanon so as to secure the release of the remaining French hostages there. Such was the power of the Prime Minister during this period that, for the first time under the Fifth Republic, the Prime Minister was able to ally with government Ministers against the President, so that the latter was unable to intervene in policy preparation.

(3) **Ministerial Government**

Ministerial government has been described as the situation where the government 'has remained a federation of departments, each of which jealously guards its own political and administrative autonomy'.[34] In this case, the Minister is the chief policy maker in his/her particular area and, when compared with the variants analysed previously, the role of the President and the Prime Minister is much reduced. In contrast to previous theories, Rigaud has argued that the presidencies of de Gaulle and Pompidou saw the golden age of ministerial government in the Fifth Republic.[35]

In France there is little collective Cabinet authority.[36] The two institutions which could, in theory, serve as the basis of a system of Cabinet government are, in practice, peripheral to the policy process. The first of these institutions, the *Conseil de Cabinet,* a meeting of the government chaired by the Prime Minister in the absence of the President, used to meet regularly under Debré's premiership, but has met only rarely ever since. A short-lived attempt by Fabius and Chirac to revive it was quickly abandoned. The second institution, the Council of Ministers, a meeting of the government chaired by the President, is mentioned in the Constitution and meets weekly. However, meetings are short; there is little majority voting; Ministers rarely intervene outside of their portfolio areas; and substantive policy decisions are rarely taken. It ratifies policy decisions taken elsewhere.

By contrast to the absence of any collective Cabinet authority, Ministers are in a relatively strong position to influence policy in the areas for which they are responsible. This situation is partly the result of the country's Jacobin and Bonapartist past. Ministers have the support of a loyal set of personal advisers, the *cabinet.* They also stand at the head of Ministries which are generally characterised by a highly centralised permanent administration. In addition, some Ministers enjoy the support of a highly developed system of field services which play a major role in policy implementation. Other Ministries without these services can rely on the support of departmental Prefects to assist them in their work.[37]

Ministers also enjoy certain legal powers. For example, they appoint the departmental *directeurs d'administration*, although these appointments have to be made in the Council of Ministers and need the approval of the President and Prime Minister. In addition, Ministers are rarely subject to parliamentary scrutiny. For example, the Foreign Affairs Ministry is able to prepare treaties without parliamentary interference. Also, Ministers enjoy the right to make delegated legislation in areas agreed by Parliament. Thus, they can issue decrees which have the force of law. Whilst these decrees are scrutinised by the GSG and the Council of State, Ministers generally control the content of the decree.

The potential for ministerial government in France has also been helped because of the political stability of the governments of the Fifth Republic, at least when compared with their Third and Fourth Republic counterparts. Governments have remained in power for longer in the Fifth Republic and some Ministers have been able to develop a certain expertise and authority by remaining at the head of a Ministry for considerable periods of time. For example, at the time of writing, apart from the two-year gap during *cohabitation*, Lang has been Culture Minister since 1981.

The result of the strength that Ministers individually possess is that they control policy making in the area under their jurisdiction. Thus, for example, the Interior Ministry is responsible for matters of terrorism; the Foreign Affairs Ministry determines the position of France in disarmament negotiations;[38] and the Finance Ministry plays a major role in the annual preparation of the budget. Individual Ministers become personally identified with laws that they have drawn up. For example, Gaston Defferre was identified with the 1981–82 decentralisation reforms, as was Jean Auroux with the workers' participation laws in 1982.

It can be argued, therefore, that Ministers control their own areas of competence, even if they are unable to influence decision making in other policy areas. This situation leads to a compartmentalisation (*cloisonnement*) of the policy process. Ministers defend their own policy turfs.[39] The result is one of conflict between departments as interests collide. Interministerial committee meetings are the site of this conflict between different ministerial interests. Ministries will only unite when they have a common interest to do so. Even then, they will be uniting against other Ministries or coalitions of Ministries with opposing interests.

This situation is typically the one in which the President and, in particular, the Prime Minister are called upon to arbitrate. The arbitration function is fundamental to the role of the Prime Minister under a system of ministerial government. The Prime Minister will often have to decide between the conflicting demands of the various Ministers. The classic example of this arbitration function can be seen with the preparation of the annual Finance bill and the disputes between spending Ministers and the Finance Ministry. For the most part, the Prime Minister's decision will be final. On some occasions, however, an unlucky Minister may 'short-circuit' the Prime Minister and appeal to the President, so as to reverse the Prime Minister's initial arbitration. Thus, under ministerial government there is a hierarchy of arbitration with the President's decision being final.

(b) Bureaucratic Co-ordination Model

The final model of core executive operations to be examined is the bureaucratic co-ordination model. Studies of the French bureaucracy are legion. However, in the main, these studies are either sociological investigations of the higher administration, or attempts to construct a general élite theory of the state based on the peculiarities of the administrative training system. Whilst, therefore, there is no existing conceptual model of bureaucratic co-ordination, such as there is for Britain, it is possible to construct such a model for the French case.

The key element of the bureaucratic co-ordination model is that the political elements of the core executive have little or no control over the content of policy decisions. Instead, policy choices are determined by the bureaucratic elements of the core executive. In France, it might be argued that policy decisions are made by senior civil servants in the permanent administration and by members of ministerial *cabinets*. Thus, although the President, Prime Minister and senior Ministers seem to exercise control over the policy process, in fact, they are only articulating information processed beforehand by the higher administration. The political input in the policy process is small. The bureaucratic input into this process is great.

One of the key elements of the bureaucratic co-ordination model is the existence of a highly developed *cabinet* system in France. In the last chapter, the functioning of the Prime Minister's *cabinet* was described. However, the Prime Minister is not the only person who enjoys the support of such an organisation. Both the President and Ministers also have their own set of personal advisers who, whilst neither being permanent, nor technically civil servants during their period of employment, play a key role in the preparation of public policy. Ministers have up to ten advisers, whilst the President's team, like the Prime Minister's, may number up to fifty.[40] Members of ministerial *cabinets* confine their activities to the affairs of their own department.

The fundamental role of *cabinet* members is to provide their political mentor with substantive policy advice. Thus, they are in a position to regulate the information which Ministers receive about policy. They also have the opportunity to make policy decisions themselves. The first stage of the policy preparation process, interministerial reunions, is staffed largely by *cabinet* members alone. Members of the permanent administration may be present, but Ministers are not. As was noted in Chapter 1, these meetings are the site of substantive policy decisions. Although these decisions are usually of a technical, or juridical nature, they often determine the general orientation of legislation. Thus, *cabinet* members are well placed to determine the substance of government policy. In this respect, they are helped by their close relations with the permanent administration and by the traditionally powerful role enjoyed by the French bureaucracy.

The plausibility of the bureaucratic co-ordination model is increased by the nature of the French political culture. As described under the previous model, French political culture is state oriented.[41] At the national level, government departments are divided up into *directions* which are subdivided into *bureaux*. The head of each *direction* and *bureau* is a senior civil servant with expertise in and influence over his or her particular domain. Thus, whilst in France there is not the tradition of powerful permanent secretaries as there is in Britain, there are a host of senior administrators who hold a vital position in the policy process. It is their responsibility, in liaison with members of their Minister's *cabinet*, to prepare legislation and to co-ordinate the implementation of policy once it has become law. Therefore, the influence of Ministers in the policy process is slight. They are not well placed to question the policy recommendations which are presented to them by their *cabinet* members and by their departmental civil servants. The influence of the technocrats in the Finance Ministry is an example of this model at work.[42]

The strength of this model is further enhanced by the plethora of interdepartmental committees which play a crucial role in the policy process. In France, there is no system of permanent Cabinet committees as there is in Britain. Instead, there is a highly developed system of committees, commissions and secretariats each of which co-ordinates inter-departmental policy in a particular area, such as the SGCI, or the SGDN. In addition, there is the GSG, which provides secretarial assistance to the government and whose head is the Prime Minister's senior legal adviser. The expertise that these organisations have accrued over the years and the central position they enjoy in the policy process means that ministerial control of decision making is further reduced. This situation extends to the security services over whom politicians have little or no control.[43]

As in the British case, there are two variants of the bureaucratic co-ordination model. The first emphasises the relatively homogeneous nature of the French senior administration.[44] Top civil servants tend to be the sons and daughters of senior administrators. They come mainly from the Paris area. They also share a common educational background with a disproportionate number having studied at the Institut d'Etudes

Politiques in Paris, followed by the Ecole Nationale d'Administration, or the Ecole Polytechnique with a subsequent passage in one of the prestigious *grands corps*. These characteristics create a homogeneity of views and a shared approach to problem solving. Moreover, this background creates the possibility of linkages between administrators in government departments and between the administration and people of a similar background in the wider public and private sector.

The second variant stresses the impact of the bureaucracy, but denies that it is homogeneous.[45] Many senior administrators do not share this common background and of those that do there is competition between them. Rivalries between departments are so great and competition between *grands corps* is so fierce that the administration does not articulate any single view. Instead, temporary alliances will form between different Ministries and services in order to force through the policy that is in their common interest at that time. On other occasions the same Ministries and services may find themselves in conflict with each other when their interests diverge. The common aspect to both variants of this model is the absence of political control over the decision-making process.

Conclusion

It is possible, therefore, to identify six different models of core executive operations in France. Under each model the role of the President, the Prime Minister and the different components of the wider central government apparatus was seen to vary. However, as they are presented here, these models are mutually exclusive. There cannot be both presidential government and prime ministerial government, or both ministerial government and bureaucratic co-ordination at the same time. That is to say, the President cannot be exercising monocratic power at the same time as the Prime Minister. Similarly, if Ministers are able to dominate policy making, then the civil servants in their departments are not able to do so as well. If one institution is dominant, then all other institutions must be subordinate.

The question remains, therefore, as to which model of core executive operations best captures the relative influence in the policy-making process of the President, Ministers, bureaucrats and, particularly in the context of this study, the Prime Minister. Is there one model of core executive operations which captures the role and influence of the Prime Minister in the political system of the Fifth Republic? It is the task of the remainder of this book to find a suitable answer to this question. Indeed, in the final chapter, the six models of core executive operations identified above will be reconsidered in the light of the evidence derived from the case studies. It is necessary now to turn to these case studies and to examine the level of prime ministerial influence not in theory, but in practice.

3 Broadcasting Policy

The first set of case studies to be examined is in the area of broadcasting. Broadcasting is a particularly suitable candidate for study. As with any area dealing with fundamental public liberties, it is of considerable popular and political sensitivity. The problems surrounding the issues, options and governmental cleavages are, thus, accentuated. At the same time, throughout the course of the Fifth Republic, it has been an area in which the Prime Minister has been able to intervene directly, unlike other areas, such as foreign affairs, which have generally been controlled by the President. Moreover, the post-1981 period provided an excellent opportunity for comparative study as there were a number of important laws passed which fundamentally reorganised the broadcasting system.

For the first set of case studies, three of these laws have been chosen for study. The preparation and passage of the July 1982, September 1986 and January 1989 broadcasting acts will be examined. The three laws will be considered in turn, starting with the July 1982 broadcasting act. Once the examination of these laws is complete, some preliminary conclusions will be drawn as to the nature of the Prime Minister's influence in the policy process.

The July 1982 Broadcasting Act

Prior to 1981, French broadcasting was subject to strict central government control.[1] For example, there were no official private radio or television companies; the state broadcasting system was for the most part publicly financed; the system was administered by a large, bureaucratic organisation (called the ORTF from 1964–74), the subject itself of government control; the government appointed all of the top figures in the broadcasting organisation; and the Minister of Information would intervene directly to change the content of news broadcasts and other programmes when he saw fit.

The first major change to the system came with the election of Giscard d'Estaing as President and the passage of the 1974 broadcasting act. This law abolished both the Ministry of Information and the ORTF. The latter was split up into its constituent parts, so as to form seven independent organisations, with a degree of competition being introduced between them. Whilst this law did symbolise a break with the past, it was an ambiguous reform that left few people satisfied with the resulting situation. The Communist Party and some gaullists were nostalgic for the ORTF. The socialists, however, felt that the changes were merely cosmetic and that the government's ability to control the system was still as strong as ever. In addition, there were many malcontents within the broadcasting profession itself, with the loss of certain privileges enjoyed under the ORTF being the main grievance. It was against this background that in his 1981 presidential election campaign Mitterrand announced that a reform of the broadcasting system would be one of his legislative priorities. With the election of Mitterrand in May 1981 and the appointment of Pierre Mauroy as Prime Minister, the preparation of this reform began.

Much of the legislation passed during Mauroy's time as Prime Minister was derived from Mitterrand's 110 Propositions for Government, which formed the basis of his electoral campaign. However, only one of these propositions, number 94, dealt with broadcasting. Here, it was stated that:

> Television and radio will be decentralised and pluralist. Public service local radio stations will be allowed to be freely created. Their statutory obligations (*cahiers des charges*) will be set out by local authorities. A National Broadcasting Council will be created on which the representatives of the State will be in a minority. The rights of CB users will be recognised.

Clearly, these vague promises were no basis for a major reform of the broadcasting system.

The only other pre-election foundation for the bill was the report of one of the Socialist Party's internal policy commissions headed by François-Régis Bastide. However, for the most part the Bastide report was a critique of the 1974 reform, rather than a blueprint for any new law. Thus, with neither the 110 Propositions, nor the Bastide report going into any detail about the content of any future reforms, the new government and its Communications Minister, Georges Fillioud, had little basis from which to draw up the new bill.

In early June, an interministerial committee for broadcasting was created. Chaired by one of Mauroy's *cabinet* members, Jérôme Clément, the *conseiller technique* for broadcasting affairs, it included representatives from the Elysée and from the Ministries of Communication, Culture, Telecommunications, External Relations, Interior and the Budget. It held weekly meetings at Matignon and its official function was set down as follows:

The group will carry out the necessary technical and political syntheses. It will prepare the arbitrations which the government will have to make.[2]

Its task, therefore, was not to draw up the wording of the bill itself, but to co-ordinate the work of others. One of the first decisions taken by the committee was to set up five working parties, each one specializing in a different policy sector. These working parties were given the task of drawing up detailed legislative proposals for the government to act upon. Each working party had on average 12 members nominated by Mauroy in consultation with Clément and Fillioud, as well as the Culture Minister, Jack Lang, and the President's *cabinet*. Whilst most of those appointed had connections with the broadcasting industry, the majority were now also members of ministerial *cabinets*, suggesting their allegiance to the government. Moreover, a large number had also been associated in the past with the ORTF.

The committee also decided to set up a *commission de réflexion et d'orientation* under the aegis of the Prime Minister. The idea for such a commission originally came from Fillioud's *cabinet*, but it was quickly accepted by all the protagonists involved. Chaired by Pierre Moinot, a former member of the Court of Accounts, television scriptwriter and good friend of Jack Lang, the commission's function was to synthesize the conclusions of the working parties and to produce a detailed report for the Prime Minister. The nomination procedure for the commission's other 12 members involved the same people as for the working parties, with the addition of Moinot himself. The result was an experienced set of people, coming predominantly from the PS, PCF and MRG and which, therefore, reflected the composition of the governmental coalition.

The commission's report, however, did not simply reiterate the government's priorities, nor did it simply present a list of proposals which it knew that the government would favour. For example, many of its recommendations did not find their way into the final text of the bill. In fact, the commission was able to draw up its proposals relatively free from governmental interference. It was allowed to do so, firstly, because the government had little idea at this early stage of exactly what it wanted to see in the report and, secondly, because Moinot was sufficiently independent of mind and strong of character, so as to be able to complete his report without too much governmental intervention.

These early stages of the bill's preparation showed that the issues involved were much more complex than had originally been foreseen. Consequently, Fillioud abandoned his original plans to see the bill debated in Parliament in November and, instead, the details of the text were finalised by the government over the winter. At this stage the bill was being prepared by the different sets of ministerial advisers. For example, Lang's *cabinet* concentrated upon the clauses which concerned the cinema, while Louis Mexandeau's *cabinet* at the Telecommunications Ministry dealt with the new role of Télédiffusion de France (TDF). However, the Communications Ministry was responsible for the vast majority of the bill, while it also supervised the work of Lang's and Mexandeau's advisers. By contrast, Clément's role was more general. His interventions were not confined to any specific areas and he was free to intervene when and where he saw fit. A similar role was played by the President's advisers and, indeed, by Fillioud himself, as the Minister responsible for the bill as a whole.

Over the winter of 1981–82, Fillioud conducted a series of meetings with the representatives of the broadcasting unions. However, in an internal note to the Prime Minister, Fillioud stated that the aim of these meetings was to make the unions feel that they were involved in the decision-making process, rather than to make them in any way the co-authors of the bill.

> This consultation seems to me to be absolutely indispensable if we are to avoid the accusation by the trades' unions that we acted in a technocratic way and so that they do not find an excuse to oppose the reform for this reason.[3]

Indeed, it must be noted that the impact of the broadcasting unions on the content of the bill as a whole was small.

The interministerial committee chaired by Clément continued to meet throughout the course of the bill's preparation. In addition to these official intragovernmental meetings, there were also numerous unofficial meetings, or encounters. Both Cotta and Estier have described meetings to which they were invited at the President's country retreat along with Lang, Fillioud, Clément, Mexandeau, Fabius (the Budget Minister) and André Rousselet, Mitterrand's *directeur de cabinet* where the broadcasting bill was discussed.[4] Lang had at least one lunch with the communist Health Minister, Jack Ralite, during which the main subject of conversation was this bill.[5] Similarly, the contents of the bill were discussed on more than one occasion during the course of Mauroy's weekly meetings with the President and at the weekly breakfasts between these two and the leaders of the PS. The confidential nature of these meetings, particularly the latter two, makes it difficult to ascertain whether they served merely as an exchange of ideas, or as a place where policy decisions were taken. It was clear, though, that their importance was not negligible. The bill also passed through a series of other mandatory preparatory stages. There was a hearing before the Council of State; a presentation to the Council of Ministers on the 31st March 1982; and a debate in both the National Assembly and the Senate. In addition, the bill was submitted to the Constitutional Council which ruled against several minor clauses, meaning that the Act was finally promulgated on the 29th July 1982.

The Preparation of the 1982 Broadcasting Act

The July 1982 law was long and complex. It contained 110 articles covering the whole gamut of broadcasting issues. Even if it were possible, it would be impractical for the present study to examine each article individually, so as to identify the Prime Minister's influence. Therefore, whilst it is argued that the Prime Minister, either personally, or through his advisers, was involved to some extent in the preparation of all of these articles, it is only possible for this study to concentrate on certain key areas. Four such areas have been chosen, namely, the fate of the main public television companies, the composition and powers of the new independent regulatory authority, the Haute Autorité, and the question of whether or not advertising should be permitted on local radio stations. Each area will now be considered in turn, starting with the fate of the main public television companies.

The reform of the two main television companies, TF1 and A2, and of the country's only production company, the Société Française de Production (SFP), was always going to be of particular professional, political and public interest. In the end, it transpired that the debate surrounding these three organisations was typical of that on the bill as a whole.

The Moinot report recommended that TF1, A2 and the SFP be brought together under one company to be called the Société Nationale de Télévision (SNT). In fact, this proposal was a compromise between the two main tendencies to be found within the working parties and the Moinot commission and, indeed, within the PS, the government and the administration. In order fully to understand the exigencies behind this part of the 1982 broadcasting act, it is necessary to examine these two tendencies in detail.

The supporters of the first tendency, who may be called the 'statists', wanted to see a reconstruction of the ORTF. The supporters of the second tendency, or 'liberals', preferred to see a decentralisation of the broadcasting system. The two tendencies represented coalitions of different interests and ideologies.

The communists favoured the statist approach. This attitude can be ascribed to ideological reasons and the PCF's desire to see the state controlling the flow of information reaching the public. It can also be ascribed to pressure from the communist controlled trades-union confederation, the CGT, which had seen its bargaining power severely weakened as a result of the break up of the ORTF in the 1974 Act. Similarly, the Jacobin inspired component of the PS also favoured this approach, as it strengthened the role of the state.

/ Conversely, the PS's *autogestionnaire* component favoured the second tendency, as it was more consistent with its beliefs. Some government members also privately favoured the liberal approach precisely because it weakened the unions. They feared that a left-wing government would not be immune to future industrial action and that immediate steps had to be taken to minimise its effects. In the permanent administration, notably amongst the members of the Service Juridique et Technique de l'Information (SJTI), there was also a strong liberal trend which favoured the advent of private broadcasting companies and which saw this bill as the opportunity to take the first steps towards this aim.

These two tendencies were present in the Moinot commission. The former ORTF employees on the commission naturally favoured its reconstruction, whilst other elements, notably amongst the representatives of the permanent administration, were opposed to this measure. The proposal to create the SNT was a compromise between the two tendencies. Thus, instead of a complete return to the ORTF, the Moinot commission proposed the creation of what amounted to a mini-ORTF. This idea, however, received a mixed reaction from members of the government. Over the summer of 1981 Fillioud had made veiled references to the creation of an organisation which would harmonise the programme schedule of TF1 and A2. His statements had led people to believe that something akin to the ORTF was about to return.[6] However, the creation of anything akin to such an organisation, including the SNT, was opposed by certain key elements within the government. For example, Jérôme Clément was in favour of the more liberal approach, as was his close friend and presidential adviser for broadcasting, Jean-Louis Bianco. Two other figures at the Elysée also favoured this approach, Jacques Attali and Rousselet. In addition, the staff of the SJTI were vehemently opposed to any return to the ORTF.

This latter group played an important role during the preparation of the law. Although officially under the control of the Prime Minister, the SJTI was effectively managed by the Communications Ministry. In 1981, it was headed by Bertrand Cousin, a gaullist sympathiser who later became an RPR deputy before taking up a post in the Hersant press empire. Cousin, backed by the rest of the SJTI, not all of whom were gaullists, set out to oppose the statists with the desire to 'vendre une thèse', namely, that of the liberal viewpoint.[7] Despite the hostility between Fillioud and Cousin, at this stage the latter was indispensable to the new Minister because of his wealth of legal and technical knowledge of broadcasting matters and because of the loyalty of the rest of the SJTI to him. However, Cousin's knowledge was used by the SJTI to provide juridical arguments against the statist viewpoint and to have the bill worded in a way which was compatible with its beliefs. Indeed, their knowledge was used by Clément in a similar way to similar ends.

Faced with opposition from several members of the interministerial committee, the idea of the SNT was quickly rejected. However, a compromise still had to be reached which would satisfy Fillioud and the unions. The compromise which was finally agreed upon involved nationalising the SFP and agreeing new production contracts between the SFP and both TF1 and A2. Therefore, the public sector's role was increased, but within limits which were acceptable to Clément and the others.

Whilst the changes described above were important, the major innovation contained in the bill was the creation of an independent regulatory agency, the Haute Autorité. It was designed to act as a buffer between the state and the broadcasting companies and its creation was testimony to the government's desire to cut the infamous umbilical cord between the government and the broadcasting system. The idea of setting up the Haute Autorité was well received by almost all concerned.

The idea of creating an authority of some sort was mooted even before the 1981 elections. The Bastide report proposed the creation of a *Conseil national* with certain independent decision-making powers, where professionals and official representatives could meet and discuss policy. The idea of a smaller, more autonomous organisation, however, came from the Moinot commission's working parties and was adopted by Moinot as one of the central propositions of his report.

The idea of such an authority did not fall prey to the debate between the statists and the liberals. It was accepted by all, either enthusiastically, or because its symbolic value was high and because the Moinot report had created expectations which it was injudicious to disappoint.[8] One of the concomitant problems, however, concerned the composition of the future authority. There was no magic formula which suited everyone and each person had his own pet solution (see Table 3.1). It is noticeable that Moinot, the least political of the above, suggested the most apolitical of all the options. All of the others to a varying degree ensured that the left

Table 3.1   *Proposals for the composition of the Haute Autorité*

Name	Proposal
Moinot	3 President, 3 *grands corps*, 3 *Conseil National de l'Audiovisuel* (CNA)
Beck[9]	2 President, 2 National Assembly, 2 Senate, 3 CNA
Fillioud	3 President, 1 National Assembly, 1 Senate, 1 CNA, 1 broadcasting personnel
Attali [1]	3 President, 3 National Assembly, 3 Senate
Attali [2]	3 President, 1 National Assembly , 3 *grands corps*, 1 Senate, 1 *Conseil Economique et Social*
Mauroy	3 President, 4 Parliament, 2 *grands corps*

would be in a majority due to the make up of Parliament at that time. In a note to the President, Fillioud stated:

> The composition must be modified so as to guarantee both its independence and its 'political legitimacy'. On the one hand, Parliament and, on the other hand, representatives of the profession are effectively marginalised according to the proposed outline. It would be best, therefore, to reintroduce them in order to ensure a better fit between the composition of the Haute Autorité and the political majority in the country.[10]

The desire to ensure a favourable governmental majority was also one of Clément's objectives.[11] Thus, while he may have put forward the liberal viewpoint on some issues, this approach was complicated by his desire and the desire of others not to let the broadcasting system fall into the hands of the opposition. As one person stated, 'arbitrations don't happen by chance', pointing to at least one machiavellian motivation behind the government's decisions.[12]

Normally, when no common agreement could be found to a particular problem, it was up to the Prime Minister to arbitrate between the conflicting demands. However, given the importance of this issue and given the Prime Minister's own involvement, the only person left to arbitrate was the President himself. Indeed, the President paid close attention to the preparation of the text as a whole. It is clear that this matter was discussed at the Elysée on several occasions. Cotta tells of a dinner there in March 1982, which she attended alongside Clément, Rousselet and Fillioud, where the decision was taken to give the authority the same composition as for the Constitutional Council.[13]

This decision was an astute tactical move by Mitterrand. At the time the Council was accused of having an anti-governmental bias by some PS deputies because of its recent decisions concerning the government's nationalisation programme. Naturally, opposition deputies defended the Council's role. By choosing this configuration, therefore, Mitterrand effectively stifled any future opposition criticism that the Haute Autorité would be biased towards the government as, by extension, such an accusation would be a criticism of the Constitutional Council as well.[14] However, Fillioud did not change the text of the bill in line with this decision before it was presented to the Council of Ministers on 31 March 1982. Consequently, the traditional image of these meetings as being occasions to ratify decisions taken elsewhere was broken as, during the meeting, the President insisted upon returning to the formula agreed over lunch a few days earlier.

Usually presidential decisions are final, yet not so this one. On this occasion, the opposition majority in the Senate received the bill particularly well. Via their spokesman, Charles Pasqua, they let the government know that they would pass the government's text if only the Haute Autorité's composition were to be changed, so as to balance out the political forces within it. Once again Mitterrand had to decide and he agreed to Pasqua's proposal, feeling that a common text voted by both Chambers would increase the consensual appearance of the bill. By chance, however, at the same time, Gaston Defferre, the Minister of the Interior, announced the law splitting up Paris, Marseille and Lyon into separate *arrondissements*. This bill was seen, quite rightly, as an attempt to weaken Chirac's hold over Paris as mayor. In retaliation, therefore, the RPR leader ordered Pasqua to withdraw the deal and to vote against the broadcasting bill. Pasqua duly complied. As a result, the Haute Autorité's composition returned to the formula agreed in the Council of Ministers.

The question of what powers the new authority was to have was also of great importance. One of the interesting aspects that this question highlighted was that of the role of the Council of State and the Constitutional Council in the policy process. The former is usually ignored in any study of policy preparation, while it is only recently that the latter has been the subject of any detailed study. Their influence on the wording of this law, however, cannot be ignored.

Fillioud had proposed that the Haute Autorité should be allowed the power to grant airspace to broadcasting companies. However, the Council of State argued that airspace could only be conceded by the government directly and recommended that the proposal be withdrawn from the text. The Council of State arrived at this decision because it considered airspace to be immaterial and that organisations other than the government had previously only been allowed to grant concessions for material things. Although the government was not obliged to abide by the recommendations of the Council of State, on this occasion the Prime Minister decided to let the matter drop, rather than pursue the matter any further and risk a confrontation with the Council of State.

The role played by the Constitutional Council was also important. One of the main criticisms of the Act following its passage was that the Haute Autorité had few powers to sanction broadcasting companies which ignored their statutory obligations as laid out in their *cahier des charges*. This lack of powers, however, was not due to any intention on the government's part to create a weak authority, but because of the fear that the Constitutional Council would strike down any such powers if they were included in the bill. At that time, the only agency which had been given such powers was the Commission des Opérations de la Bourse. This commission, however, had been set up under the Fourth Republic and neither the jurists within the SJTI nor the ministerial *cabinet* members knew whether or not under the Fifth Republic's Constitution such powers were permissable. As a result, it was decided to play safe and the government watered down the Haute Autorité's sanction powers, providing a perfect example of *autolimitation*.[15]

As for the other powers of the new authority, it was quickly apparent that the recommendations of the Moinot commission went too far for the government. In a note to the President, Fillioud stated:

> adopting the proposed outline would make it impossible ever to be able to draw up and put into effect a coherent governmental broadcasting policy.[16]

Even those people usually associated with the liberal stance, such as Clément and Bianco, were not keen to accept Moinot's proposals in their entirety. Bianco, for example, refused to accept the proposition that the Haute Autorité be given the power to share out the licence fee revenue amongst the public television companies.

This consensus within the government formed shortly after the publication of Moinot's report. The *cabinets* of the leading Ministers, the Prime Minister and the President were all generally in agreement about the amount of power to be accorded to the authority. It was agreed that the authority's powers should be relatively modest. As a result of this consensus at the highest level, this aspect of the bill was dealt with almost entirely in interministerial reunions where the only people present were *cabinet* members. Indeed, it did not even figure on the agenda of the interministerial committee chaired by the Prime Minister in the presence of the relevant ministers. Whilst it did crop up during a meeting at the Elysée, the President did not intervene, preferring to leave the matter to his advisers.

In contrast to the previous example, the question of whether advertising should be permitted on local radio was debated primarily in the higher échelons of the government. The conflict centred upon the diverging opinions of the Prime Minister and Communications Minister. Despite the fact that the Moinot report came out in favour of advertising, Mauroy and Fillioud had already hardened their positions over the summer of 1981. The speed with which the two protagonists formulated their arguments followed on from the decision taken in June 1981 to draw up a bill dealing with the local radio issue separately from the main broadcasting bill so as to legislate on this issue more quickly. The local radio stations act was passed in November 1981. The passage of this act meant that a preliminary presidential arbitration on the question of advertising was necessitated in the summer of 1981. This arbitration went in Mauroy's favour. The preparation of the July 1982 act, however, provided an opportunity for Fillioud to reverse this decision and the matter was discussed again.

Fillioud was in favour of allowing advertising. He felt that it was essential if the stations were to survive financially. He was supported by the advertising companies. Mauroy, however, was opposed to this measure. In part, his decision was motivated by ideological reasons. There was a long-term and widespread belief within the PS that advertising on radio or television lowered the cultural quality of programmes. Mauroy identified with this tradition and once in power he reiterated it, talking of '*radios-fric*' to describe the resulting situation. Equally important, however, was the coalition of local interests which formed around the Prime Minister's viewpoint. This coalition consisted of representatives of the local and regional press, whose financial survival was closely linked to their existing advertising agreements. The previous few years had seen an explosion of local radio stations and the press felt that if advertising on them were to be allowed, then its future would be in doubt.

One of the most important figures in this coalition was Gaston Defferre, the Minister of the Interior and mayor of Marseille, who had a controlling interest in much of the area's press. Mauroy, too, as mayor of Lille, was not unconcerned personally by the matter. Their insistence, backed up by the close relations both of them shared with Mitterrand, meant that Fillioud was unsuccessful. Giesbert recounts the meeting at the Elysée:

You are quite right, the President said to Fillioud, but in a matter such as this I cannot go against the wishes of the Prime Minister.[17]

Consequently, the 1982 law made no provision for advertising on local radio and it was only later that the coalition against it weakened, thus making it possible.

The September 1986 Broadcasting Act

In many respects the 1982 act represented a watershed in the history of French broadcasting. Once it had been passed, for example, the support for a return to the ORTF came only from certain isolated elements within the PCF. Moreover, the existence of an independent authority was widely recognised to be an essential component of the system. Nevertheless, major disagreements did remain about the future of broadcasting. These disagreements were exacerbated by the arrival on the scene of new media issues from 1982 onwards.

Between 1982 and 1986, the old media debate centred primarily around the role of private television within the broadcasting system. The creation of Canal + by Rousselet in 1983 with Mitterrand's benediction effectively ended this debate. Indeed, in 1985, Mitterrand announced the formation of two further private stations, channels 5 and 6. Their franchises, however, were awarded to industrialists close to the PS and the opposition was enraged. Their anger was also directed at the Haute Autorité, partly because the government had a clear majority on it, but also because it lacked the powers to assert itself, even on those occasions when it wished to do so. Combined with other latent difficulties, such as the SFP's continuing budget deficits, a major reorganisation of the system became one of the opposition's legislative priorities in the run up to the 1986 legislative elections.

This traditional area of difficulties, however, was combined with problems surrounding the new media. The 1982 cable television plan had been a financial and organisational disaster and the progress of satellite broadcasting was slow. Both of these issues highlighted the interrelationship between policy and technology. New media initiatives were costly, involved numerous national and international industrial concerns and, in the French case, were dogged by sometimes less than expert bureaucratic intervention. Therefore, having committed itself to a new law, Chirac's government was faced with a variety of complex problems in the area of both old and new medias.

When it came to power in March 1986, the right-wing government was generally much better prepared than the socialists had been in 1981. This situation was particularly true in the area of broadcasting. In May 1984, Chirac delivered a major speech, mostly drafted by Bertrand Cousin, in which he detailed his own policy objectives. Then, throughout 1985, the opposition parties worked together to produce the 1986 election platform. This platform included specific engagements to privatise two television companies and to embark upon a complete reform of the telecommunications sector. In charge of the opposition's pre-election working party on broadcasting was Xavier Goyou-Beauchamps, ENA graduate and former adviser to Giscard d'Estaing as President. His work led to Giscard himself proposing a private members bill in January 1986, in which he outlined his plans for the broadcasting system.

The March 1986 elections saw the appointment of François Léotard as Minister for Culture and Communications. Although he was not at his first-choice Ministry, Mitterrand having vetoed his appointment as Defence Minister, Léotard still ranked fourth in the governmental hierarchy and was determined to make an impression at his new job. He was backed up by Philippe de Villiers as Secretary of State for Communications, but Léotard's ambition meant that at no stage during the bill's preparation did de Villiers play anything other a minor role.[18]

Instead, Goyou-Beauchamps was appointed by Léotard, slightly reluctantly but on Giscard's insistence, to help draft the bill. Nominated on April 1st, Goyou-Beauchamps immediately called upon the SJTI's expertise in order to draw up the law. On this occasion, the SJTI provided classic administrative support to the Minister and his advisers and did not attempt to influence the wording of the bill, despite the fact that the head of the organisation, Marc-André Feffer, had been appointed by the socialists. Goyou-Beauchamps's starting point was Giscard's January bill, although this was quickly abandoned as it proved to be insufficiently detailed.[19]

One of the first decisions to be taken was that of dropping the proposed telecommunications reform. This decision was taken by Chirac personally after a meeting at the beginning of April with André Bergeron, the head of the trades' union confederation, the Force Ouvrière (FO), in which he made it clear to the Prime Minister that any hasty reform would be likely to result in strike action.[20] With Chirac remembering the 1974 strike by telecommunications workers, which he had had to face when Prime Minister before, and with only two years until the presidential elections, he abandoned the idea of any immediate reform.

As part of the preparation process, Léotard arranged four meetings with professionals from the broadcasting industry in mid-April. However, these meetings had no real outcome on the bill as a whole and served merely as a media exercise.[21] In fact, the first draft of the bill was drawn up by Goyou-Beauchamps and leaked to the press on April 24th. This leak was not at all appreciated by Chirac whose advisers still had to go through the project and whose arbitrations were still to come. The Prime Minister refused to be put before a *fait accompli*, something which was affirmed the next day by Denis Baudouin, the government spokesperson. As a result, there followed numerous interministerial reunions chaired by José Frèches, Chirac's adviser on broadcasting affairs, until only major disagreements remained. When these meetings were completed, a series of interministerial committees were held. These committees were chaired by Chirac himself. As with the 1982 law, it must be noted that there were also many informal meetings, organised by Léotard alone, or by Chirac and his advisers, where the bill was discussed and whose influence on the final wording cannot be dismissed.

As the bill went before the Council of State on June 5th and then to the Council of Ministers on June 11th, the one thing notable for its absence throughout the whole process was any presidential intervention. Mitterrand did not intervene personally during the preparation of the bill, except after the Council of Ministers to say that he feared for the bill's effects on basic freedoms. Neither did his advisers attend any preparatory meetings, or even try to contact government members, or their advisers. They kept the President informed of the bill's progress, but were not implicated at any stage in its preparation.

During the Council of Ministers, the Prime Minister decided to call an extraordinary parliamentary session so as to allow the bill to be passed during the summer, rather than waiting for the normal parliamentary recall in October. The bill was examined firstly by the Senate. It was poorly received, especially by the Senate's special commission. There, the RPR's spokesperson, Adrien Gouteyron, proposed over 120 amendments on the commission's behalf. In all, over 1,800 amendments were drafted by the Senators, the vast majority by the PS/PCF minority in an attempt to delay the bill's passage. It was finally passed on July 24th after 180 hours of debate, the longest in the history of the Senate.

The debate in the National Assembly was much shorter, starting on August 4th and finishing four days later due to Chirac's authorisation of the use of Article 49–3 of the Constitution to truncate discussion. After the meeting of the parliamentary mixed parity commission, the bill was finally passed on August 12th. The PS deputies, however, then placed it before the Constitutional Council, whose decision came a month later in which several important points were struck down, causing anger in the government ranks.

The Preparation of the 1986 Broadcasting Act

Given the range of issues covered and the complexity of the questions involved, it proved to be impossible to keep the text of the bill short. In the end, the law contained 110 articles, the same number as in 1982. Once again, it is impossible to study all of these articles and so three of the act's major reforms have been chosen, namely, the composition of the regulatory agency which replaced the Haute Autorité, the choice of which television channel to privatise and the conditions under which this privatisation was to take place. These reforms are representative of the problems faced during the preparation of the text as a whole.

In a press conference in 1984, Chirac had already stated that it was his intention to replace the Haute Autorité and he even suggested a name for the proposed new authority, La Commission Nationale de la Communication et des Libertés (CNCL). The Haute Autorité's fate seemed to be sealed when Giscard's private members bill in January 1986 also proposed its replacement. However, just before the March 1986 elections, Chirac suddenly changed his mind and told Michelle Cotta, the Haute Autorité's president, that he had dropped any plans to abolish it. Cotta recalled a conversation she had at this time with Chirac in which he said:

> I believe in institutions. This is one and it has proved itself. I see no reason to change it.[22]

Once in power, however, the new Prime Minister came under pressure from both Léotard himself and from the parliamentary majority once again to replace the Haute Autorité with a new agency. Chirac, faced with their insistence and not believing this to be an issue on which he felt strongly enough to assert his authority, bowed to their pressure and agreed to have the Haute Autorité replaced.

As in 1982, one of the most difficult problems facing the government was the composition of the new agency. In 1984, Chirac had proposed that the President of the Republic should appoint one member with six others to be nominated by the *grands corps* and the different Académies. On the other hand, in January 1986, Giscard suggested that it should consist only of representatives from the *grands corps* and, consistent with Goyou-Beauchamps's original directive, it was largely this formula that figured in the first draft of the bill in April 1986. Here, three people were to be appointed by each of the three *grands corps*, namely, the Council of State, the Court of Appeal (*Cour de Cassation*) and the Court of Accounts. These three people would then co-opt three professionals from the broadcasting sector and these six would proceed to co-opt one further member.

This proposal, however, met with opposition from Matignon, most notably from Maurice Ulrich, Chirac's *directeur de cabinet*. Ulrich's position meant that he had a overall view of the policy process, but he followed the passage of this bill with particular interest because of his long experience of the broadcasting system, notably as head of A2 until 1981. While Ulrich was not opposed to the presence of the *grands corps*, he felt that the agency would lack legitimacy without any political representation.[23] Not being a decision, however, which could be agreed upon at the level of interministerial reunions, the matter was discussed at an interministerial committee in May 1986. This meeting was chaired by Chirac in the presence of other senior ministers and Ulrich. At this meeting Ulrich's viewpoint prevailed. Léotard was unwilling to insist upon the formula as outlined in the first draft of the bill, preferring to compromise on this issue so as to win on others. It was decided, therefore, that the President of the Republic and the Presidents of the two parliamentary Chambers would each appoint one person to the CNCL. Three people would be named by the *grands corps*, whilst these six would then co-opt three others. Not only did this formula give the agency more legitimacy, but it was also designed to give it a right-wing majority due to the traditionally conservative nature of the *grands corps* and the right wing parliamentary majority at that time. This was the formula adopted in the Council of Ministers on June 11th.

Immediately, however, the government came under pressure to alter the composition. Both the RPR and the UDF groups in the National Assembly had set up their own working parties to study the bill and both reached different conclusions to the government and to each other as to the best formula. More importantly, on June 12th, Chirac received a letter from three members of the Académie française formally requesting that their organisation be represented on the CNCL. This initiative was inspired by a dual motivation. Firstly, the Académie was seen as the guardian of French culture and, therefore, it would not be out of place on the CNCL. This argument was popular amongst those people who were worried by the prospect of cultural standards being lowered following the privatisation of TF1. Secondly, the people who proposed the idea and those who were behind the proposal, notably Academicians Alain Peyrefitte and Edgar Faure, were close to the Hersant press and broadcasting group. The proposal was one way in which Hersant could be assured of a voice on the CNCL. Indeed, the implications of this proposal were not lost on at least one adviser at Matignon.

From this point on, two things were clear: firstly, neither Chirac nor Léotard was willing to battle on this question[24] and, secondly, the naked intention of at least the parliamentarians was to ensure that the CNCL would be endowed with a right-wing majority. The matter came to a head in early July with the examination by the Senate of the CNCL's composition. The special senatorial commission on broadcasting had two options which it preferred to the government's. The first involved a commission of nine members: three appointed by the three Presidents as before, three by the *grands corps* and one by the Académie française, with these seven to co-opt two others. The second was that of a 12-member commission with the same formula, but with the Presidents naming six people between them. The matter was finally decided over a lunch at Matignon on July 3rd in a meeting which brought together senior government Ministers and leaders of the parliamentary majority.

At this meeting and despite Ulrich's opposition, it was first of all decided to accept the introduction of a member nominated by the Académie française. This proposal made the Hersant group happy and it would be likely to lead to a right-wing appointment. However, the parliamentarians were not sure that this measure by itself would ensure a right-wing majority. They believed that the *grands corps*, after five years of socialist rule, might elect people unfavourable to the government. It was remarked, for example, that the President of the Court of Accounts, André Chandernagor, was a socialist and that both he and the vice-President of the Council of State were known to frequent the Elysée from time to time. In order to be sure of a right wing majority, therefore, it was decided to follow the Senate's second option and to double the number of people appointed by the three Presidents and to increase the number of people co-opted to three, bringing the number of members up to thirteen.

The above example is a good illustration of the nature of the Prime Minister's role during *cohabitation*. In all of the decisive meetings concerning the composition of the CNCL, it was the Prime Minister's arbitration which was final. There was no higher authority which could question his decision. There was no person to whom those people who had been defeated could turn in order to try and have the decision reversed. In this way, the Prime Minister's role during this period was reminiscent of that of the President previously. While, this situation represented a sea change in the policy making process of the Fifth Republic, it was the norm between 1986 and 1988.

The choice of which television channel to privatise was an equally divisive issue. The metamorphosis of the traditionally state orientated gaullists into fully fledged neo-liberals took place progressively throughout the early part of the 1980s, at least at the level of the party leadership. One of the earliest manifestations of this transformation was Chirac's 1984 press conference during which he proposed the privatisation of two television companies, one of which was to be FR3, though the other was not specified. A similar commitment to the number of companies to be privatised was contained in Giscard's January 1986 bill and in the March 1986 RPR-UDF election platform. Once again, Goyou-Beauchamps took Giscard's bill as his starting point and he proposed the choice, with Leotard's full approval, of A2, plus a complete reorganisation and a partial privatisation of FR3. However, within a month of coming to power, conflicting positions had formulated within the government and the choice of the number of channels to be privatised proved to be highly controversial.

Two questions were discussed in interministerial committee meetings. Firstly, the number of channels to be privatised and, secondly, which channels were to be chosen. Meetings were held on the 12th and 14th May to decide these questions. At these meetings Chirac (the chairman), Ulrich, Léotard, Longuet, Balladur (the Finance Minister), Madelin (Industry), Juppé (Budget), Cabana (Privatisation), Pasqua (Interior) and Chalandon (Justice) were present.

Ulrich was in favour of privatising only one channel. As early as January 1986, he had written to Chirac to warn of the dangers of a full-scale reform of the broadcasting system.[25] The lack of time before the 1988 presidential elections and the social problems that such a reform would induce were the main reasons for his fears. In this view he was backed up by Frèches and by a significant part of the RPR, particularly in the Senate. This latter group represented the traditional tendency within the party which preferred to see changes amongst the public sector personnel, rather than a reorganisation of the system. They made their views known to Chirac before the interministerial committee meetings were held.

At the same time, it had become clear even amongst Léotard's closest advisers that the mechanics of privatising a television company were much more difficult than had at first been thought. The problems involved were highly complicated and a different procedure to the government's other privatisations would have to be adopted. As a result, Leotard did not insist upon the immediate privatisation of two channels, but only on a long-term commitment to a second. Despite Léotard's liberalism and the opposition's electoral commitment, therefore, it was decided to privatise only a single company.

The decision as to which company to choose was much more difficult. Léotard and his Republican Party (PR) colleagues, Gérard Longuet and Alain Madelin, had publicly come out in favour of A2. To choose anything other than this channel, therefore, would be to embarrass the Minister who supposedly had responsibility for the bill. It would also create an unfavourable climate between the RPR and the PR and, indeed, the UDF as a whole, because behind the scenes Giscard had supported Léotard's choice of A2. Having refused the privatisation of two channels and with Chirac wanting to count upon the full support of the UDF at any future second round presidential election ballot, the Prime Minister could only go against Leotard's option with great difficulty.

Chirac's own advisers, however, were strongly in favour of the choice of FR3 and had been lobbying the Prime Minister to this end for several weeks. Ulrich felt that FR3 represented the least destabilising option and that it would also rid the state of the station's enormous financial deficit which had accrued over the years.[26] Others, more cynically, believed that Ulrich was trying to protect his former interests at A2. In any case, Ulrich was supported by Frèches and, indeed, by Hersant who saw the opportunity here to increase his influence.[27] Unfortunately for this group, the technical problems associated with a privatisation of FR3 were even greater than those of any other station because of its decentralised structure. In addition, a week before the interministerial committee, Chirac had met with representatives of the regional press lobby and, having mooted the possibility of privatising FR3, found that they were strongly opposed to the measure, seeing their interests threatened.[28]

At the first interministerial committee meeting, both Ulrich and Léotard put forward their respective views and neither were willing to back down. Towards the end of the meeting, first Balladur and then Madelin suggested that as a compromise TF1 ought to be considered. This proposal came too late to be fully discussed and another meeting was scheduled for two days later. In the meantime, Ulrich addressed another letter to the Prime Minister in favour of FR3, whilst Léotard contacted Giscard who between them decided that either TF1, or A2 would be acceptable, although their preference was for the latter.[29]

The second meeting followed the same course as the first with neither Ulrich nor Léotard changing their views. In the face of a renewed attempt at a compromise in favour of TF1 by Balladur, Chirac came to see this solution as a way out of the impasse and it was accepted by Léotard.

Although clearly a compromise, TF1 was chosen for seemingly sound financial, technical and political reasons. It was losing as much money as FR3, therefore, the government's budgetary problems would be eased; its privatisation was technically easier than that of FR3; it was already a generalised, commercial channel, which was likely to make it appealing to investors; it was sufficiently important so as not to be seen as a snub to

Léotard; and its chairman was Hervé Bourges, a socialist, who would be obliged to leave once privatised. Therefore, although a compromise, there was reasoning behind Chirac's arbitration.

Apart from discontent within the company itself, the choice of TF1 was not well received by everyone within the governmental coalition. The question came up for discussion again during the debate on the bill in the Senate. The existence of a conservative element within the RPR senatorial group has already been noted, but the senatorial majority as a whole was highly critical of the text. They argued that it had been drawn up in haste and that they had not been consulted by Léotard. The result was that a large number of amendments were proposed and the bill advanced only very slowly.

After two weeks of the extraordinary parliamentary session and with only 30 articles having been examined, Jean-Pierre Fourcade, president of the senatorial commission, asked Chirac to convoke a meeting at Matignon to discuss the bill's future.[30] At this meeting it was proposed on behalf of the senatorial majority that, in order to speed up its passage, the bill should be split into two parts, namely, the privatisation of TF1 and the rest. It was also proposed that the examination of the first part should be delayed until the autumn. While Frèches was in favour of this option, Léotard was violently opposed.[31] The Minister had already been criticised for his handling of the bill in the Senate and saw this proposal as undermining his authority even further. The Prime Minister arbitrated in Léotard's favour, fearing Léotard's immediate resignation and electoral repercussions by the UDF at the next elections if he did not. Chirac was also aware of the technical difficulties involved in cutting up such a complex bill. In return, the Senate's standing orders were scrutinized and a way was found to accelerate the passage of the bill without resorting to it being split up.

Once the choice of channel had been made, the problem remained as to how it should be privatised. One of the most difficult sections of the bill concerned the privatisation procedure for TF1. The mixture of technical and political difficulties that the government faced led to what one adviser called '*un débat sanglant*'. These difficulties started immediately after the government's formation, even before the decision over which channel to privatise had been taken.

As Finance Minister, Balladur had been given the responsibility of preparing the bills for all of the companies chosen by the government for privatisation. Naturally, he assumed that his brief would include that of the chosen television company as well. Léotard, however, informed Chirac that, as Culture Minister, he ought to control this process. His request was formally put to the Prime Minister on 24 March 1986:

> The preparation and implementation of legislation concerning certain bodies and businesses in the communication sector are clearly a matter for my Ministry. Anything else would have the practical effect, given the government's programme, of taking away the 'communication' dimension from my department.[32]

In part, this demand was an example of the normal jockeying for position that occurs at the start of any new administration. Ministers generally know that if they lose control of a certain sector at the start, it is very difficult to win it back later on. Here, two Ministers were engaged in competition for the control of the same sector, thus necessitating a Prime Ministerial arbitration. Chirac's decision favoured Balladur. This decision was consistent with the logic of the other privatisations, but it also reflected the Finance Minister's close ties with the Prime Minister, something that was also shown in the budgetary negotiations at this time. All witnesses asserted, therefore, that the details of TF1's privatisation were largely controlled by Balladur and Jacques Friedman, his economic adviser.[33] In all humility, Léotard now asserts that his Ministry would not have had the administrative resources to draw up these details by itself.[34] At the time, therefore, he was obliged to work alongside Balladur.

Once the choice of TF1 had been made, Balladur was able to start detailing the manner in which it would be privatised. It was immediately clear that TF1 was a special case and that a different procedure to the other privatisations would be necessary. In fact, the final text was a mixture of the normal privatisation procedure as adopted by the government for the rest of its programme and the assurance that the cultural obligations required from a national television company would be respected. This mixture was testimony to the specificity of TF1, but also reflected the way in which Léotard and his *cabinet*, along with Frèches, worked alongside Balladur and Friedman.

For every other privatisation, an independent commission set the minimum share price of the company, with the Finance Minister then being free to offer the shares at whatever price he saw fit, so long as it was not below the minimum level. Usually, the price was not fixed far above the minimum, so that a large number of potential investors would be willing to put in a bid. The government then allotted a fixed percentage of shares to be placed in the hands of a stable set of investors, or *noyau dur*, personally selected by Balladur.

With regard to the privatisation of TF1, there was never any question that the Privatisation Commission would not be called upon to fix a minimum price. The first difficult decision, however, was whether the government, or the CNCL should appoint the *noyau dur*. In fact, this matter was resolved rather quickly, as all were agreed that to avoid giving the impression that the government still controlled the system, it should be the CNCL.

Much more divisive was the question as to what the criteria were to be by which the CNCL chose the stable set of investors. There were those people who wanted to see the application of a purely financial criterion, whereby the group that offered the most amount of money for the channel would be awarded it. This proposal was described as the '*mieux disant financier*' option.[35] Then, there were those people who argued that the decision should be based on a different criterion, such as the group's obligations to the amount of educational programmes it would broadcast, or its commitment to children's programmes, for example. Instead, Léotard himself invented the notion of the '*mieux disant culturel*', whereby the CNCL would choose the group which met or bettered the minimum price, but which also committed itself to the maximum number of cultural obligations. This decision was inspired by the desire to avoid the accusation that the channel would simply go to the highest bidder and was designed to show that privatisation did not necessarily entail a decline in cultural standards. This formula was accepted by Chirac and Balladur and was laid down in Article 64 of the law.

The other major decision involved the maximum percentage of shares that any one person could hold in the company. The original ordinance laying down the general rules for the privatisation programme was very vague on this point. No maximum percentage was specified. Therefore, it was up to the government to fix the limit in each case. With regard to TF1, the debate centred around the competing proposals of Léotard and Balladur. Léotard, in conformity with a recognised principle of company law, put forward a threshold of 33.3 per cent, or the minimum amount which provides a veto over company policy decisions. Balladur, on the other hand, wanted a widespread dispersal of capital, with a maximum of 15 per cent. Indeed, this was the figure that appeared in Goyou-Beauchamp's first draft of the bill, reflecting Balladur's influence over the privatisation details. When Léotard challenged this figure, however, Chirac was again called upon to arbitrate. Indeed, the Prime Minister accepted a suggestion made by Ulrich.[36] Namely, that a compromise figure of 25 per cent should be chosen, whereby both Ministers would be satisfied. This figure also represented the level at which the majority shareholding for the other privatisations had been fixed.

The January 1989 Broadcasting Act

In the short period between the promulgation of the *Loi Léotard* and the May 1988 presidential elections, the main problems in the area of broadcasting surrounded the CNCL itself. Its right wing majority was immediately criticised by the opposition once the names of its members were made known. It suffered internal problems due to a divisive presidential contest between two of its members, Gabriel de Broglie and Jean Autin. One of its first decisions was the highly controversial reattribution of the franchises of the fifth and sixth television channels, La 5 and M6, to people broadly associated with the new government, with the former largely coming under Robert Hersant's control. It was accused of pro-governmental bias in its handling of the 1987 New Caledonian referendum. In addition, its reputation was badly tarnished when one of its members, Michel Droit, the representative of the Académie française, had to leave due to allegations that he had illegally awarded franchises to certain local radio stations in which he had an interest.

It was against this background that Mitterrand called the CNCL, *'peu digne de respect'*, in a newspaper interview in late 1987. In his election manifesto, the *Lettre à tous les Français*, Mitterrand pledged that, if re-elected, the CNCL would quickly be abolished. He added, rather ironically, that the CNCL, *'aura eu le mérite de montrer ce qu'il ne fallait pas faire'*. After the elections, a new Communications Minister, Catherine Tasca (a former, but untarnished, CNCL member and presidential confidante), was appointed with the responsibility for drafting a new law aimed at replacing the ephemeral CNCL.

Even more than most election manifestos, the *Lettre à tous les Français* was a relatively vague and undetailed document. The fact that in the letter the section on broadcasting only dealt with the replacement of the CNCL seemed to rule out any major reorganisation of the system. Similarly, any plans to renationalise TF1 also seemed to be ruled out due to the presidential commitment to the 'ni – ni' principle of neither further privatisations nor nationalisations. However, the letter did suggest a name for the new authority, the Conseil Supérieur de l'Audiovisuel (CSA), but there was no mention of its future structure or powers. It did stress, however, that the CSA should, if possible, become part of the Constitution, thus putting an end to the chop and change of authorities. As a result, despite the desire expressed in some quarters of the PS, Tasca made it clear from the outset that the new law would confine itself to the creation of a new regulatory authority and little more.

This decision was confirmed at the end of a meeting of the Council of

Ministers which was devoted almost entirely to this subject on 4 July 1988. This meeting also accepted the joint proposition of Tasca and Lang (Culture Minister), backed up by the new Prime Minister, Michel Rocard, to set up a commission of experts to recommend to the government the powers that the CSA should be given. This proposition was inspired partly out of the government's desire to legislate in a different manner to Léotard, who drew up the 1986 law *'dans le secret du cabinet'*,[37] and partly out of the desire to draw more people into the preparatory process. In this way, it was thought that the bill would stand a greater chance of winning enough support to allow it to enter the Constitution. This proposition was also consistent with the *'méthode Rocard'*, whereby any major bill should be preceded by a commission set up to study the problems involved and to suggest a consensual way forward.[38]

Despite these motivations, it was also clear that there was to be no repeat of the Moinot Commission. The group was given instructions to study the problems surrounding the creation of a new authority, but not to embark upon an overall critique of the broadcasting system. It consisted of only seven members and there were no sub-commissions, or working parties. The members were appointed by the Prime Minister, in close consultation with Tasca and Lang, and included eminent jurists, such as Pierre Avril, and also Françoise Giroud, a Minister during Giscard's Presidency.

The commission met, on average, four times a week, although on numerous occasions only three or four of its members were present. It met at the Communications Ministry, in the presence of one of Tasca's advisers, Bertrand Delcros. Its work consisted of interviewing representatives from the broadcasting industry and of asking them how they would set about creating a new authority. By the end of August it had seen nearly 100 people and Delcros had summarised its findings in a short report which was then presented to Tasca.

During this time there were also several interministerial reunions. Chaired by Sylvie Hubac, Rocard's adviser on broadcasting affairs, they involved only a small number of people, such as Delcros, Dominique Meyer, a member of Lang's *cabinet*, and Bruno Chetaille from the Elysée. In fact, it was in these meetings, before the commission's report, that most of the important decisions were taken. Or rather, these meetings ratified agreements made between the same people beforehand in unofficial meetings, encounters and telephone conversations.[39] Such was the agreement between those present at the reunions, that only one informal interministerial committee was needed on this subject, although on several occasions there were informal meetings and lunches at the Elysée in the presence of Mitterrand.

In the desire to draft a bill that would win sufficient support for it to go into the Constitution, the Prime Minister arranged a series of highly publicised meetings with representatives of all of the major parties. They were invited to come to Matignon and to discuss the project with the Prime Minister, Tasca and Lang. Between the 20th–29th September, Mauroy (PS), Méhaignerie (CDS), Marchais (PCF), Juppé (RPR), Léotard (PR) and the former Prime Minister, Raymond Barre, all took up this offer. These meetings, however, had little effect on the wording of the text and once again they served mainly as a media exercise.[40] Indeed, in private, the government had already given up hope of seeing the bill enter the Constitution, at least immediately.

The bill was examined by the Council of State on October 6th and only minor changes were made. It was presented to the Council of Ministers on 12 October and put before the Senate two days later, with the Prime Minister having declared the bill to be of urgent importance. Discussion in the Senate took place between November 8th–10th where important amendments were passed by the opposition majority. In the National Assembly, however, the government's text was largely restored, although several concessions were made to the centrist group, the UDC, in order to try and win its support. With the PS only having a relative majority and with the PCF having declared that they would not support the text, the government needed the UDC's support so as to pass the bill without recourse to Article 49–3, something that it wished to avoid. On the bill's first reading the UDC abstained allowing it to pass. On December 21st, at the second reading, however, the UDC line hardened, with Méhaignerie imposing conditions for his group's support that the government could not accept. Therefore, the use of Article 49–3 was necessitated. The bill was submitted to the Constitutional Council the next day and its decision was delivered on 17 January 1989 with only a few minor points were struck down. The next day the bill became law.

The Preparation of the 1989 Broadcasting Act

In contrast to the two previous texts, this law contained only 30 articles. In this respect, it is easier to focus upon the most important debates without losing sight of the contents of the bill as a whole. However, as before, there is insufficient room here to study everything and so two areas of decision making have been chosen. These areas deal respectively with the composition and the powers of the CSA.

The *Lettre à tous les Français* only obliquely hinted at the future composition of the CSA. In its eulogy of the Haute Autorité, it went into detail about the way in which its members were appointed. Whilst it did not commit the new government to this particular formula, it was a clear hint as to what the preferred presidential option was to be. Nevertheless, during the preparation of the bill numerous different solutions were put forward, although no-one was willing to commit himself strongly to any particular formulation.

By contrast, the commission of experts did come up with a suggestion which won favour with certain people in government circles. They proposed the same composition as for the Haute Autorité, but with the members' names being simply announced by the President of the Republic after secret consultations had taken place with the Presidents of the National Assembly and the Senate. It was hoped that this solution would avoid the members being branded from the outset as representatives of a particular person or party, whilst still guarding the authority's political legitimacy.[41]

However, Tasca was opposed to this solution. She favoured a simple return to the 1982 situation.[42] She asked for her proposal to be endorsed by the President during a lunch at the Elysée where the bill was to be discussed. Also present were Alain Simon, a former member of Fillioud's cabinet and a presidential friend and author of the broadcasting section of the *Lettre à tous les Français*; Gilles Ménage and Jean Kahn, both presidential advisers; Tasca; Hubac; and Roger Lesgards, Tasca's *directeur de cabinet*. Of these people, Simon favoured the proposal of the commission of experts, Mitterrand, however, did not and he arbitrated in Tasca's favour.[43]

During the passage of the bill through the Senate, the text was changed by the opposition majority, so as to allow the *grands corps* to appoint three of the nine members. This proposal was rejected by the government. In the National Assembly, however, this question was one of the major points of discussion with the UDC with a view to winning their support and avoiding the use of Article 49– 3. Jacques Barrot, one of the leading UDC members and an important figure in the parliamentary commission examining the law, was in favour of his group supporting the text in return for the government's acceptance of a series of amendments. In the parliamentary commission he worked closely with Jean-Jacques Quéyranne, the PS spokesperson, and obtained several quite substantial concessions. Rocard and Tasca were willing to accept these concessions in return for the UDC's support, still with an eye to the bill's entry into the Constitution at a later date. One of the points, however, on which neither Rocard nor Tasca would cede was the CSA's composition. This was a presidential arbitration and could only be reversed by Mitterrand himself. The President was unwilling to do so.

The UDC, however, still insisted that the CSA's composition be altered. Even its most conciliatory members were unhappy to support a bill which would be likely to leave the authority with a socialist majority. Moreover, the UDC had already just supported the law installing the *Revenu Minimum d'Insertion* and had voted with the government to pass the 1989 budget. To support the government again would be to anger even further the RPR and UDF, whose support the group needed at the municipal elections in March 1989. Méhaignerie, seeing the need to dissociate his group from the government, insisted that it vote against the bill. Barrot, still favouring an agreement and aware that the government would withdraw hard fought concessions if it were forced to use Article 49–3, was still conciliatory. He publicly argued that there was no magic formula and that the present one was as good as any.[44] As Barrot himself stated, however:

> Unfortunately I was not supported . . . by certain members of my group who called into question the composition of the CSA. As a result, we arrived at a negative vote.[45]

Barrot's fears were realised as the government refused to compromise. The UDC voted against the bill and the use of Article 49–3 saw the disappearance of several of Barrot's amendments.

The range of powers that the new authority would enjoy was another of the major issues that the law addressed. These powers covered three main topics. Firstly, the powers it should have to set production quotas for both the public and private television companies, sponsorship rules and limits to the number of films made for the cinema to be broadcast on television. Secondly, the role that it should play with regard to the public stations, whether it should appoint their managing directors, or whether it should share out the licence fee itself. Thirdly, whether or not it should have the same wide range of responsibilities as the CNCL, over telecommunications, for example.

While there were many different arguments involved with these problems and many different interests involved, it is possible to study them all together. What united them was that they raised a single, but fundamental issue that divided the government and Parliament alike, namely, the distribution of these powers between the government and the CSA.

Within the government, it was clear that there were two opposing tendencies. On the one hand, there were those people who felt that the CSA should be given as wide a range of powers as possible. This was the position of Hubac at Matignon and Delcros at the Communications Ministry. On the other hand, Tasca, Kahn and Leroy, the head of the SJTI, were all in favour of the CSA policing the system, but of the government drawing up the rules.

This cleavage could be seen on the question of production quotas, for example. In order that the government's influence over the system be seen to end, Hubac argued that the CSA should fix them. Tasca, however, was opposed, arguing that the economic and industrial implications of these quotas meant that they were too important to be fixed by anyone but the government.[46] The same positions were held over who should set the *cahiers des charges* of the public television companies. Hubac felt that the CSA could happily fulfil this task, whereas Tasca felt that, given the CSA's powers to sanction the companies, this proposal would make it both judge and jury. Tasca also argued that, because the state funded the public stations, it had the right to determine what they should and should not be doing.[47]

The debate between the two sides, however, was nowhere near as 'bloody' as it had been in 1986. Neither Hubac nor Tasca defended these positions to their logical extremes. Jean Kahn's initial suggestion that, because the CSA was not to be responsible before Parliament, it should not be given any powers of note was quickly rejected by Tasca.[48] While at no time did Hubac envisage that the CSA would be allowed to share out the licence fee revenue between the public channels. Due to the experience of the last decade and the political situation in which the government found itself, the protagonists were generally aware of the limits within which they had to remain. Within these limits, however, people argued their case tenaciously.

Interesting, here, is the SJTI's role. Similar to the 1982 situation, the head of the SJTI, Thierry Leroy, appointed in July 1988, had his own particular blueprint for the CSA. At the same time, his particular view of a top civil servant's role was that he should not simply administer orders given to him by the Ministers responsible, but that he should tell the government what he, as an expert, thought policy should be.[49] Thus, in debates, such as the one over who should fix the production quotas, the SJTI's role was far from neutral. As someone close to Lang, Leroy's proposals were certainly better received by the government than were Cousin's suggestions in 1982.

Policy conflict, however, meant the need for arbitration. There were three distinct levels of arbitration. For the most difficult questions, the President was called upon to decide. Thus, it was he who resolved the problem of who was to set the *cahier des charges*. Here, both tendencies were unable to agree a solution without the President's intervention. It is important, however, to dispel the notion that, in 1988 at least, broadcasting belonged to the reserved domain of presidential interests. His direct involvement was confined to an Elysée lunch. Broadcasting was considered to be too base an issue for him to deal with in his second term of office.

The Prime Minister arbitrated a second level of problems. For example, the question of whether the CSA should authorise installations in the telecommunications sector, as the CNCL had done before. Paul Quilès, the Minister of Telecommunications was opposed to this measure, Tasca was in favour and the Prime Minister was called upon to decide between them, with Quilès winning the day.

However, by far the greatest number of decisions were taken in the interministerial reunions. It is worth noting that in these meetings the role of the presidential advisers, in conformity with an unwritten rule of Mitterrand's second *septennat*, was to observe and then to inform the President, rather than to take an active part in the discussions on his behalf.

More often than not, the result of these arbitrations, at whatever level they may have taken place, was a compromise. Victory was rarely total for either one side or the other. As one adviser rather idiosyncratically put it: '*Un arbitrage, ce n'est pas un arbitre, quelqu'un sur son trône, mais une salade.*'[50] An arbitration was a compromise arrived at through bargaining, rather than a royal proclamation. So, for example, on the question of the production quotas, it was agreed that the government would issue a decree fixing them, but that this decree would be examined by the CSA whose opinion of it would consequently be made public. A similar agreement was reached for the *cahier des charges*.

It must also be noted that some of the things which influenced the final outcome of the above decisions were unforeseeable at the start of the process, or were independent of the arguments of those involved. For example, one of the major factors that resulted in arbitrations generally favourable to Tasca's viewpoint was the strike in the public sector broadcasting service that started in September 1988. The strike was particularly disruptive and it was the government's responsibility to try and end it, with Matignon leading the secret negotiations to do so. This strike brought home to the government just how implicated it was in the running of the public sector system and it was realised that this situation would not change even if the CSA's powers were to be as great as possible. Without this strike the result of the arbitrations may have been very different,[51] whilst one contemporary newspaper close to the PS summed up the situation as follows:

In a certain way, events have arbitrated: when there is a crisis people always turn to the otherwise much decried State. In the end Rocard came down in favour of Tasca, against the advice of his own councillors, who wanted the Conseil Supérieur de l'Audiovisuel to have all the power.[52]

Exogenous factors, such as this strike breaking out when it did, will always add an element of unpredictability to the policy process.

So far, we have presented the governmental side of the process. Parliament's role, however, must not be underestimated. Parliament's influence varies according to the political circumstances of the day. In December 1988, these circumstances were in Parliament's favour. As a result of the Prime Minister's desire to see the law passed without the use of Article 49–3, the government accepted several UDC amendments. Barrot met with Delcros, Tasca, Lang and Quéyranne to negotiate their wording.[53] For example, the issue of production quotas was reopened. Barrot was still favourable to the CSA fixing them. A compromise was duly reached whereby the government would continue to fix them for 18 months after which time the CSA would do so. A similar agreement was reached over the telecommunications issue, where the Prime Minister went back upon his earlier arbitration and allowed the CSA to guard its responsibilities in this area until the passage of a new law.

As with the previous example, however, Méhaignerie's unwillingness to vote the bill meant that some of these concessions were withdrawn. Méhaignerie made it one of his conditions for the UDC's support that the CSA be given responsibility for the production quotas right from the outset. With the government unwilling to accept his conditions as a whole, the UDC refused to support the bill. The government then withdrew the amendment it had agreed with Barrot and the CSA lost all powers in this area.

Conclusion

The three case studies considered above enable some preliminary conclusions to be drawn about the nature of the policy process in France and about the influence of the Prime Minister within that process. Although at this stage these conclusions will necessarily be incomplete, they provide a background from which better to approach the chapters to come.

The above case studies threw into relief the mechanics of the policy making process. In essence, there were two parts to this process: the intragovernmental part; and the extragovernmental part. The former refers

to the bargaining which took place between government members, largely
before the wording of the bill was finalised. The latter refers to the
influence of extragovernmental actors in the process, such as the Council
of State and Parliament.

The intragovernmental part of the policy process typically consisted of
three stages, namely, reunions, committees and councils. As was seen in the
case of the 1982 broadcasting bill, these three stages may be complemented
by a special commission, or informal encounters. However, these three sets
of meetings were the occasions when arbitrations occurred. In this sense,
together they were the site of the decision-making process.

There was a clear hierarchy of meetings. Reunions were followed by
committees, which in turn were followed, if necessary, by councils. At
reunions only members of ministerial *cabinets* were present, as well as
senior members of the permanent administration, such as the SJTI. At
committees Ministers were present, while senior *cabinet* members were
also occasionally invited to attend. Committees were chaired by the
Prime Minister personally. At councils the same people were present
as for committees, except for the President who attended and chaired
the meeting. The only time when this process was disturbed was during
the period of *cohabitation* when there were no councils, as the President
was absent from decision making.

This series of meetings acted as a filter system for the decision-making
process. Reunions served to decide technical matters, or non-controversial
political issues. Thus, for example, it was at this stage during the preparation of the 1989 broadcasting act that many of the details of the CSA's
powers were agreed upon. Committees were held to resolve matters where
there were interministerial disputes. Here, the Prime Minister was called
upon to arbitrate, for example in the dispute between Tasca and Quilès
in 1989. Councils were the top tier of the arbitration process where the
President had to intervene on issues which were either too important to be
decided upon in committees, such as the over the composition of the CSA
in 1989, or where the Prime Minister's arbitration had been challenged,
such as on the question of advertising on local radio in 1982.

It is important to stress, however, that at all three stages of
the intragovernmental decision-making process, the arbitrations which
occurred were not haphazard. The arbitration process was a bargaining
process. It involved negotiations and compromises between all the protagonists concerned. For example, in 1982 the decision not to set up the
SNT was counterbalanced by new production agreements between the SFP
and the broadcasting companies. Similarly, in 1986, the decision to privatise
TF1 was arrived at as a compromise between the conflicting demands of

those people who wished to see A2 chosen and those who wanted it to be FR3. Along with the observation that the policy process was a bargaining process, involving negotiations and compromise, goes the assertion that the influence of the Prime Minister cannot be considered in isolation, but that it must be judged alongside the influence of the other protagonists. This point will be considered again in the chapters to follow.

In addition to the intragovernmental part of the process, there was also an extragovernmental element. That is to say, the situation where extragovernmental organisations intervened to try and change the wording of a bill. These organisations usually intervened after the resolution of the intragovernmental series of meetings and, thus, their influence was an element exogenous to the governmental policy process.

In the case studies, several different organisations were identified which had such an influence: the Council of State, the National Assembly, Senate, Constitutional Council and various pressure groups, such as the Hersant group. In the case of the parliamentary actors and the Hersant group, the government was again obliged to engage in a process of bargaining before the final version of the bill was agreed upon. In the case of the two judicial actors, their decisions were either unchallenged, in the case of the Council of State's influence on the 1982 law, or unchallengeable, in the case of the Constitutional Council. Just as above it was concluded that the influence of the Prime Minister can only be appreciated alongside the influence of the other governmental actors, so the influence of the government can only properly be appreciated alongside the influence of these extragovernmental organisations. Again, this proposition will be reconsidered in future chapters. However, it is now necessary to turn to the second series of case studies, namely, budgetary politics.

4 Budgetary Policy

The second area of policy to be considered is that of budgetary politics. As in the previous chapter, three case studies will be taken, namely, the preparation and passage of the 1985, 1987 and 1990 budgets. While the preparation of the budget is an annual event and there are many similarities in the process from year to year, these three budgets do provide three separate case studies. The differences in the overall political situation and in the policy content of the three examples mean that they may be considered as three distinct case studies.

Due to the complexity of the French budgetary process it will be necessary, first of all, to give a general account of this process. Having done so, the three case studies will be examined in detail.

The French Budgetary Procedure

In most liberal democracies the preparation and vote of the budget is the centrepiece of the economic and political year. France is no exception. All Ministries take part in its preparation. It is the bill which regularly commands the most public and journalistic interest. It is the bill on which, in Parliament, the allegiances of all party groups are judged. As Prada notes:

> It is clear that the budget is probably the government's major act, since it expresses better than any other the government's responsibility for drawing up a policy in which virtually all of its component parts are implicated.[1]

The centrality of budgetary politics to the political system as a whole makes it a suitable candidate for a set of case studies. After all, the influence of the Prime Minister will be judged to a large extent upon his role in the preparation and passage of the most important bill of the legislative year. However, it is also a prime candidate for investigation as it is an annual process. The budgetary procedure changes very little from one year to the next. While the circumstances of each budget are different, the opportunities for comparison between one case study and another are

70

Table 4.1   The preparation in the year n − 1 of the budget for the year n

Month	Stage
Jan.–Feb.	Preparation of the *budget de réconduction*
March–April	Interministerial committees Changes agreed by the Finance Minister, Prime Minister and President
Mid-April	*Lettre de cadrage*
May–June	*Conférences budgétaires* for expenditure items
July	Final prime ministerial spending arbitrations
Mid-July	*Lettres plafonds*
July–August	Finance Ministry prepares revenue items of the bill
Late August	Prime ministerial arbitrations on the revenue component after meetings with the President
Early Sep.	Bill presented to the Council of State
Mid-Sep.	Bill presented to the National Assembly Examined by the Assembly's Finance Commission
Mid-October	Debated by the National Assembly Vote on the budgetary equilibrium level Votes on individual ministerial spending items
Mid-Nov.	Vote on the revenue component of the bill
Early Dec.	Examination by the Senate (same procedure as for the National Assembly)
Mid-December	*Commission mixte paritaire* Possible recourse to the Constitutional Council
Late December	Definitive adoption of the bill

maximised. It is necessary, therefore, to outline the budgetary procedure in general before turning to an examination of the case studies in detail.[2]

The French financial year runs from January 1st to December 31st. Therefore, the budget for 1985, for example, was prepared wholly during the course of 1984. The preparatory process for the budget of year n starts in January of the year n − 1 (see Table 4.1). Throughout January and February, one of the services within the Finance Ministry, the *direction du Budget*, starts to prepare a draft budget for the year n. In general terms, the previous year's budget is taken and its continuing items are identified (*services votés*), so that a basic expenditure figure may be calculated. At the same time, the most recent economic indicators are used so as to provide a rough estimate of the level of government income, once again based on the provisions of the previous year's budget. To these figures are added various new measures which the government has passed and any other items whose adoption is felt to be unavoidable during the course of the year. Once this information has been fed into the computers of the *direction du Budget* and the econometric models completed, there emerges a detailed draft of the coming year's budget (*le budget de réconduction*).

It is usually in early March that the *directeur du Budget* presents this draft to the Finance Minister and the Budget Minister. They scrutinise it, making any changes to it that they feel to be necessary, or possible, at this stage. In fact, these changes are usually proposed not by the Ministers themselves, but by the *directeur du Budget* himself and by the *cabinets* of the Finance and Budget Ministers in close consultation with the Prime Minister's and President's economic advisers. The resulting document is then usually discussed at the interministerial level in a meeting of ministerial advisers, full Ministers and the Prime Minister.[3] This meeting determines the government's overall budgetary priorities, such as the level of the deficit, for example.

The result of this meeting is the *lettre de cadrage* that the Prime Minister sends to every Minister. As the former *directeur du Budget*, Michel Prada, notes:

> This letter, besides giving a reminder of the government's basic economic policy, is made up of the central elements of its budgetary strategy which vary from one government to the next and from one situation to the next.[4]

It is at this stage in the process that the Prime Minister's influence is considered to be at its greatest as he is closely involved in the choices of the government's overall budgetary strategy, which form the central components of the *lettre de cadrage*.

The appearance of this letter is followed by the interministerial expenditure part of the process. Each Minister is called upon to prepare a list of continuing items (*mesures acquises*) and of new demands (*mesures nouvelles*). It is these latter items which are usually the source of greatest debate. Ministers generally wish to spend more than those preparing the budget are willing to accept. Ministerial demands are discussed in a series of *conférences budgétaires*.

These *conférences* take place at a number of different levels, depending on the gravity of the dispute. The first level brings together one of the sub-directors of the *direction du Budget*, the permanent ministerial budgetary representative, ministerial advisers and various members of the different sub-sections of the *direction du Budget*.[5] Whilst many matters are agreed upon in these meetings, problems often still persist, in which case there is an appeal procedure through which the Minister may go. Firstly, the Minister will meet the *directeur du Budget* himself. If problems persist there will be further meetings between the Minister and the Budget Minister, followed, if necessary, by a meeting with the Finance Minister and, if all else fails, with the Prime Minister. Although, in private, the President and his advisers may also be called upon to intervene, their arbitration is usually reserved for the major budgetary orientations, rather than relatively minor spending differences.

By mid-July the final spending arbitrations have been made and the Prime Minister sends out a *lettre plafond* to each Minister. Unlike the *lettre de cadrage*, the *lettres plafond* are different for each Ministry and they formalise the points agreed upon in the *conférences budgétaires*. These letters represent the final stage of the governmental preparation of expenditure items and only in exceptional circumstances are they changed to any significant degree.

The next stage deals with the revenue side of the budget. Here, the preparation process is usually confined to the *direction du Budget* and the budgetary advisers of the Finance Minister, Budget Minister, Prime Minister and occasionally the President. These consultations continue until the end of August, when the bill is ready to go before the Council of State and then the Council of Ministers. By the end of September the bill is ready to sent to Parliament to be voted upon.

The parliamentary stage is strictly governed by a set of constitutional and legal limits.[6] Article 47 of the Constitution states that Parliament has 70 days in which to pass the budget and that, if it fails to do so, the government is automatically authorised to proceed by ordinance. Firstly, the Finance bill is discussed for a period of up to 40 days by the National Assembly. Then the Senate has 20 days to examine it, with the remaining 10 days being set aside to iron out any differences between the two Chambers. Article 40 also states that any amendment proposed by a deputy which results in an increase in expenditure, or a decrease in revenue is considered to be *ultra vires*. Only the government has the power to propose such amendments and so deputies have to convince the Finance Minister and the Prime Minister that their amendments are well-founded.

The Finance bill is considered first of all by the National Assembly's Finance Commission. It then proceeds to the floor of the Chamber where there is a discussion and vote on each article of the revenue section, followed by a vote on the overall budgetary equilibrium level. This is the first major vote. It is followed by an examination of the expenditure section of the bill, which involves a debate and vote on each of the different ministerial budgets, followed by the adoption of the *services votés* and finally a vote on the Finance bill as a whole. This procedure is repeated in the Senate, where the bill is likely to undergo a different series of amendments. As a result, a mixed parity commission of the two Chambers is normally required, in order to agree upon a common text. If the commission reaches agreement then there is a further vote by both Chambers. If no agreement can be reached, then the National Assembly has the final say. Due to this process and following any examination by the Constitutional Council, it is not rare to see the bill become law on December 31st just in time for the new financial year.[7]

Following this brief general account of the normal budgetary procedure, it is now necessary to examine the case studies in detail.

The 1985 Budget

The first case study to be considered concerns the preparation and passage of the 1985 budget. Following the procedure in the previous chapter, the case study will first of all be put in context. For the 1985 budget, it is necessary to outline the economic and political conditions under which it was prepared. Having done that, an examination of the expenditure component of the bill will then be undertaken before turning to the revenue side. Conclusions will be drawn once the examination of all three case studies has been completed.

The budgetary choices facing the government in 1984 were still being determined by the nature of the policies pursued in 1981 and 1982. The effects of the 1981 post-election spending boom have been well chronicled elsewhere.[8] In short, however, the unilateral decision to increase government spending during a time of world recession created an enormous budget deficit, currency problems and an ever increasing debt repayment bill fuelled by high interest rates.

The effects of the government's economic policy were felt not only economically, but socially and electorally as well. Thus, gradually, throughout 1982 the government changed tack. First of all, it announced a pause and then introduced a half-hearted austerity programme. This process culminated in the third devaluation and severe austerity plan of March 1983, which signalled the end of the French socialist economic experiment and made financial and budgetary rigour the two core subjects of the government's economic policy curriculum (see Chapter 6).

The 1983 and 1984 budgets made the first and most difficult policy changes. Spending was reduced and, more symbolically, the number of government employees was reduced, going directly against one of the

110 Propositions considered until then to be amongst the most sacrosanct, namely, the creation of 200,000 jobs in the state sector. The government-engendered recession that followed served to make budgetary policy-making all the more difficult. For example, government income from VAT fell, which in turn reduced revenue and necessitated further expenditure cuts for fear of seeing the budget deficit increase even further. Elementary economics showed that the government was in a vicious circle from which it did not have the means to break out.

In 1984, the government's room for manœuvre was small. In such a situation, the influence of the *direction du Budget* became ever greater. As one ministerial adviser noted:

In 1984, we were still in a period of severe budgetary restriction. There weren't all that many choices as to how to conduct budgetary policy.[9]

In contrast to its anomalous role in 1981 when it had to recommend additional spending plans to a government which did not possess sufficient ideas about how to spend public money, in 1984 the *direction du Budget* had to draw up a long list of spending cuts. As a result, the role of the Prime Minister and the Finance Minister was reduced. They become more reliant than usual on the administrators of the budget division. One adviser stated:

The mark of a Prime Minister depends very much on the financial room for manœuvre of the period. In 1985 and 1986, there wasn't the slightest financial margin. Therefore, both the Prime Minister's and the Finance Minister's ability to take the initiative was very limited.

This restriction could be seen at the time of the *lettre de cadrage*. In 1984, the major budgetary orientations were effectively set for the Prime Minister by the overall economic situation and by the proposals of the *direction du Budget*. In addition, Parliament's already subordinate role was further reduced. With regard to the 1985 budget one person in the *direction du Budget* at that time, stated: 'I don't believe that it had an important role to play'.[10] The mid-1980s, therefore, saw a diminished role for the budget's political actors and an increased role for the administrative ones.

This general statement has to be nuanced, however, and one political figure who had a very clear influence on the 1985 budget was the President. Quite exceptionally, he publicly laid down two conditions that the budget had to abide by. The first concerned the general level of mandatory tax deductions (*les prélèvements obligatoires*) and was announced during a television interview on TF1 on 15 September 1983: 'Next year, when the 1985 budget is being prepared, tax levels will be reduced by one percentage point.' This measure was announced without any prior warning being given to Mauroy, or Jacques Delors, the Finance Minister. Its overall effect on the state budget and the social security budget was to necessitate savings of around 80 billion francs in 1984. The budgetary exercise was made doubly difficult by the further presidential announcement that the budget deficit would not be allowed to exceed 3 per cent of the GNP. The main role of the President's budgetary advisers throughout 1984 was constantly to inform the government that these decisions were irreversible, despite the harsh budgetary choices that they necessitated.[11]

The other major occurrence in 1984, which had certain effects on the budgetary process was the change of Prime Minister. Laurent Fabius officially replaced Pierre Mauroy as Prime Minister on July 17th 1984. At the same time, Jacques Delors left the Finance Ministry to be replaced by Pierre Bérégovoy, although Henri Emmanuelli remained as Budget Minister. In addition, there was a near complete change of ministerial *cabinets*. Few of Mauroy's advisers remained to work under Fabius and the same was true at the Finance Ministry.

What was striking about the members of the new budgetary team, however, was the close working relationship that they immediately struck up. Relations between Delors, Emmanuelli and Mauroy, including their advisers, had not been altogether harmonious. The same was not generally true amongst the members of the new government. Fabius and Bérégovoy worked together particularly closely, whilst a large proportion of their budgetary advisory staff consisted of former *inspecteurs des finances* who had previously enjoyed close personal and professional contacts. More than one person interviewed stated that the familiarity between advisers and Ministers facilitated the task of taking the most difficult decisions. There was a mutual confidence between those involved.[12]

Equally important was the different approach that Fabius brought to the premiership, at least with regard to the budget. In terms of policy outlook, little distinguished Mauroy from Fabius. The new Prime Minister, however, had experience of the budgetary process, whereas Mauroy was a *notable*. When asked about the relative influence of the two Prime Ministers, one adviser noted that in terms of policy:

The difference is that Mauroy is a politician as is Fabius, but Fabius is also a technocrat. He gets to grips with technical dossiers more easily.[13]

In addition, it should not be forgotten that Fabius was the Budget Minister himself between 1981 and 1983. This familiarity with the subject contrasts strongly with Mauroy's lack of budgetary expertise.

It is clear, therefore, that there were a number of important economic, political and personal factors present throughout the 1985 budgetary process that had a bearing on the final contents of the bill. These factors have been considered in some detail here, partly because they help to explain the case studies to follow, but also because the preparation of any budget is such a vast project that the number of detailed case studies able to be examined is necessarily very limited. However, the expenditure component of the 1985 budget will now be considered.

With the President having ordered a cut in taxes and a stabilisation of the deficit, the government was left with no option but to cut spending. As all governments in all countries know, however, such a task is not at all easy. Ministers fight their corners, pressure groups defend their interests and the public rarely take kindly to a loss of services. In France, it was particularly difficult to cut spending because of the vast number of continuing items of expenditure (*services votés*). Each year, these items represent around 90 per cent of the total spending component of the Finance bill. Each year they are renewed quasi-automatically and appear in their near entirety in the *budget de réconduction*. They consist mainly of the government wage bill and basic running costs and mean that the opportunity to make cuts lies only at the margins, unless the government is willing sharply to cut back on services and personnel. Any government would find this difficult to do, but particularly so the socialists after 1981 as their level of support amongst public sector employees was great.

Faced with this situation, in 1984 the aim of the *direction de Budget* was to minimise the increase in new spending (*les mesures nouvelles*). According to one former Budget Minister, this is the situation where the *direction du Budget* is generally at its most powerful.[14] Each spending Ministry has its expenditure closely monitored by a sub-section of the Budget division. In many cases, the Budget division, because of its greater technical and human resources, knows the subject matter better even than the budgetary experts in the Ministry itself. This expertise means that, during the *conférences budgétaires*, the representatives of the Budget division are in a position to refute the spending demands of the Ministry in question. In 1984, the *direction du Budget* was particularly vigilant and recommended that only the most urgent proposals be accepted. In this period of budgetary restraint, the Prime Minister and Finance Minister had little option but to agree and, indeed, they did so not ungratefully, as they were the ones who were ultimately responsible for cutting spending so as to meet the President's conditions.

This cut back on the new items, however, was not enough to balance the budgetary equation. Having foreseen this difficulty, in March the *directeur du Budget* had already personally proposed a 1 per cent across-the-board cut in administrative personnel: 'The proposed solution was brutal, summary, simplistic. The same rate for everyone.'[15] This proposal was accepted by Delors and Mauroy in preference to the other option which would have involved setting up a commission of enquiry to recommend cuts for each individual Ministry separately. This 1 per cent across-the-board cut was combined with a 2 per cent cut in spending and they were both revealed to Ministers in the *lettre du cadrage* sent out on March 30th.

At this point the strategy of Delors and Mauroy was to shock the spending Ministers into accepting the cuts. As one newspaper noted: 'First of all, each Ministry's spending is pared right down. Then, if necessary, negotiations take place'.[16] As everyone realised, however, some Ministries had better grounds than others to escape the sweeping cuts and, during the round of prime ministerial arbitrations in June, certain departments were prioritized.

Firstly, there were those areas which the President considered to be a priority, notably defence and the Research Ministry's budget. The Prime Minister fully agreed with the President's choice. Secondly, there were the areas in which the President showed a personal interest, such as the Culture Ministry's budget. Thirdly, there were areas, such as education, where the lobby was powerful enough to overturn the cuts. Finally, there were several areas where it was considered to be prudent to avoid cuts, so as to ward off any possible social discontent. For example, the level of overcrowding in prisons meant that the Justice Ministry's budget was spared, while Rocard at the Agriculture Ministry also avoided the cuts.[17] It is interesting to note that all the people interviewed insisted that Rocard had been favoured because of the specificity of his Ministry and not because of his important position within the party. The battle between the *courants* in the PS became influential only at a later date. While the Prime Minister was personally responsible for taking these decisions, it would be unrealistic to suggest that he initiated the choices. They emanated mainly from the President and from economic and social factors largely beyond his control, even if, in many cases, he agreed with the resulting decision.

The final spending arbitrations were made by Mauroy in the first week of July. It was clear to him at this stage, however, that he was going to be replaced as Prime Minister. Therefore, he refused to sign the *lettres plafond* leaving this responsibility to Fabius.[18] The latter, however, not being content with accepting Mauroy's arbitrations, proceeded immediately to review the decisions. In consultation with Bérégovoy and their two *cabinets*, he changed a number of budgets, notably reducing the spending of the former communist Ministries who had been slightly favoured by Mauroy in order to keep them in the government. The other major change was to increase the amount given to Fabius's successor at the Industry Ministry.

The parliamentary stage saw few important changes to the expenditure side of the budget. There were no demands for greater spending from the PS and the government was never going to accept similar communist demands given their recent departure. The *provision parlementaire*, however, should be noted. This item is the sum which is allocated each year by the government to accommodate some of the parliamentarians' demands. Around 0.1 per cent of the budget is set aside for this purpose. In 1984, this amount was between 200–300 million francs. In 1984, only the National Assembly benefited from the *provision parlementaire*, the government feeling that it was not necessary to include the Senate because of its opposition majority and its limited role in policy making. Whilst this item should not be ignored, it is an annual occurrence and, in overall budgetary terms, the amount of money involved is small.

On the income side of the budget, one of the most difficult decisions concerned a reform of the *taxe professionnelle*. This was a business tax set up in 1976 whose rate varied according to a firm's capital. Naturally, the business peak association, the CNPF, had always been opposed to it, calling it a tax on investment. From 1981 onwards, the opposition parties, too, were in favour of reducing, or even abolishing it. More importantly, Mitterrand himself was on record as saying that it was a '*taxe imbécile*'.

In 1984, the government saw that the promise to reduce the level of *prélèvements obligatoires* presented a perfect opportunity to abolish this generally unpopular tax. Its abolition, however, proved to be more difficult than was at first envisaged. The debate between those in favour of its abolition and those opposed can be seen at two different levels within the government. The higher level set Delors against Mauroy and Emmanuelli. The former, on the advice of the *direction du Budget* and his *cabinet*, was in favour of reducing the tax, but not of abolishing it. Mauroy, also on the advice of his advisers, preferred to see it abolished. At this level, however, according to one adviser: 'There wasn't a serious debate'.[19] The Prime Minister and the Finance Minister appeared to follow rather blindly the advice of their advisers, out of loyalty and not personal conviction.

The debate was much more serious between Hervé Hannoun, one

of Mauroy's budgetary advisers, and Jean Choussat, the *directeur du Budget*. Hannoun was fervently in favour of seeing the tax abolished: 'He considered it be his mission to see the *taxe professionnelle* abolished'.[20] Accordingly, he drew up a series of complex proposals to abolish it and replace it with any number of different options. It was the very complexity of the solutions that was Choussat's main argument against its abolition. One former Minister recounted how his own proposals were rebuffed by the *direction du Budget*:

> There were people who passed us notes every day saying that what we wanted to do was impossible. It was like that. I had done my own outline, but it was too difficult.[21]

Choussat was able to convince Delors of the folly of abolishing the tax because of his and his division's greater technical knowledge of the subject matter. One adviser stated:

> A Finance Minister is always attached to existing taxes. He is under pressure from his administration. Politicians don't understand anything. Which is true in fact. Talking about taxation is much more difficult than talking about spending. The experts have a great weight in the debate.[22]

For Mauroy and Emmanuelli the abolition of the tax was highly symbolic politically, but this argument was one which those opposed to the reform at the *direction du Budget* could easily rebuff because of the complexity of the problem. It was stated that:

> Pierre Mauroy never really understood the administration. He thought that you could abolish a tax in a week.[23]

Thus, the debate was largely conducted at a technical level between Hannoun and Choussat. The former was unable to put forward any simple counter-arguments to the latter. Despite being a former *inspecteur des finances*, he did not have the resources to outsmart the *direction du Budget*.

Nevertheless, the question was raised in a formal meeting with the President before Mauroy's departure in early July. Mitterrand arbitrated in Delors's favour and a 10 billion franc reduction was agreed, although it is unclear how strongly the Prime Minister argued his case. When Fabius was appointed one of his first decisions was to confirm this arbitration.[24] Meanwhile, Hannoun, now at the Elysée, did not press for the decision to be overturned.[25]

The 1987 Budget

The change of government in March 1986 and the upturn in the state of the French economy after 1985 meant that the situation facing the budgetary actors in 1986 was noticeably different to the circumstances in 1984. Therefore, while procedural similarities remain between the two budgets, they are sufficiently different in policy content so as to allow useful comparisons to be drawn between them.

The legislative elections and the subsequent change of government in March 1986 provoked an initial delay in the budgetary process. Whilst the *direction du Budget* had carried out its normal preparatory calculations at the beginning of the year, Chirac was appointed around the time when ordinarily the *lettre de cadrage* would have appeared. Moreover, the new government, with its Finance Minister, Edouard Balladur and Budget Minister, Alain Juppé, decided that the preparation of the 1987 budget would have to take second place to the 1986 *collectif budgétaire*, or mini-budget.

The preparation of a mini-budget during the course of the budgetary year is something that occurs almost annually. Governments find it propitious to adjust their initial calculations according to the changing economic and political environment. In 1986, the mini-budget was used as a way of quickly passing a series of important economic reforms promised in the election platform. Most of these reforms, such as the abolition of the wealth tax, had been prepared before the election by special opposition working parties. Once in power, the most important reforms had to be passed immediately, so that their effects would be felt before the 1988 presidential election.

The Ministers and their *cabinets*, therefore, spent the first three weeks in office preparing the *collectif budgétaire*. Only once this law was voted by the National Assembly in early May could work on the 1987 budget properly start. Due to the work already completed by the *direction du Budget* and due to the budgetary policy consensus that reigned between Chirac, Balladur and Juppé, the delay was quickly made up. The *lettre de cadrage* was sent out by Chirac on May 30th. It was immediately followed by the *conférences budgétaires*, which were completed by the beginning of July, so that the *lettres plafonds* were sent out between July 15th–19th. The revenue side of the bill was prepared during August, with the major policy decisions being taken around August 22nd and the final arbitrations taking place on 25 September. The bill was then sent to Parliament on the normal prescribed date where it was passed and promulgated on December 31st. Apart from a slight initial delay, therefore, the 1987 budget followed the same timetable as any other. However, the manner in which it was prepared does differ significantly to the 1985 budget. As with the 1986 broadcasting act, the most fundamental change was the absence of any presidential influence in the preparatory process. The unwritten rules of *cohabitation* applied as much to the budget as to any other bill. Apart from Ulrich's relations with Bianco, the only people authorised to have any contacts with the Elysée were Balladur's *directeur de cabinet*, Jean-Claude Trichet, and Juppé's, Daniel Bouton. However, these contacts served merely to inform the President's advisers of the budget's progress, rather than to bargain over its contents. Both Chirac's and Balladur's economic and budgetary advisers attested that there was no interference from the Elysée during this period.[26]

The other major change also resulted from the specificity of the *cohabitation* period and concerned the allocation of responsibilities between Chirac, Balladur and Juppé. The Prime Minister, with the 1988 elections in mind, wanted to cultivate a quasi-presidential image for himself and, therefore, decided that he should not be seen to intervene in the details of policy preparation, but would remain above this process setting only the general policy directions. With regard to the budget, he was unwilling to meddle in the spending and revenue arbitrations. This decision was also inspired by the fact that the cuts to be made were severe and it was felt to be prudent that the Prime Minister should not be seen to be personally responsible for them.[27] Following a suggestion from Balladur, Chirac agreed to give the Finance Minister '*une délégation totale*'.[28] He was to be responsible, therefore, for the vast majority of budgetary arbitrations. This extra responsibility for the Finance Minister also led to a more important role for the the Budget Minister, as will be demonstrated below.

Such a situation was brought about by *cohabitation*, but also because Chirac had '*une confiance totale*'[29] in both Balladur and Juppé. Both were senior members of the RPR, both had worked closely with Chirac in Paris and all three shared the same economic credo. The result was that, whilst the Prime Minister guarded his influence over the major policy decisions, he was less present in the budgetary minutiae than, for example, Fabius had been previously. The same was true for his economic and budgetary advisers, Emmanuel Rodocanachi and Gérard Rameix. As one of Balladur and Juppé's budgetary advisers stated:

I told them what was going on. I passed papers on to them. They were aware of what was happening, but they were rather more spectators than actors. What I am saying is a little extreme, but it was a bit like that. They were there so that if they knew that the Prime Minister attatched a particular importance to such and such a point then the Finance Minister would be made aware of the fact.[30]

The Prime Minister, however, was in no way unable to intervene. He regularly met with Balladur and Juppé, both separately and as part of the frequent meetings of the majority. He was personally informed of the budget's progress by one of the Finance Minister's advisers, Jacques Friedman, who was the go-between between him and Balladur. Rodocanachi had weekly meetings with the Finance Minister and all the junior Ministers under his authority, whilst he was also present at the arbitrations presided over by Balladur. Rameix attended the arbitration meetings that Juppé organised. Moreover, as will be seen, on occasions Chirac did intervene personally and he did sign the *lettre de cadrage* and the *lettres plafonds*, thus accepting political responsibility for them. Therefore, his withdrawal from the budgetary process is more a sign of strength than of weakness. Having put the budget in context, the expenditure side of the bill will now be examined.

The RPR-UDF election platform contained little detail about the then opposition's spending plans. It was much more precise about its commitment to cut the budget deficit and about its fiscal policy. It was clear, however, that in order to meet its promises, significant cuts in government expenditure would be required. In the *collectif budgétaire* cuts amounting to 10 billion francs were agreed upon. The harshness of the cuts came as a shock to some government members, but it was a deliberate signal to the spending Ministries that the new administration was going to keep to its election promises and that, consequently, further cuts would be necessary.

In fact, the 1987 budget contained a 40 billion franc spending decrease. This figure was included in the *lettre de cadrage* and was arrived at as a balancing figure once the calculations had been made about the reduction of the budget deficit and tax cuts.[31] In an attempt to find areas of saving, Juppé's *directeur de cabinet*, Daniel Bouton, proposed that each Ministry should undergo a so-called '*exercice de budget base zéro*'. This exercise obliged each Ministry to reconstruct and justify its spending needs down to the last franc, rather than simply automatically renewing its projects from one year to the next. Bouton used his new found influence upon Juppé to have the exercise accepted, although he would have proposed it to the socialists had they been re-elected in March 1986.[32]

The results of this administrative exercise were patchy. In some cases important areas of saving were identified. However, the spending patterns of some Ministries were not suited to this sort of procedure. One example was the Telecommunications Ministry, which proceded to make personnel cuts, but not as a result of this exercise.[33] The Culture Ministry refused even to participate in it, arguing that it had a minimum level of budgetary requirements and that it could only reconstruct its needs from this figure upwards.[34] As one adviser noted generally about the exercise:

This story of zero budgeting began within the *direction du Budget* and we, in the *cabinet*, didn't really take it up. It was more of a reference which was there in the dossier and which allowed us to proceed to arbitrations which were relatively classical in nature.[35]

There are two reasons, however, as to why the 1986 *conférences budgétaires* were slightly anomalous. Firstly, there was a large degree of consensus within the government that drastic spending cuts had to be made. At least on the expenditure side of the budget, the disagreements within the government on economic policy were small. Most people gave top priority to tax cuts and reducing the budget deficit and they were aware that this policy entailed spending reductions. As one of Balladur's budgetary advisers stated: 'There was general agreement that spending had to be cut so as to enable the budget deficit to be reduced and above all so as to enable taxes to be lowered'.[36] This consensus facilitated the task of Balladur and Juppé. It must also be noted that, since 1981, the right had consistently criticised the socialists for overspending and, thus, once in office, they were likely to want to reduce expenditure.

Secondly, in at least one case, a Minister, guided by his liberal beliefs, proposed to cut spending by more than the amount asked of him at the arbitration meeting. Alain Madelin, Industry Minister and leading member of the economically neo-liberal Republican Party, wanted to slash the level of subsidies his Ministry accorded to industries in trouble. Such zeal is certainly atypical of the classical arbitration process. A reduction in such subsidies was already government policy, but Madelin went much further than Balladur and Juppé had proposed. Needless to say, they accepted further cuts.

In general, however, despite these provisos and the base budget exercise, the spending arbitrations reflected the normal bargaining process that takes place each year between the parsimonious Finance Minister and the profligate spending Ministers. One person who was in the *direction du Budget* at the time described this process as: '*une dialectique de négociation entre quelqu'un qui demande beaucoup et quelqu'un qui a peu à offrir*'.[37] As usual, the *direction du Budget* organised the preliminary round of arbitrations. The next stage, however, saw an increased role for the Budget Minister. Juppé had the consent of Balladur and Chirac to arbitrate personally on all but the most important points of disagreement, rather than simply preparing the dossiers that the Finance Minister would decide upon. He received each Minister in the presence of the *directeur du Budget*, Fabre, Bouton, Blanchard-Dignac and Rameix. One of those present notes: 'I had the feeling that the Budget Minister tried to settle as many things as possible at his level'.[38] Around 50 per cent of all budgetary arbitrations were made at this level. This figure is much higher than normal and includes, for example, an agreement on the Education Ministry's budget, something almost unheard of at this early stage.

One of the reasons for the high success rate is the privileged information to which Juppé had access. The *direction des Impôts* calculated that the income from taxes, especially corporation tax, was likely to be higher in 1986 than had been forecast in the *budget de réconduction*. Therefore, Juppé was left with a leeway that he would not otherwise have possessed:

A lot of budget's were sorted out at Juppé's level because there was a certain leeway. Notably, there was a big surprise, namely an increase in governmental receipts which took place during the year. The Budget Minister had been informed about this and gave a little of it away at his level.[39]

The spending Ministers, however, were ignorant of this windfall and, thus, when Juppé agreed to certain items that they originally feared would be cut, they agreed to let other matters drop. From a position of strength, Juppé kept within his spending targets.

However, there were limits to Juppé's authority and Balladur was called upon to arbitrate in a number of different areas, although, in most cases, with the notable exception of the Culture Ministry, only one or two outstanding points in any particular budget were left for him to decide upon. There were several reasons why these problems could not be fixed at Juppé's level. Some Ministers refused to accept the level of cuts that the Budget Minister had demanded. For example, this was the case of the Culture, Telecommunications, Transport and Employment Ministries. For others, it was felt to be politic that they be seen to be arbitrated by Balladur. For example, Méhaignerie, the leader of the CDS, fell into this category. The same was true for the Minister of the Interior, Pasqua, whose budget caused no problems, but who, nevertheless, saw Balladur. While other budgets, such as that of the Co-operation Ministry, were considered to be too important strategically for Balladur not to look at them. Whilst the delegation of responsibility to Balladur was certainly great, some budgets inevitably found their way up to Chirac himself. The Prime Minister had made it clear from the outset that he would deal personally with the Agriculture budget. This decision reflected the Prime Minister's interest in and knowledge of the subject as a former Agriculture Minister. Similarly, he indicated his desire to study the budget of the DOM-TOM Ministry, again reflecting a personal interest. In both of these cases, however, it should also be noted that they were sensitive political issues, French farmers having a seemingly spontaneous tendency to riot, while the New Caledonian problems were of the gravest order.

Another budget which Chirac arbitrated was that of the Defence Ministry. Normally, defence is considered to belong to the President's reserved domain, but during *cohabitation* the Prime Minister assumed at least a joint responsibility in this area. Whilst the President was informed of the details of the Defence budget, observers agreed that the final arbitrations belonged to Chirac and not Mitterrand. The same was not necessarily true, however, for the preparation later in the year of the *loi de programmation militaire*, with which the President was closely associated.

The Culture Ministry's budget was the only other to be arbitrated at Matignon. Here, there were particular problems over the *grands travaux*, such as the Bastille Opera, the Louvre project and the Villette science park. The Finance Minister felt that at least one of these ambitious schemes should be scrapped. He focused on the Bastille Opera, work on which had only just started and which, if stopped immediately, would entail the waste of only a relatively small amount of money. Léotard, however, was violently opposed to this proposal and, indeed, to any of his spending plans being dropped.[40] His meeting with Juppé was perfunctory and his meeting with Balladur was inconclusive. Chirac, therefore, was called upon to arbitrate. The tactics used by the Culture Ministry were classical. Léotard threatened to resign; he evoked the importance of his position as leader of the PR; and he made a concerted effort to show how the *grands travaux* would be of benefit to Chirac and Juppé at the Parisian level. While several minor issues were lost, for the most part Chirac arbitrated in Léotard's favour. Even then, some of the lesser items were regained as part of the *provision parlementaire*, as his budgetary advisers cleverly lobbied deputies.

Turning to the revenue side, even before the March elections there were difficulties between the RPR and the UDF over the future government's fiscal policy. The UDF, led by the supporters of Raymond Barre, the *barristes*, favoured a large reduction in the budget deficit, whilst the RPR and a section of the UDF, notably the PR, wanted substantial tax reductions. The election platform was a compromise between these two demands. It was agreed that there should be an equal reduction of both.

The *collectif budgétaire* was used by the new government to fulfil a number of electoral promises, but the preparation of the 1987 budget was the first major opportunity to debate exactly which policies ought to be adopted. For much of the time, however, it was a very one-sided debate within the government. The *barristes*, because of their leader's objections to the very existence of *cohabitation*, had refused any senior government posts. Only Méhaignerie agreed to head a largely technical Ministry. The RPR, however, held the most important economic and budgetary posts. During the early stages, therefore, the *barriste* input was negligible.

Juppé proposed a plan to reduce the budget deficit by 15 billion francs each year for three years, so as to wipe out the deficit apart from interest charges. This plan was accepted by Balladur and subsequently by Chirac. Indeed, this process is typical of the preparation of fiscal policy. The Prime Minister was involved in the definition of global policy options, but the detailed work was then undertaken by the Finance Ministry. One of Juppé and Balladur's advisers stated:

> Really, it was Balladur and Juppé who sorted out the fiscal side. I didn't get the impression that the Prime Minister was involved. The same goes for his *cabinet*.[41]

In 1987 the only detailed fiscal questions decided by the Prime Minister were farming tax regulations. Nevertheless, the Prime Minister was always in the position to refuse a particular proposal when he saw fit. One adviser noted:

> Taxation policy is something which is normally delegated to the Finance Minister. The Prime Minister intervenes in a political sense to set the major fiscal guidelines. However, once these have been set, it is so technical that it is out of the Prime Minister's hands.[42]

The Prime Minister's role, therefore, is important at the beginning of the preparatory process, but also at the end when the details have been drawn up. At this stage they will be presented to him for his acceptance, or rejection. It was this double intervention that characterised the 1987 budgetary process.

Despite the electoral promise, it was decided by Balladur and Juppé that tax reductions should take priority over a reduction of the budget deficit. This decision was made largely for economic reasons, although political considerations were not absent. It was decided to reduce the deficit by 15 billion francs and taxes by 27 billion francs, a much higher figure than was originally thought possible and which was facilitated by the windfall receipts from which the government benefited in July and August 1986. The main debate then centred around how to divide the tax cuts between individuals and companies. The election platform had committed the government to a substantial cut in personal taxation and both Balladur, Juppé and the influential liberal trio, Léotard, Longuet and Madelin, were all in favour of this measure for economic and political reasons. The *barristes* and the non-PR component of the UDF, however, favoured substantial reductions in company taxation and/or investment incentives.

The debate once again centred on the *taxe professionnelle*. The *barristes* favoured reducing it, in return for an increase in the level of *crédits d'investissement*. Balladur was resolutely opposed to this latter proposal. The debate was largely technical and focused on economic reasons for and against the particular measures, rather than political ones. On the one side, the *direction du Budget*, Balladur, Juppé and their *cabinets* were all opposed to any idea of abolishing the *taxe professionnelle* and preferred to take steps to reduce the level of corporation tax, rather than increase the level of *crédits d'investissement*. Their view was supported by the liberals who had several meetings to co-ordinate their ideas and to decide how best to go about convincing the Finance Minister to stick to his line. On the other side, Barre put forward his case in newspaper articles and speeches, rather than in meetings with the government. Personal contacts were left to Méhaignerie who had the easiest access to Balladur and Juppé, but also to Bruno Durieux, a UDF deputy who met with Juppé on several occasions in the latter stages of the preparatory progress. Also present were Edmond Alphandery, the UDF's budgetary spokesperson in the National Assembly, and Michel d'Ornano, the President of the Assembly's Finance Commission.

Balladur and his supporters were adamant that the economic arguments in favour of increasing investment subsidies were poor, but realised that it would be politically difficult to insist upon only a small cut in the *taxe professionnelle* as well. Therefore, he accepted the proposal from one of his advisers to cut the latter by five billion francs, an amount sufficiently substantial so as to quieten the *barriste* lobby. Chirac accepted Balladur's recommendation.

This measure alone, however, did not satisfy the UDF. One of the principal figures at this stage was d'Ornano. On a number of occasions in September, d'Ornano met Juppé and Balladur and argued for further measures in favour of companies. The level of the reduction in the *taxe professionnelle* was partly due to his insistence. This pressure, however, continued and was accentuated when the bill was placed before the National Assembly. D'Ornano conducted meetings with the parliamentary majority and found a favourable response to his proposals. Therefore, during the meeting of the National Assembly's Finance commission he proposed two important amendments that the government felt obliged to accept at the cost of around two billion francs. While the government was not opposed in principle to the amendments, they would not have been passed without d'Ornano's insistence. One adviser noted:

> We accepted a certain number of costly parliamentary amendments. D'Ornano was extremely tough. We had to back down on quite a number of issues. He was the only person who mattered.[43]

Indeed, d'Ornano deliberately upped the ante knowing that in the political climate that reigned he was likely to succeed.[44] From his experience in 1981, Chirac knew that in any future second ballot of a presidential election he would need the full support of the *barristes* in order to beat Mitterrand. Therefore, he could not afford to alienate them. He was also aware that the government had only a slender parliamentary majority and that to pass its legislation it needed the full support of the UDF. D'Ornano exploited this situation to the full and obtained certain concessions, in return for which he assured that there were no dissenting votes within the majority. In each parliamentary vote the majority was solid and the budget passed with little difficulty.

The 1990 Budget

Following his appointment as Prime Minister in May 1988, Michel Rocard immediately had to immerse himself in budgetary arbitrations that were already at a rather advanced stage. The preparation of the 1990 budget, therefore, was the first for which he was completely responsible. In practice, this responsibility was shared with the Finance Minister, Pierre

Bérégovoy, and the ebullient Budget Minister, Michel Charasse. As might further be expected, *cohabitation* having ended, the President's role was not insubstantial and, consequently, the Matignon, Bercy (new home of the Finance Ministry), Elysée axis was the dominant political force in the preparation of this budget.

This budget saw a number of minor, but not unimportant procedural changes. The initiative for these changes belonged mainly to the *direction du Budget*, but they were fully endorsed by both Rocard and Mitterrand. The first change came on April 13th with an extraordinary meeting of all government Ministers to discuss the government's overall budgetary strategy. Normally, discussion in this period is confined to the Finance Ministry, the Prime Minister and the President and, indeed, in March and April these three had discussed at length all of the different options available. The April 13th meeting, however, did much more than just rubber stamp decisions taken elsewhere and a full debate about budgetary policy took place. A proposal was made to follow Bérégovoy's recommendation and reduce the budget deficit by 10 billion francs to 90 billion francs and was accepted by all those present.

A further innovation followed the day after with the appearance of the *lettre de cadrage*. In previous years there had been only a single letter, a copy of which was received by each Minister. This year the letter was individualised. Each Minister received a separate letter outlining the major budgetary orientations for the year to come, but also fixing a spending limit for his/her particular department. In practice, this strategy pre-empted the *lettre plafond* and reduced the Minister's capacity for overestimating his/her spending needs in the *conférences budgétaires*. The result was also to reduce the involvement of the Prime Minister in the arbitration process, as he was signalling the limits within which Ministers had to keep in April, rather than two months later after the final arbitrations.

The *direction du Budget* was behind this reform, but Rocard readily accepted it. In 1988, he had been forced to arbitrate each department's budget down to the last million franc project. Rocard considered this to have been an unnecessary and time consuming process and an experience which he was not going to repeat.[45] As with 1986 changes, this reform should not be seen as reducing the Prime Minister's influence. Instead, it shifted it to an earlier stage in the process, upstream of the detailed spending arbitrations. Although, even here he remained the person to whom all Ministers appealed.

As usual, the final spending arbitrations took place in mid-July, after which the revenue side of the budget was prepared. These arbitrations took place in early September and the bill was passed by the Council of

Ministers on September 20th. The PS parliamentary group, however, was unhappy with the fiscal measures in the bill and its pressure meant that the government was forced to amend the bill substantially after its final and decisive meeting with the party on October 17th. This aspect of the bill will be studied in detail below.

As with the passage of the 1989 broadcasting act, the absence of a PS parliamentary majority meant that the passage of the bill through Parliament was more complicated than usual. In 1988, the government had been able to pass the budget without recourse to Article 49–3 because on each vote it had won the support of either the PCF, or the UDC. In 1989, this course of action proved to be impossible. The UDC leader, Méhaignerie, declared in early October that his group would vote against the bill. The same was true for the PCF with whom no acceptable deal could be agreed, even after negotiations between the leader of the parliamentary group, André Lajoinie, and one prominent PS Finance commissioner.[46]

Despite the opposition of these two groups, the Prime Minister's parliamentary advisers were still confident that Article 49–3 could be avoided. They had received assurances from a sufficient number of individual UDC and independent deputies, so that they believed they would not have to resort to a no-confidence vote. However, the leader of the PS parliamentary group, Louis Mermaz, refused to accept this strategy and insisted that Article 49–3 be used. He felt that it would be better for the PS's image to resort to this article, rather than relying on a few cobbled-together centrist votes.[47] The preparation of the PS's party congress a few months later was certainly the main inspiration behind Mermaz's decision. As a result, Rocard was obliged to use 49–3 twice in order to pass the bill. After a referral to the Constitutional Council the bill became law on 30th December 1989.

The first major expenditure choices were signalled with the appearance of the *budget de réconduction*. Here, the Finance Ministry estimated that the GDP would increase by 5 per cent in 1990. This became the guideline figure which to a large extent determined the ministerial spending levels in the *lettre de cadrage*. This figure was set as the level for the overall increase in public expenditure. If some Ministries were felt to be in need of an increase greater than 5 per cent, then others would have to see their spending increased by less than this amount. In fact, four categories of Ministry were identified by Matignon and Bercy.[48]

The first category consisted of the prioritised departments. They would be allowed to increase spending by more than 5 per cent. In fact, these priorities were not fixed by Rocard, or Bérégovoy, but were outlined in Mitterrand's 1988 electoral campaign. He made very clear public commitments to large spending increases in the budgets for the Education, Research and Co-operation Ministries. One of the most important roles that the President's advisers played after 1988 was to ensure that these priorities were abided by. In interviews with people at Matignon and Bercy, however, it was confirmed that at no time was it ever a question of them ever trying to change these priorities, or even of not keeping to them. Rocard's unwritten contract with Mitterrand included the clause that he would faithfully execute the President's mandate. These budgets did, however, go to the Prime Minister for arbitration. He was to decide how far over the 5 per cent limit they were to be set, with Bercy in favour of a smaller overshoot than the Ministers. It was up to Rocard to arbitrate, although he did so in close liaison with the Elysée.

In the second departmental category spending increased only in line with inflation, then running at around 3 per cent. This increase affected, for example, the Telecommunications, Justice and the Interior Ministries. Whilst in the third category spending was only allowed to remain at the previous year's levels and, thus, did not account for the increase in inflation over the year. In these two categories the Prime Minister played a much greater role. He was in the position to decide which Ministries would be included in which category, although it was in no way an individual decision and again Bercy and the Elysée were closely involved.

Even in these two categories, the President personally intervened during the final arbitrations in July to demand an increase in spending for a number of budgets. This was the case notably for the Culture Minister, Lang, and the Housing Minister, Delebarre. Lang's close personal links with Mitterrand and the President's intense interest in the grand cultural projects of his second *septennat*, meant that, while not amongst the priorities listed in the *Lettre à tous les Français*, the Culture Ministry was able to enjoy a larger than average budgetary increase. Moreover, Lang was very clever to exploit his relations with Mitterrand, so as to appeal directly to the President and short-circuit the Prime Minister in the appeal process.[49] He wrote several letters to the President appealing for more money and, while he was not systematically granted it, he did benefit on a number of occasions.

Delebarre's situation was slightly different. Although the overall increase in his Ministry's budget was only 5.3 per cent, only slighter higher than the average figure, spending on special low cost housing projects (*le logement social*) increased by 17 per cent. This increase came at a very late stage in the arbitration process. It was due to two reasons. Firstly, the Finance Ministry greatly underestimated the Housing Ministry's basic needs in its initial budgetary calculations in March. This mistake was identified during the budget conferences and Delebarre's budget increased accordingly.[50] Secondly, Mitterrand took a personal interest in the social housing question. In a speech during the summer to the HLM federation, he announced that the government had to make a greater budgetary effort in favour of social housing. Moreover, in the light of the liberal changes necessitated by European economic integration, particularly in the fiscal domain, Mitterrand insisted that further social measures be taken to redress the balance. Rocard had no option but to comply with the President's wishes, although the opposition to this measure came more from Bérégovoy and Charasse, than from the Prime Minister.[51] Consequently, on July 26th, the Prime Minister announced that 2.3 billion francs would be added to the social housing budget.

The fourth and final category consisted of the Defence Ministry's budget. This budget was set apart as a special case because 1989 also saw the preparation of the revised *loi de programmation militaire* for 1990–93. To a large extent, the Defence budget for 1990, therefore, depended on long-term strategic defence decisions, which in turn depended on the international situation and also on the government's other long-term priorities. The most notable of these priorities was the 24 billion franc increase in the Education Ministry's budget over five years and an annual 15 billion franc tax reduction due to European economic harmonisation. These constraints put pressure on the government and the President to decrease spending on the military programme which was set to cost the country 470 billion francs in five years' time.

The initiative to cut the military programme in order to fund the government's other priorities came from the Finance Minister. He suggested a 70 billion franc cut, something that the Defence Minister, Jean-Pierre Chevènement, violently opposed, as it would mean the abandonment of one his Ministry's prestige projects. Chevènement was willing to accept a 30 billion cut coming from personnel reductions, but he wished to leave the major projects intact. These two contrasting proposals were presented to Rocard in an arbitration meeting in late June. However, the Prime Minister was aware that he did not have the authority personally to arbitrate. With the Prime Minister refusing to take the side of either Chevènement, or Bérégovoy, the matter was settled in a defence council meeting at the Elysée where a figure of 45 billion francs was agreed upon.[52]

In fact, the tactics used in the bargaining process over this budget were typical of the arbitration process as a whole. The Finance Minister argued that the government's budgetary calculations would be shattered if the level of cuts he proposed were not made. The Defence Minister proposed certain reductions, so as to appear conciliatory, but on the main and costly issues he was insistent, even threatening to resign if any major projects were cut.

In the other budgetary negotiations, the process was very similar as were the tactics used by both sides. The Prime Minister, however, was better placed to arbitrate. It should be remembered, though, that the President always reserved the right to intervene when he considered it to be necessary. It should also be remembered that the Prime Minister was sometimes weakened in relation to the Finance Minister. Matignon does not have the administrative resources to question the figures that are presented to it by Bercy. Therefore, it is not unheard of for Bercy deliberately to underestimate the government's economic leeway, so that the Prime Minister feels obliged to be very strict with Ministers in the arbitrations with which he is faced. This was the situation in 1989.[53] In fact, the level of public spending rose by only 4.7 per cent, less than originally foreseen in the *lettre de cadrage*.

On the income side, the major influence on the government's fiscal policy was the impact of European economic harmonisation. In 1984 and 1986, its effects had been slight. In 1984, the prospect of the Single European Act deterred the government from raising VAT, even if it did not lead to any reduction. In 1986, the reduction in corporation tax was consistent with economic harmonisation, but it was mainly due to political circumstances and Balladur's economic philosophy. In 1989, economic integration was imminent and the government had to take steps to prepare it.

Bérégovoy was particularly anxious to take the necessary steps to harmonise France's fiscal policy with that of its EC partners. One of the first changes needing to be made was an increase in the incentives to save (*la fiscalité d'épargne*). This same topic had been the subject of a detailed report by the PS deputy, Christian Pierret, published in June 1989. In the propositions delivered to Rocard in August 1989, Bérégovoy included several of the report's recommendations, although he went further than Pierret had considered to be prudent.

Another area in which it was essential to make changes was the VAT structure. France had a very high top rate of VAT, which needed to be reduced in order to align the country with the rest of Europe. Both Bérégovoy and Rocard were agreed that steps had to be taken, although they and their advisers differed over the details of the reform. Rocard favoured a reduction of the top rate on cars only, whereas Bérégovoy favoured an across the board reduction for simplicity's sake and as a sign of France's European commitment. The Prime Minister agreed, unwilling to make this issue a divisive one.

The third measure which Bérégovoy wanted to introduce was the most controversial. He proposed a reduction in the level of corporation tax from 39 per cent to 37 per cent for companies which reinvested their profits. This proposal met with opposition from the Prime Minister, who felt that priority should be given to reducing the level of tax on dividended profits, aligning the two at 39 per cent. Bérégovoy, however, insisted that his proposal was consistent with the President's desire for economic harmonisation and he also wanted to give the financial markets a sign that the country was helping business activity.

Consistent with the usual process, the President was called upon to endorse these changes. Whilst his electoral mandate unequivocally outlined his commitment to European integration, he was concerned that these reforms smacked too much of liberalism. Therefore, he agreed to accept them only if the government would increase the social aspect of the budget, proposing an increase in the wealth tax and increased spending on social projects.[54] The government agreed. In voicing his concern at the liberal aspects of the budget, however, the President was articulating the worries of a large part of the PS. In fact, the most concerted opposition to these reforms came from the PS parliamentary group and the party itself.

Parliament's interest in and its influence on the revenue side of the budget are generally much greater than on expenditure matters. Revenue questions are more highly publicised than their spending counterparts. The public impact of changing the tax structure is much more immediate and the debate surrounding it is often couched in much more political terms. In 1989, the debate between the party and its parliamentary group and the government centred around fiscal policy. It was difficult, however, to distinguish between the influence of the party and the influence of the PS group. This was because the leading figures in the group all held important positions in the party and because the leading party members were all deputies.

The most important figures in the debate with the government were Dominic Strauss-Kahn, the President of the National Assembly's Finance Commission; Raymond Douyère, a leading commissioner; Alain Richard, the group's budgetary spokesperson; Louis Mermaz, leader of the PS group in the Assembly; Pierre Mauroy, PS first secretary; and Henri Emmanuelli, number two in the party. The problems between the government and the party were caused by two main reasons. Firstly, there were genuine policy disagreements. Strauss-Kahn, for example, was opposed to the government's reforms on economic grounds. Secondly, there were institutional problems between the party and the government.[55] The government's legislative co-operation with the UDC over the preceding 18 months had left the PS with the feeling that its influence had decreased to the point where the government took little notice of it when drawing up policy. With the knowledge that the party conference was only a few months away, party leaders were determined to try and influence the budget where they felt it to be necessary.

Strauss-Kahn was opposed to the reduction in the VAT level for sound economic reasons. He believed that any such reduction would only increase the level of imports and would create a balance of payments problem as French industry would not be able to cope with the subsequent increase in demand. The government, however, presented the party with a *fait accompli*, announcing the reduction in the Council of Ministers on 6 September 1989. Whilst all agreed that, once decided, the reform had to be put into effect immediately, the party was angry that it had not been included in the discussions surrounding it and that it had learnt of the decision at the same time as the public.[56]

The party was even more aggrieved when the government used the same strategy to announce the corporation tax reduction on September 13th as part of Rocard's second employment plan. As one parliamentarian noted:

It was a good strategy to get the reform passed, consisting of a *fait accompli* by the Finance Minister if not the government.[57]

Whilst the Finance Commission could have refused to accept both of these reforms, it could only have overturned them with the government's agreement, as the Constitution prohibits any parliamentary amendments which reduce the level of government income. Bérégovoy, however, would not contemplate reversing these measures. For him the matter was an issue of confidence. He was behind the reform and, now that they had been announced, if he backed down it would be a sign of weakness to which the markets would react adversely. In a particularly stormy meeting with the PS group on October 3rd, Bérégovoy threatened to resign if the party did not accept the reduction in corporation tax.[58]

Faced with this ultimatum, the party decided to agree to the reform and it was passed by the Finance Commission on October 11th. In return, however, the group started to formulate a list of demands which it would insist upon in the final government/party arbitrations later in the month. Matters came to a head at the final arbitration meeting on October 17th at Matignon. Representing the government were Rocard, Bérégovoy, Charasse and Poperen, the Minister for Parliamentary Relations. The PS was represented by Mauroy, Emmanuelli, Strauss-Kahn, Richard and Douyère.

The party had a list of demands that it presented to the government. In return for lowering corporation tax, Strauss-Kahn wanted the government to increase the level of death duties. Bérégovoy was absolutely opposed to this proposal saying that it would undermine business confidence and would be electorally unpopular. However, he proposed to set up a commission to study the matter in time for the 1991 budget. He also suggested an increase in the wealth tax as a compensatory social measure. Whilst the Prime Minister had publicly opposed any further increase in this tax the previous year, on this occasion he realised that he had to agree to it in order to pacify the party. As one of Rocard's advisers states: 'You have to compromise. That's politics. It was necessary to give something up to the group'.

The group also proposed a significant increase in the level of taxation on the profits of both companies and individuals derived from the appreciation on property and other items. The group argued that this measure was necessary in view of the exigencies of European fiscal harmonisation, France's levels being rather low. This rather ironic argument was strengthened because Strauss-Kahn had previously secretly contacted the heads of various leading companies asking them if any such increase would effect their investment plans. The response was that it would not.[59] Bérégovoy, therefore, was deprived of using this argument and agreed to increase the level of taxation on companies from 15 per cent to 19 per cent, on condition that the level for individuals remained the same.

The group was also able to pass an amendment reforming the *taxe professionnelle*, so that it favoured lower income earners. Bérégovoy also agreed to set up studies similar to the one on death duties for this tax, as well as for the *taxe d'habitation* and the *Dotation Globale de Fonctionnement*. The overall result of the meeting was a compromise between both sides, but it was particularly instructive in that it put clearly into focus some of the dynamics of the decision-making process.

For example, although a compromise was reached, the successful arguments put forward by the group were based on soundly researched economic principles. Also, the government, normally seen as the dominant partner in its relations with the party and its parliamentary group, was clearly forced to cede on a number of issues. This situation was due to a number of reasons. The position of the Finance Ministry was weakened due to a debilitating tax-collectors' strike. Their claims were regarded sympathetically by a large part of the PS. By refusing to give in to the tax-collectors, Bérégovoy reduced his bargaining power on budgetary matters. Similarly, by insisting on the reduction in corporation tax, Bérégovoy built up resentment within the PS and found his room to manœuvre on other issues reduced. He was also faced with a noticeable lack of overt support from the President and Prime Minister. Whilst on a South American tour with Mitterrand in early October, Mermaz had urged the party to insist on its own reforms. Given their timing, these comments were taken to have the President's support. Similarly, Rocard, while in favour of the reduction in corporation tax, was unwilling to enter publicly into a damaging debate.

The ulterior motive behind many of these positions was the forth-coming party congress. For example, whilst there always tends to be a certain institutional antagonism between the Finance Minister and the President of the Finance Commission, the relations between Bérégovoy and Strauss-Kahn in 1989 were not helped by the fact that the former was a *fabiusien* and the latter a *jospiniste*. The conflict between the two reflects the breakdown of the *mitterrandiste courant* in the PS after 1988. Similarly, Rocard was unwilling publicly to intervene because he was trying to create the image of himself as a potential unifier of these two factions at some future date. The party congress, however, served to confuse the institutional debate between the government and the party, rather than aggravating it because the different factions were present in the government just as they were in Parliament. It also may have served to defuse the debate at certain times, as well as to envenom it at others. For example, Strauss-Kahn argued that the party failed to force through the change in death duties because: '*les fabiusiens nous ont lâchés*'.[60] Bérégovoy made this issue into a factional one, precisely so as to ensure that the followers of the former Prime Minister would be obliged to support him and not Strauss-Kahn.

Conclusion

The dynamics of the budgetary policy-making process provide a good illustration of the politics of the governmental decision-making process. Although there are special procedures which are unique to the preparation of the budget in France, the process still resembled to a large extent the one which was encountered in the previous chapter. Policy outcomes were the result of a hierarchical arbitration process in which the Prime Minister's role was central.

Indeed, many of the forces which, in the last chapter, were seen to impinge upon the policy process were also present in the case studies presented in this chapter. For example, just as in the preparation of broadcasting policy the bureaucrats of the SJTI had a certain influence, so in the preparation of budgetary policy the role played by the *direction du*

Budget was also important. Indeed, arguably the influence of the permanent administration was greater in the case of the budget, because of the fact that the preparation of budgetary policy necessitates the co-operation of all government Ministries and because of the technical nature of many of the decisions which have to be made.

Similarly, in both policy areas, although the Prime Minister played a central role in the arbitration process for both expenditure and revenue items, the influence of the President must also be noted. On several occasions during both the preparation of the 1985 and 1990 budgets, the President intervened directly and publicly in the policy process to demand that certain policy decisions be taken. On these occasions, the Prime Minister and the Finance Minister had no option but to acquiesce to the President's wishes. Clearly, the exception to this observation occurred during *cohabitation* when the President played only a residual role in the policy process.

At the same time, however, this chapter provided certain other insights into the dynamics of the policy process which were not apparent from the study of broadcasting policy. Firstly, the impact of the international economic environment upon the domestic decision-making process in France must be noted. It was clear that government's room for manœuvre and, hence, the capacity to influence policy of the domestic actors and, therefore, of the Prime Minister were constrained during periods of international economic recession, such as in 1984. However, in periods of international economic expansion, such as 1989, the scope for governmental and prime ministerial intervention was much greater. It was also noted that the role of the bureaucracy was greater during periods of recession than periods of expansion.

Secondly, in contrast to anything which was seen in the previous chapter, the impact of intra-party disputes had a profound effect on the outcome of the 1990 budget. The importance of the disputes within the PS increased throughout the period under consideration and became noticeably more virulent in the run up to the 1990 party congress at Rennes. Whereas the study of the 1985 budget could be undertaken with only slight reference to intra-party rivalry, the preparation of the 1990 budget was greatly influenced by this problem. Indeed, the Rocard's actions were, on several occasions, determined by his perception of how best to operate in the face of these rivalries.

Finally, the impact of individual personalities was more apparent in this chapter, notably, during the preparation of the 1985 budget. The change of Prime Minister during 1984 at the height of the budgetary arbitration process, highlighted the differences between Mauroy, with his background as a *notable*, and Fabius, with his training in the *Inspection des Finances* and his experience as Budget Minister. This is not to say that Fabius was a technocrat, but undoubtedly their differing backgrounds helped to account, in part, for their different approaches to and influence on the budgetary policy process. However, the constraints of the wider system within which they operated must also be noted.

5   Crisis Policy-Making (I): The Devaquet Higher Education Bill, 1986

In this chapter and the next, instead of embarking upon another analysis of routine decision-making, the influence of the Prime Minister is examined during a period of crisis. Periods of crisis policy-making have been chosen, because they concentrate most clearly the issues at stake in the policy process and clarify the interests of the actors present. As one of the most central of these actors, the role and influence of the Prime Minister will be put into relief.

Therefore, two public policy decisions which were made during periods of governmental crisis have been chosen for study. The first case study examines the period of governmental difficulty in November and December 1986 when the wave of student protests against the Chirac government's higher education reforms was so acute that it provoked the resignation of the Minister for Higher Education, Alain Devaquet, and forced the withdrawal of the bill in question. The second study deals with the problems surrounding the devaluation of the franc in March 1983, when both the future of the Prime Minister in office and of the franc in the European Monetary System were in doubt.

It must be appreciated, however, that the concept of a political crisis is itself highly problematic. Therefore, in this chapter and the next, before embarking upon a detailed examination of the crisis period itself, the type of crisis period in each case will briefly be outlined.

A Period of Crisis: November–December 1986

Dunleavy and O'Leary have argued that a political crisis may take three different forms: a terminal crisis; an endurable crisis; and a curable crisis.[1] The problems surrounding the Devaquet bill fell into one of the latter two categories. That is to say, a period of chronic political difficulties and sub-optimal performance, or, conversely, a period of short-run political problems which could be resolved.

Opinions differed as to the precise nature of the governmental crisis in November–December 1986. Student leaders felt that something approaching the former definition was more appropriate, whereas representatives of the government tended to downplay the situation, arguing that something approaching the latter was accurate. At least there was agreement, however, that there was a crisis of some sort during this time. This is also the conclusion of Michel Dobry who has made a particular study of political crises.[2] He argued that:

> We witness, therefore, a disintegration of the routine logic of the political game; the usual points of reference, the ways of anticipating the future, of calculating, of predicting the efficiency of actions all collapsed and, for a very short period, things became uncontrollable and there was a good deal of political fluidity.[3]

By common consent, therefore, there was a time of political crisis during some part of November and December 1986.

In fact, this chapter concentrates upon the events in the period between the outbreak of the first student strike which was called on November 17th and the decision by Chirac to withdraw the bill on December 8th. While not all of this period could be considered as exhibiting the characteristics of a crisis, it did incorporate the most unstable period just before the bill's withdrawal. It also included the events leading up to this decision which provided the necessary background context for the crisis period.

Before embarking upon a detailed examination of this three week period, a brief chronological account of the complex series of events which led up to the withdrawal of the bill will be given. Having done this, the government's reaction to the student protests will be examined and the role played by the Prime Minister analysed.

A Chronology of Events Surrounding the Devaquet Bill

On 4 April 1986 in a speech to the National Assembly, Chirac announced his government's intention to draw up a bill which would reform the higher education system. In this speech there was little detail. The Prime Minister mainly reiterated the pledge contained in the RPR–UDF election platform promising greater autonomy for French universities. Alain Devaquet, an academic and Parisian RPR deputy, was given the responsibility for drafting the bill. His responsibility was immediately challenged, however, when Jean Foyer, an RPR deputy, tabled a private members bill designed to reorganise completely the university system. Foyer proposed a series of reforms that were much more radical than those envisaged by Devaquet and which were inspired by the work of a set of neo-liberal academics and deputies in the GERUF group. Foyer's bill aimed to introduce market forces to the higher education system by giving universities almost complete autonomy to run their own affairs. For example, they would be able to set their own level of tuition fees; they would decide their own entry requirements; and they would be able to deliver their own degrees, in place of the existing national degree system.

Devaquet was fiercely opposed to the ideas of the GERUF group and to the content of Foyer's bill. Consequently, the first draft of the government's bill bore little relation to the Foyer text. In fact, Devaquet's first draft was drawn up very quickly and was ready by May 18th. The speed of its preparation was criticised during the crisis period by students and others who felt that they had not been consulted over its contents. Devaquet insisted, however, that there had been ample consultation especially in meetings after the first draft and that the bill had subsequently been amended to accommodate the objections raised in these meetings.[4]

Once prepared the bill went through a series of interministerial reunions which began in mid-May. One of the key figures at these meetings was the academic Yves Durand. He was a leading figure in the GERUF group and had been appointed as Chirac's adviser on university affairs in March 1986. The relations between Devaquet and Durand were strained right from the start. Durand used his position to try and alter Devaquet's text in a way consistent with GERUF's ideas:

> Throughout these months, I came to the unfortunate conclusion, either through my own experiences or those of my advisers, that Durand was acting as the vigilant and committed representative of the organisations to which he belonged, resolutely determined to get their ideas and principles adopted.[5]

Moreover, Devaquet was also heavily criticised in Parliament by the RPR group which accused him of betraying the Prime Minister and the party's electoral platform. They called for the introduction of major amendments. The antipathy between Devaquet and Durand and the mistrust between the Minister and a section of his own parliamentary group was to have a significant influence on the events in November and December.

Due to the influence of Durand and Foyer the bill was altered in a number of respects, notably at a meeting chaired by Chirac on June 3rd. However, by the end of the month it was sent before the Council of State and it was approved by the Council of Ministers in a form acceptable to Devaquet on July 11th. Devaquet and his advisers hoped that the bill could be debated over the summer as they feared student protest against it if it were delayed until the autumn session.[6] There had already been some very minor protests outside of Paris in April and May. This request, however, was refused by the UDF Minister for Parliamentary Relations, André Rossinot. He gave preference to Méhaignerie's housing bill in the National Assembly, while the Senate was busy slowly rewriting Léotard's broadcasting bill. The university reform bill, therefore, had to wait until October to be debated.

The Senate finally debated the bill between 23rd–29th October. It was passed with little difficulty and encountered criticisms from only a few socialist senators. There had been little press or public interest in the debate. The different student organisations, however, had started to try and mobilise their members against the bill. On October 21st, 400 students launched what came to be known as the '*appel de Caen*', which called for a total withdrawal of the bill. As yet, however, student action was confined to a small group of union militants who had little impact on the mass of students who had just started the new academic year.

The first main student initiative came at the university of Paris XIII at Villetaneuse on November 17th. Although the principle of going on strike had been passed four days earlier, it was on this date that the students there voted by a large majority to strike and to try and extend it to students at other faculties. In fact, by November 22nd the strike had spread to students in a series of other universities in the Parisian region and outside. Moreover, the strike had also spread quickly amongst the *lycéens* and from the 21st onwards their numbers were to swell considerably the ranks of the student protestors.

On November 22nd the long-arranged *Etats généraux* of the main students' union, the UNEF-ID, were transformed into the *Etats généraux des étudiants en lutte* and a demonstration was announced in Paris on the 27th.[7] Also on the 22nd the movement received the support of President Mitterrand who said, whilst on an official visit to Auxerre: '*Comment voulez-vous que je me sente déphasé par rapport à eux (les jeunes)*'. Furthermore, the 28th saw the long-planned rally in Paris of the FEN which announced its support for the students. This demonstration was much larger than the government had expected and, indeed, the government consistently underestimated the movement's strength over the next fortnight.

The national student demonstration on the 27th also proved to be a great success and by this time disruption was widespread in most of the country's universities. Another demonstration was fixed for December 4th. In an attempt to calm the situation, on the 28th the government announced the

Table 5.1   *Chronology of events: November 17–December 8, 1986*

Day	Event
Monday 17th	Strike vote at Villetaneuse
Saturday 22nd	Creation of the *Etats généraux des étudiants en lutte*
Sunday 23rd	FEN demonstration in Paris (100,000 attend)
	Mitterrand's declaration at Auxerre
Thursday 27th	First national student demonstration
Friday 28th	*Renvoi en commission* of the bill
Saturday 29th	Internal problems within the UNEF-ID
Sunday 30th	Chirac appears on *Questions à Domicile*
Monday 1st	Darriulat alleged to have met Monory
Tuesday 2nd	Election of student delegation to meet Monory
Wednesday 3rd	Thomas meets Toubon
Thursday 4th	Second national student demonstration
	Student delegation meets Monory
	Rioting in the evening
Friday 5th	Government crisis meeting (morning)
	Chirac and Mitterrand leave for London
	Monory's television appearance (evening)
	Devaquet writes resignation letter
	Rioting and death of Malik Oussekine (night)
Saturday 6th	Beginning of two day RPR festival
	Chirac and Mitterrand return from London
Sunday 7th	Chirac has an audience with Mitterrand
Monday 8th	Bill withdrawn

postponement of the bill's examination by the National Assembly. Chirac then personally announced on November 30th that the government was aware of the opposition to the bill and that it would spend the next couple of weeks re-examining it and making any changes that were felt to be necessary.

This promise did not deflate the movement and was seen by the students as an attempt to buy time by Chirac with the hope that the protests would die down. In fact, the student organisations, buoyed by favourable television coverage and opinion polls, did their best to ensure that the demonstration on the 4th was to be an even greater success. For UNEF-ID, the demonstration was the most potent weapon against the government and its success depended on the number of people joining the marches.[8]

The demonstration on the 4th proved to be a great success with between 500,000 and 700,000 protestors marching in Paris alone. The government, however, refused to back down. Monory, the UDF Education Minister and Devaquet's superior, had already agreed to meet a delegation of striking students on the evening of the 4th. This meeting, however, was a failure with neither side either wanting to negotiate, or being allowed to do so when an attempt was made. Instead, the demonstration degenerated into violence between the police and students and a night of rioting ensued. The students blamed the police and the police blamed *casseurs*, who the police claimed were deliberately provoking violence from within the student ranks.

The next day was marked by intense governmental activity which culminated in a rather unapologetic television broadcast by Monory. It also saw the overnight resignation of Devaquet in response to the transfer of responsibility for the bill to the Education Minister and the violence that had occurred the previous day. Worse was to follow when during the night of the 5th–6th rioting again broke out. In the police operation to disperse the crowds a student, Malik Oussekine, was chased by two policeman and was struck. He died of his injuries in hospital a few hours later.

During the next two days the crisis was at its height. Chirac, however, had gone to London the previous day and there appeared to be a lack of governmental leadership. The student organisers called for a further demonstration on the 10th. There were clear signs that the protest was spreading to other non-student unions. Moreover, certain members of the government gave the impression of being less than sympathetic to what had happened during the night. In a speech to the RPR's 10th anniversary festival on December 7th, Charles Pasqua, the Minister of the Interior, suggested that the student movement was trotskyist inspired and that the government would never give in to street violence. While there had been violence and while trotskyists were present in the national delegation, this was a view which seemed caricatural to the mass of ordinary students and their parents alike.[9]

Behind the scenes, however, there was intense pressure on Chirac to withdraw the text. Government solidarity had never existed in private over what to do and now divisions were appearing in public as certain prominent Ministers called for the text to be withdrawn. On the morning of the 8th, Alain Madelin, the Industry Minister, publicly condemned Oussekine's death and said that the bill should be scrapped. Faced with pressure from within his government Chirac decided to end the escalation of violence and at 1 p.m. on December 8th it was announced that the bill had been withdrawn.

The repercussions of this troubled period for the government did not end there. On the 9th Chirac announced a pause in the government's reform programme. There was a silent student demonstration in memory of Oussekine on the 10th. Both the National Assembly and the Senate set up special commissions of enquiry which produced voluminous reports and provoked charges of a government cover up.[10] The two policemen involved in the death of Malik Oussekine were acquitted only in 1990. This study, however, will concentrate on the events between November 17th and December 8th. First, the response of the government to the student protests during this period will be examined.

Machinations within the Government

In this section, the focus will be upon two things in particular. Firstly, the divisions within the government over whether or not the bill should be maintained. Secondly, the different governmental strategies that were adopted to combat the crisis. In both cases, the role of the Prime Minister will be identified and the extent to which he determined the government's response to the student protests will be highlighted.

From the first weekend of the crisis onward (22–23 November), it was possible to identify three different attitudes within the government. There were those people who refused to alter the text and wanted to defend the unamended version; there were those who wished to modify it to a greater or lesser extent in an attempt to appease the students; and there were those who wished to withdraw the text immediately and unconditionally. During the crisis period there was a gradual shift from the first position to the second and then finally to the third. However, in no way was this progression linear. Opinions were relatively slow to move until the death of Malik Oussekine. It was only on Monday 8th that the pressures to withdraw the bill became so strong as to convince the Prime Minister that it had to be abandoned.

The strategies adopted during the crisis period could largely be seen to correspond to the divisions within the government. At the beginning, when there were only a few voices calling for the bill's withdrawal, the government adopted several of what might be called 'classical' strategies: media appearances to explain the bill, public meetings with the protestors to put forward the government's case; and the collation of information by the *renseignements généraux*. As the crisis spread, so the measures taken to deal with it became less routine. The *renvoi en commission* was an example of this point. Finally, during the period of greatest fluidity it became difficult to talk of a governmental strategy at all. At this point the action of government members was more inspired by private rivalries, personal initiatives and finally open rebellion, rather than by any pre-determined strategy.

Although the strike at Villetaneuse was called on November 17th, it was not until the weekend of the 22nd–23rd that any exceptional action was taken. In part this delay was not surprising. Opposition to the bill during its passage through the Senate had been no greater than for any other bill. Similarly, although the strike did spread quickly, it was not until the 22nd that there was any national co-ordination. Moreover, on the 17th itself, Devaquet had fulfilled a long-arranged meeting with Phillipe Darriulat, the leader of UNEF-ID, where the contents of the bill were discussed, but where it was never suggested to the Minister that it was unacceptable to the union, or that it should be withdrawn. Instead, discussion centred around some rather technical amendments and Darriulat was content merely to state his opposition to the contentious parts of the bill.[11]

It was only during the weekend of November 22nd–23rd that the situation became at all worrying for the government. The *états généraux* of UNEF-ID were transformed into the *états généraux des étudiants en lutte*; Mitterrand made his comments at Auxerre in support of the movement; and the demonstration by the FEN proved to be a great success. The first person within the government to appreciate the potential seriousness of the situation was Charles Pasqua. He was particularly shocked by the number of people who attended the FEN demonstration:

> Two days earlier, during a reception at the Elysée, Charles Pasqua boasted in front of several journalists. 'There'll only be ten thousand of them'.[12]

In fact 100,000 people turned up to demonstrate many of whom were students. Pasqua immediately ordered the services under his control to gather information about the student movement and its likely strength. The results were alarming and on the 24th at the first government meeting held on the student problem Pasqua shocked everyone by calling for the bill to be withdrawn. He stated:

> We'll never be able to hold our own in the face of this wave of discontent. Whatever we do, we'll be forced to abandon this project. If we do it now we can still save face. It will soon be too late.[13]

Pasqua's suggestion, however, was rejected. For the Prime Minister and the rest of the government it appeared to be a premature reaction and, moreover, Pasqua had only recently been embarrassed in the Chalier affair which had lowered his bargaining power amongst the other government members.

There were further government meetings on the 25th and 26th where the student issue was brought up. At these meetings Pasqua reiterated his views, but found some support only from Pierre Méhaignerie, the leader of the CDS. The centrists had been careful to make and maintain contacts with SOS-Racisme who were very close to one of the three major factions within the UNEF-ID, *Questions socialistes*.[14] Through his contacts Méhaignerie had come to the same conclusions as Pasqua about the nature of the problem.[15] In a meeting of the CDS leaders in the evening of the 24th, Méhaignerie proposed that the passage of the bill should be delayed and that changes should be made.[16] It should be noted that Monory, however, also a member of the CDS, was not present at this meeting.

In the few days preceding the first national demonstration on the 27th, the govenment had a number of different strategies which it pursued simultaneously. Devaquet and Monory started to appear much more frequently on television and radio to explain the intentions that lay behind the bill. Moreover, they argued that there had been a misunderstanding over the bill's contents which was due in part to a deliberate misinformation campaign by student activists at all levels who were engaged in a systematic distortion of the bill's provisions.[17] Monory also began calling *chefs d'établissements* and *recteurs* on a twice daily basis in order to keep himself informed of the state of the movement.

In addition, the government started to enter into secret negotiations with representatives of the UNEF-ID leadership. In the days before the national student demonstration in Paris on November 27th, one of Devaquet's advisers was in regular contact with Alain Bauer, a member of UNEF-ID's majority faction. These contacts allowed the two sides to exchange information about the previous day's events, but also for Bauer to suggest what action the movement might consider as acceptable if it were to be proposed by the government. As Bauer pointed out:

> There wasn't only an exchange of information. It was very complex. I didn't negotiate. I said: 'in my opinion . . . ' etc., 'if you do this, then . . . '. I had nothing in particular to suggest except withdrawing the bill.[18]

What Bauer did suggest, however, was that the government ought to announce that the bill would be re-examined by the National Assembly's social affairs commission (*le renvoi en commission*) by 1 p.m. at the latest on November 27th, the day of the demonstration. This initiative would be taken as a positive sign by the movement and would provide the basis for further negotiations. Bauer felt that he had received an assurance from the government that this re-examination would be announced by the suggested time.

The government, however, prevaricated and the announcement did not come until the following day. Its first reaction was to argue that the demonstration had not been a success and that the number of people taking part was much smaller than the organisers were claiming. This strategy, however, was clearly insufficient as television pictures showed that there had been a large turnout. Instead, the Prime Minister decided to drop the amendments of the National Assembly commission which would have hardened the bill. This decision served to get rid of at least one possible source of provocation and was one with which Devaquet was in agreement. Chirac also proceeded to consult his coalition colleagues about which course of action to take. Once again, however, only Pasqua and Méhaignerie suggested that the bill should be withdrawn.

Pasqua's advice, however, did have an influence on Chirac. The following morning (Friday 28th) Chirac met Monory, Devaquet and Maurice Ulrich to discuss the next course of action. At this meeting, Chirac proposed that the bill should be abandoned. The two Ministers, however, were strongly opposed to this. Giesbert recounted the conversation:

> For Chirac, who had consulted a lot of people in the last few hours, there were three solutions and they were all problematic: withdrawal would be considered to be a surrender; maintenance would lead to a test of strength; compromise would not end the protests. Because he has never liked minefields, he opted for the first solution. However, his two Ministers wanted to hear nothing of it. They cordially detested each other, but on this occasion they were in agreement.[19]

Feeling that he could not go against the two Ministers responsible for the bill, Chirac agreed to back down. However, it was clear that something had to be done and the Prime Minister decided to delay the passage of the bill by having the National Assembly's commission re-examine it and to announce that it might be amended to meet the students' demands.[20]

Instead of sending a clear signal to the students that it understood their worries and that it would try to take their demands into account, the government's delay in announcing the re-examination of the bill was seen by the students as a delaying tactic. Indeed, Devaquet admitted that this strategy did lie behind the decision.[21] As one of the student leaders noted, however, the government's concession had come too late and the movement, flushed with the success of the demonstration, now wanted more than vague promises of amendments:

The government always acted too slowly. It agreed to send the bill back to the commission, but it did so the next day. In a day, a lot of things happened. There was a delay between the decision being taken and it being implemented.[22]

The students, led by the *Questions socialistes* faction and their spokesperson, Isabelle Thomas, decided to step up the campaign for the bill's complete withdrawal and received blanket media coverage over the weekend where this demand was constantly reiterated. Thus, when Chirac appeared on the television programme, *Questions à Domicile*, on Sunday 30th and personally announced that the bill might be rewritten if necessary, he gave the impression of having ignored the students' demands.

The government's prevarication was caused principally by its internal divisions. Pasqua and Méhaignerie wanted to see the bill withdrawn, whereas Monory and a substantial cross-section of the RPR parliamentary group and its coalition partners refused to envisage this option. There were several reasons why Chirac finally decided to follow Monory's advice rather than Pasqua's. One of the principal reasons was that on the 29th the Education Minister threatened to resign if the bill were withdrawn.[23] Devaquet also felt that if it were to be withdrawn he too would have to resign. Chirac felt that the loss of an important text and two government Ministers would have had an adverse effect on his own and the government's popularity. Just as importantly, Chirac did not want to alienate Monory in any way. He was one of the few UDF *notables* who was willing to support Chirac ahead of Barre in the forthcoming presidential election.[24] His resignation, therefore, would have been a blow to Chirac's campaign. It must also be noted that there were still only a few people at this time who wished to see the bill abandoned. Most of the coalition leaders did not want to see the government capitulate to pressure from students in the street, although they were willing to accept that the bill should be delayed and perhaps rewritten. One of the other contributing factors was the fear that the withdrawal of this bill would have a knock-on effect on the rest of the government's legislation. Notably, it was felt that the Nationality bill would be the next bill to come under pressure. Indeed, this fear was realised as the Nationality bill was one of the first casualties when the government announced a pause in its legislation on December 9th immediately after the withdrawal of the Devaquet bill.

The presence of all of these factors meant that there appeared to be a certain prevarication in the decision-making process. In part, the problems facing the government were logistical in that some leading figures could not be reached as they had already returned to their constituencies for the weekend. Mainly, however, the Prime Minister wanted to avoid rash decisions and was trying to satisfy as many of the conflicting demands with which he was faced. This situation could account for why the government seemed to be reacting slowly to the problems it faced. What is more, Devaquet argued that the events were so complicated that it would be wrong to suggest that the government had a set of options from which it chose its next strategy:

> It would be wrong to imagine us all weighing up our information, making a list of possible strategies and evaluating their consequences.[25]

According to Devaquet, decision making during this period did not seem to bear the hallmarks of a rational process.

One of the strategies that may have been adopted, however, was the decision to exclude Devaquet from the decision-making process. One of the first people to receive this impression was Bauer. He felt that after the first demonstration the Minister had been effectively withdrawn from the group of people within the government who were deciding what course of action to take. Having received this impression Bauer no longer concentrated on contacting Devaquet's advisers.[26] Instead he contacted Monory's advisers, notably his *directeur de cabinet*, Bertrand Saint-Sernin, while at the same time he was in contact with Yves Durand at Matignon.

Equally, Devaquet also felt that he was no longer at the centre of things by the end of November, although he described this feeling in a coded and poetic way:

> From December 1st onwards, the wind disappeared, mist clung to the ridge and, like a foreign body, asphyxiated everything. Total silence. I could see nothing anymore. I could no longer hear my companions. I had to sense the path through the fog.[27]

Devaquet was the first to admit that he was an inexperienced Minister and that he had made mistakes. Moreover, it was clear that the government really needed a scapegoat and that a decision to sideline Devaquet was a precursor to this action.

Devaquet's main evidence that he had been eliminated from the decision making process came with the claim that he had not been informed of the meeting that allegedly took place between Monory and Darriulat on Monday December 1st. Devaquet claimed that he had only learnt of it at the same time as everyone else, namely, when he read the report of the special parliamentary committees.[28] In his testimony to these committees, however, Monory said that he had informed Devaquet of it very soon after it had taken place. This conflict between the two Ministers only served to complicate the account of this meeting, the existence of which Darriulat has, in any case, always denied. Nevertheless it did seem clear that Devaquet played little positive role in the following week.

In fact, it was Monory in his testimony to the National Assembly's special commission who first stated that he had secretly met with Darriulat in person on December 1st at the Education Ministry with a view to negotiating an acceptable version of the bill. Durand and Saint-Sernin confirmed this version of events in their testimonies and said that they too were at the meeting. All three stated that in principle an agreement had been reached whereby Darriulat would be present in the delegation which was to meet Monory and Devaquet on the 4th. Amendments would be discussed at this meeting and the following day Darriulat would suggest that the student *co-ordination* accept them. Darriulat, however, vehemently denied to the special commission that such a meeting ever took place, claiming that Monory had invented it. Indeed, in an interview with Darriulat, three years after this testimony, he continued to deny that such a meeting ever occurred. He also denied that he had ever considered being part of the student delegation, which was confirmed in an interview with Bauer.

Despite Darriulat's insistence that this meeting never occurred, it was admitted in other interviews that Darriulat had been in contact with Matignon during this period and that he had used André Bergeron, the head of Force Ouvrière (FO), as an intermediary.[29] It was noted that Bergeron had contacted Chirac in preparation for the Prime Minister's important television interview on Sunday November 30th and that he had taken the opportunity to present himself as a go-between in order to facilitate a negotiated solution.[30] Moreover, given Bauer's contacts with the government, there was ample opportunity for negotiations to have taken place between the leadership of UNEF-ID and the government.

Whether the meeting did take place and whether Devaquet was informed of it or not, the logic of this meeting and of the other undisputed contacts was consistent with what had been decided after the first demonstration. Namely, that the bill was likely to be amended in a way acceptable to both sides after the meeting on the 4th. It was clear, however, that there was a certain amount of confusion within the government about what was going to happen. One of the themes of Devaquet's book was that information did not flow smoothly between the different centres of decision making within the government. This observation was confirmed in various interviews and, according to one politician, it could be put down partly to the strained relations between Devaquet and Durand, but also by

Monory's unwillingness to be seen publicly to be drawn into the crisis. He preferred to see Devaquet take responsibility for events.

This lack of policy co-ordination within the government was one of the reasons why Toubon, the general secretary of the RPR, accepted an invitation to meet the representatives of *Questions Socialistes* on Wednesday December 3rd. Toubon felt that the forthcoming meeting with the student delegation had to be prepared and was unaware that Monory and Durand had been conducting secret negotiations with the student movement to this end. On the advice of one of the members of his *cabinet*, Toubon agreed to meet Isabelle Thomas and two other student representatives on the evening of the 3rd. Julien Dray, the leader of the *Questions Socialistes* faction, had contacted Thomas that same morning and informed her that she should prepare to meet Toubon. The details of the meeting had been arranged between Dray and the young RPR deputy, Eric Raoult. While the two never met personally, they used their mutual contacts at the St-Maur faculty in Paris to arrange a meeting. At the meeting Thomas suggested the ways in which the bill could be made acceptable to the movement and she was given the assurance that Devaquet would be informed of her suggestions in time for the meeting with the delegation the following day. There were at least two agreements, therefore, between different union factions and different government Ministers both preparing an honourable compromise the next day.

An honourable compromise, however, did not occur. The meeting with the student delegation was a fiasco. The explanation for this débâcle lay at least in part with Monory. Devaquet in his book stated that just before they were about to meet the delegation the Education Minister did not seem inclined to talk about what course the meeting should take.[31] It was largely for this reason that Devaquet felt that he did not have the authority at the meeting to suggest the amendments to the bill that had been drawn up the previous day and which had been passed on to him by Toubon. Monory did not put forward any signs of compromise and David Assouline, the delegation's spokesperson, did not propose any amendments.

This meeting, therefore, saw an apparent reversal of Monory's strategy. The Education Minister has argued that he was not allowed to propose any amendments because Assouline had firmly taken the decision not to allow any discussions to take place.[32] However, according to the students present and according to Devaquet, the blame could be said to lie equally with the Education Minister who seemed unwilling to negotiate. In fact, Monory refused to negotiate because he felt that the situation had changed over the previous two days and that now the government might be in a position to win.

Some observers felt that the elections to the student delegation on the 2nd had marked a decisive change in the nature of the protests. These elections saw the apparent take-over of the movement by trotskyists. The newspapers talked of the movement being hi-jacked by the extreme left.[33] Isabelle Thomas had not been elected; Darriulat had not put himself forward for election; and the delegation was to be led by Assouline, a member of the trotskyist LEAS faction within UNEF-ID. Monory shared this analysis and his suspicions were seemingly confirmed by a telephone call from Assouline on the morning of the 4th where he was told that he, Assouline, and not Darriulat would be leading the delegation.[34] Matignon's immediate response was to issue a press release giving lurid details of Assouline's curriculum vitae. Many of these details were later discovered to be false, but at the time they served to confirm the impression that the extreme left now controlled the movement.

The belief in governmental and journalistic circles that there had been a trotskyist takeover of the movement was false. According to various interviews, over the course of the previous weekend the UNEF-ID majority faction and the *Questions Socialistes* faction had agreed that a student delegation should be elected to meet the government.[35] It was also agreed that they would join forces to place Assouline at the head of the delegation so as to ensure that he too would be forced into a process of negotiation to which he and his faction was still officially hostile. This mistrust of the LEAS was a constant factor during this time. One student leader voiced these doubts:

I don't know if Assouline wanted to win. There's always a doubt with the extreme left.[36]

Assouline's presence at the head of the delegation, therefore, was not a sign that the trotskyists had taken over the movement. On the contrary, it was an attempt by the other more moderate UNEF-ID factions to ensure that the movement would both remain unified and negotiate with the government.

If the movement had really been taken over by the trotskyists, then the government would have been in a much stronger position. It could have hoped to see the movement split. It could have portayed the students' demands as being extremist and it would have hoped to have won back public support by taking a firm line against them. Such a change would also have put the PS in a difficult situation as it could not have been seen to support a movement orchestrated by the extreme left. Monory seemed personally to re-evaluate his tactics in the light of these considerations and decided not to hand out any olive branches to the student delegation.

This personal initiative was confirmed the following day and provoked cries of a *coup d'état* from amongst some members of the Prime Minister's *cabinet*.[37] There was a government meeting in the morning to discuss the events of the day before. It was clear from this meeting that opposition to the bill was growing from within the government's own ranks. Notably, the liberals, Léotard and Madelin, argued that it was time to withdraw the bill. They were backed up by Méhaignerie, Juppé and Michel d'Ornano. Paradoxically, however, Pasqua now supported the text having reversed his position during the previous few days. He argued that if the government were to abandon the bill now it would be seen to be weak and as having capitulated to the mobs on the street.[38] Pasqua was supported by Monory, but also by several important figures within the RPR, such as the former Prime Minister, Pierre Messmer.

At this meeting it was decided that Monory should take charge of the situation himself. Chirac personally asked Monory to *'reprendre l'affaire en mains'*. This decision was to provoke Devaquet's resignation later that day when he was informed of it by Balladur. In practice, he had already been put to one side, but the decision was now confirmed. It was also decided that Monory should appear on television later that day and that the substance of this appearance would be fixed at a meeting in the afternoon. Chirac, however, had to leave immediately for London where he was accompanying Mitterrand to an EC summit. Balladur, therefore, chaired this meeting and he proposed that the Minister should announce that the government understood the students' demands and that it would withdraw the offending parts of the bill. Monory, however, refused to accept this proposition. At an earlier meeting with Léotard he had said:

> I am in the process of taking on board the responsibility for a dossier to which I have been denied access for nine months. Either I take things in hand or I go.

Similarly, at the later meeting with Balladur he said: 'There's no way that I can mention that word [*retrait*]'[39] Indeed, during the television appearance later that day no mention was made of withdrawing any part of the text and the impression was given that the government's position had not changed since Chirac's statement the previous weekend. This refusal to mention the word *'retrait'* was highly unpopular with many government Ministers. As one person very close to the government noted:

> When things became hot, Monory systematically tried not to defuse the conflict, but to bypass Devaquet and the government, in general, by

negotiating modifications to the bill in, shall I say, an isolated way. Without contacting either Devaquet or Matignon. He went it alone. He tried to extricate himself from the situation.[40]

It must be noted, however, that any question of Monory being disloyal to the Prime Minister during the crisis was flatly denied by the Minister and his advisers. As with the account of the meeting with Darriulat earlier in the week, there are two different and utterly contradictory versions of what happened during this period.

The death of Malik Oussekine during the night of December 5th–6th was to be the catalyst for the abandonment of the text as a whole. Although many deputies had returned to their constituencies for the weekend, it was clear from the numerous meetings and telephone calls that pressure was increasing to abandon the bill. Previously, there had been little serious talk in the government meetings about withdrawing the text as a whole because the bill also included some important changes to the structure of university governing bodies to which the students were not hostile. During the course of the crisis, therefore, both Devaquet and Monory's advisers had been drafting rewritten versions of the text, whereby the contentious articles would have been dropped, but these reforms kept. By this weekend, however, many felt that only the withdrawal of the text as a whole would satisfy the students and public opinion.

This feeling was transmitted to Chirac by several leading government figures when he returned from London on Saturday in the late afternoon. Despite the death of Malik Oussekine there were still contacts between the government and the students. On Saturday 6th, Bauer met Pasqua in the church of Saint-Etienne du Mont, Paris, while on the 7th Thomas had a second meeting with Toubon. On both of these occasions, however, the government was told that the movement was uncontrollable and that only the abandonment of the bill would bring it to an end. Bauer received the impression that Pasqua was preparing the way for the bill's withdrawal:

> At the end of the afternoon I decided that, despite everything, I had to meet my contact who had been waiting for me since 4 o'clock in a church. The Minister of the Interior. I had the impression that he had the power to take certain decisions concerning the course of events. Withdrawal.[41]

Neither Bauer nor Thomas, however, had anything to propose but the withdrawal of the text. It was clear to the UNEF-ID leadership that unless the bill was withdrawn the protests would spread to other societal groups.

At the same time there were already fears of possible public order problems during the demonstration fixed for the 10th. Natalie Prévost described the atmosphere in the offices of UNEF-ID on Saturday December 8th:

> From Saturday to Sunday [6th–7th], the offices of the UNEF-ID were plagued by the leaders of the major political and union organisations each of whom wanted to rally to the demonstration scheduled for the 10th . . . In short, according to one person close to the leadership of UNEF-ID, no-one could control the movement any longer. It was being propelled by its own force. Malik's death has transformed it into something different, enlarging it to other categories of the population.[42]

The message that UNEF-ID could no longer control the movement and that only the withdrawal of the bill would now be acceptable to the students was passed on to both Pasqua and Toubon and subsequently to Chirac.

During the course of the weekend Chirac also met various representatives of the majority, including Balladur, many of whom had now reached the conclusion that the bill had to be abandoned. The Prime Minister also had an audience with the President, although, once again, there were two mutually contradictory accounts of this private meeting. What was clear, however, was that the President supported the students and that the opinion polls were also showing overwhelming public support for them.[43]

Sunday December 7th also saw a day of frantic meetings and telephone calls. Chirac was contacted by both Bergeron and Maire, the leader of the CFDT union confederation, both of whom informed him of the discussions that they had held with Darriulat. Initially, they had both told the students that the time had come to end the protests. They were told, however, that UNEF-ID could no longer control the movement and that, if they wished to see the protests end, then they should put pressure on the government to withdraw the text. It also became clear that Raymond Barre was set to intervene the following week in favour of the students. Mitterrand would also use a long-standing radio engagement to support the movement. The Prime Minister also met Léotard and Madelin and was told by the latter that he had written an article which would appear in *Le Matin* on Monday morning saying that the bill should be withdrawn.

It was difficult at this time, however, for Chirac to abandon the text. One of the reasons for this was that the RPR's 10th anniversary celebrations were taking place over this weekend and it would not have been a propitious occasion to announce such a decision. More importantly, however, the Prime Minister still believed that Monory would refuse to withdraw the bill. The Minister had given no indication to Chirac that he had changed his mind. Over the weekend, however, the Education Minister was the target of fierce lobbying by members of his own party and from coalition partners all of whom wished to end the crisis by withdrawing the bill. It was only on Monday morning when he returned to Paris for a further crisis meeting that he informed the Prime Minister that he had changed his mind. Chirac, who had not personally decided on the best course of action to take, now found that almost all of his senior colleagues wanted the bill to be dropped. The Prime Minister, therefore, agreed that this solution would be for the best.

The delay in taking the decision led to criticisms that there was a lack of prime ministerial leadership and that throughout the crisis Chirac had been vacillating. Also, the fact that he left for London at the height of the affair was criticised by many people. According to one senior party figure, however, the Prime Minister's attitude throughout the period was consistent:

> The Prime Minister and his collaborators clearly followed events closely during the two week period and sought plenty of advice. Certainly Matignon asked many questions of itself. At the beginning the Prime Minister had certainly not taken the decision either to withdraw the bill or to maintain it. It was during the course of events that little by little he adopted his position.[44]

It was clear that the final weekend saw a major shift of opinion within the government and that Monday saw Monory change his mind. It was only at this stage, when it was clear that both Monory and an overwhelming majority of government members and senior party figures favoured the bill's withdrawal, that Chirac decided that it should be abandoned.

Conclusion

During a public policy crisis, a concentration of power within the highest ranks of the core executive might be expected, as political leaders try to assert their authority over the situation. If so, on this occasion, during *cohabitation*, there should have been an increase in prime ministerial leadership. Such an increase, however, did not occur. At no stage did Chirac take the initiative for, or be seen to take the lead in the management of the crisis. Instead, for the most part there was a form of collective leadership with the government's strategy being decided amongst a small group of senior Ministers and advisers. Although, towards the end of the period, there were also individual initiatives by senior figures, notably, Monory, Toubon and Madelin.

The main reason for this absence of prime ministerial leadership was derived from the problems arising from managing the governmental coalition. The rivalries that existed between the UDF and RPR and, indeed, between the individual components of the UDF, meant that Chirac could not take the initiative during the crisis period without the risk of seeing all or part of the coalition collapse. This placed the Prime Minister in a delicate position, particularly as he was a candidate at the forthcoming presidential election and also because his right-wing rival, Raymond Barre, was in no way associated with the government's plight. While these pressures were present in the other decisional studies, notably during the preparation of the 1986 broadcasting bill, they were greater in the above study because of the crisis nature of the situation. As we saw, the crisis exacerbated the tensions within the government and threw into relief the constraints under which the Prime Minister had to operate.

It must be appreciated, however, that while crisis periods heighten the need for political leadership, they also make it difficult for such leadership to be forthcoming. The conditions under which politicians have to make decisions at such times militate against the exercise of political leadership, even if they do not render it impossible. This is because the stakes are much higher during periods of crisis than they are during periods of routine decision-making. As a result, the consequences of any decisions are much greater. Stark choices have to be made and compromises are difficult to reach. Decisions may entail the departure of a Minister, as in this case, or the government itself, if the crisis is sufficiently acute.

Given the nature of political crises in general, therefore, and this one in particular, it is not surprising that there was a period of vacillation on the part of the government. In the situation where the benefits which would have accrued to Chirac from 'winning' were so great and where the penalties for 'losing' were equally important, then the fact that the Prime Minister allowed for a period of reflection is understandable. Nevertheless, there were serious miscalculations on the part of the Prime Minister and the government. Notably, these miscalculations concerned the strength of the student movement and, equally importantly, the speed at which the situation was developing.

Even so, despite these miscalculations, the government might have been able to weather the storm had not the death of Malik Oussekine occurred. His death coincided with the period of greatest fluidity. Not only was it impossible for the Prime Minister to have foreseen this event, short of confining all policemen to barracks, but it was also very difficult for him to have done anything else other than withdraw the bill once it occurred. This exogenous event, which was outside of the Prime Minister's control, served to introduce an unpredictable element to the decision-making process and one which was not present in the examination of the previous case studies.

6 Crisis Policy-Making (II): The Politics of Devaluation, March 1983

The fourth case study examines the debate surrounding the third devaluation of the franc in March 1983 and the decision to retain Pierre Mauroy as Prime Minister. The debate over the franc saw a clash between the people who favoured a realignment of the parities of the European Monetary System (EMS) and those people who wanted to see France withdraw from the system altogether. This debate coincided with and was the cause of much speculation about the position of Mauroy as Prime Minister. In the end, Mitterrand decided that France should remain in the EMS and he kept faith with Mauroy.

This case study differs from the previous chapters because, whilst it is an example of a policy decision, it is an example of a policy which did not require the passage of a law. Thus, the decision-making process as witnessed here is slightly different from the one which was observed in the other examples. Here, there was neither the usual process of reunions, committees and councils, nor was the Parliament or the Constitutional Council involved. Instead, policy was made in a series of informal meetings at the highest governmental levels. Nevertheless, as an example of policy making, this debate provides numerous points of comparison with previous chapters and is worthy of consideration.

A Period of Crisis: March 1983

As with the events surrounding the Devaquet higher education bill, this case study examines a period of crisis. There was a nine-day period in which the debate over whether to withdraw from the EMS or to devalue the franc within it was concentrated. This period was one of a 'curable' crisis.[1] During this time the policy process was characterised by a breakdown of the routine channels of policy preparation. This situation is typical of crisis periods. As Dunleavy and O'Leary state:

Almost by definition, crises are periods when the normally routinised operations of the bureaucracy are insufficient or cannot be relied on, when decisions have to be quickly pushed up through the chain of command, and where an unusually large and direct role in controlling policy implementation has to be taken by political leaders.[2]

Even given that this policy was one which did not require a statute, the decision to remain in the EMS was not marked by official, scheduled meetings. Nor was it characterised by unofficial meetings which brought together all of the leading protagonists. Instead, the President arrived at his decision through a series of unofficial encounters and *têtes-à-têtes* which rarely brought more than three people together at any one time. There were secret plots and there was an atomisation of the policy process.

This period also constitutes a time of crisis because of the importance of the decision which had to be made. As Dunleavy and O'Leary again state:

> Crises often mark turning points in overall patterns of policy development, because the consequences of alternative decisions can be momentous.[3]

The policies between which the President had to choose were mutually exclusive. They represented two alternative and radically opposed solutions. There was no compromise solution possible. Favier and Martin-Roland have described the decision to remain in the EMS in March 1983 as '*une orientation historique*'.[4] Giesbert has said that it is '*à cet instant que se joue le sort du septennat*'.[5]

In the previous chapter it was noted that times of crisis necessitate strong political leadership. During *cohabitation* the Prime Minister had to exercise such leadership. In 1983, it belonged to the President to do so. It is in this respect that the present case study differs from the ones previously examined. It will be seen that the Prime Minister was involved in the policy process as an actor, but not as a decision maker. The decision to remain in the EMS and the subsequent decision to retain Mauroy as Prime Minister were both taken by Mitterrand personally. Therefore, this case study provides the clearest study of presidential influence in the policy process.

In the first section the background to the March 1983 debate will be outlined and a detailed résumé of the crucial nine-day period will be given. In the second section the political and politico-economic considerations behind the decision not to withdraw from the EMS and to retain Mauroy as Prime Minister will be considered.

The 1983 Devaluation Debate

The 1983 devaluation can be placed in the logic of the socialist government's post-1981 economic policy. The two strands of thought articulated in March 1983, one supporting a withdrawal from the EMS, another preferring to devalue the franc within the system, were present within government circles from May 1981 onwards. The March 1983 debate was important because it saw the second school of thought triumph finally and definitively over the first.

In the course of the 1981 presidential election the reflation of the French economy was one of Mitterrand's main campaign issues. The PS was united in the pursuit of this policy. However, the extent of the reflation of demand and the means by which it should be achieved were a source of dispute.[6] The first manifestation of the differences of opinion within the PS on these issues came immediately after Mitterrand's election. Whilst a decision to withdraw from the EMS was quickly discounted, Mauroy and Rocard were amongst those who argued that the franc should be quickly and substantially devalued within the system, so that the proposed reflation of demand could take place under propitious conditions. Mitterrand's reaction to this suggestion is well documented and came as he and Mauroy were being driven down the Champs Elysées on 21 May 1981: '*On ne dévalue pas un jour comme aujourd'hui*'.[7] Thus, from the outset Mitterrand asserted the primacy of political considerations over economic ones.

During the course of the summer the government faced severe economic problems. The decision to reflate had been taken against an international background of high interest rates, deflation and decreasing growth. The result of French policies was to cause the country's balance of trade deficit to increase, inflation to rise and interest rates to be raised, so as to relieve some of the pressure that the franc was experiencing within the EMS. In fact, Mitterrand's unilateral decision in May only delayed a devaluation of the currency. This devaluation came on 4 October 1981.

The intragovernmental debate surrounding the October devaluation saw the first dress rehearsal of the arguments which would be used in March 1983. Jacques Delors, the Finance Minister, wanted the devaluation to be accompanied by a set of deflationary measures which would stifle rising demand. He insisted that 10 billion francs should be cut from the spending component of the 1982 budget and that a further 15 billion francs should be frozen. Delors's plan, which was supported by the Germans who had to agree to a realignment of the EMS, was opposed by Fabius, the Budget Minister, who had conducted the budgetary expenditure arbitrations largely unaided.[8] In the end, Mitterrand arbitrated in Fabius's favour, although some budgetary credits for 1982 were frozen. Despite the devaluation, the country's economic problems only accentuated. Bauchard has argued that, as a result of these problems, both Delors and Mauroy became convinced that a further devaluation was necessary and that this time it had to be accompanied by a substantial programme of deflation.[9] The economic advisers in their *cabinets* and the President's main economic advisers were instrumental in convincing them that this course of action was the only one which was economically viable. The Prime Minister ordered a plan of economic rigour to be drawn up secretly in the spring of 1982.

When this plan was presented to the President and to leading members of the government on May 28th 1982 it was opposed by Fabius, Pierre Bérégovoy, then *Secrétaire général de l'Elysée*, Jean-Pierre Chevènement, the Industry Minister, and by the communists in the government. They were opposed to any deflation and tended to support the arguments of several influential industrialists and economists who argued that France should withdraw from the EMS, so as to be able to conduct its economic policy without worrying about the constraints that the system imposed. Cameron has stated that two industrialists, Jean Riboud, the head of Schlumberger, and Georges Plescoff, the head of Suez, argued that France should temporarily withdraw from the EMS. Both were close to Mitterrand and their arguments were taken very seriously by the President.[10]

A decision as to which policy to pursue was not immediately taken, however. Mitterrand decided to use the forthcoming summit of the seven leading industrial nations at Versailles from June 4th to the 6th as the final occasion to persuade the Americans to lower interest rates and to reflate their economy. When they refused Mitterrand took the decision to devalue and Delors negotiated an agreement within the EMS which was announced on June 12th.[11]

Although the preliminary decision to devalue had been taken, the question of whether the franc should withdraw from the EMS, or whether there should be a programme of deflation paradoxically had not been resolved. At a council meeting devoted to this issue on June 13th Mitterrand finally arbitrated in Mauroy's favour, despite the absence of a majority for the Prime Minister's proposals amongst those present.[12] It was agreed that there should be a four month prices and wages freeze; employers' social security contributions were reduced; company taxation was reduced; various family allowance costs were transferred from employers to employees; and employers' VAT costs were reduced. Thus, demand was reduced and various supply side measures in favour of industry were taken.

However, these measures did not serve to alleviate the country's economic problems to any great degree. The 1982 balance of trade deficit still increased from 56 billion francs in 1981 to 93 billion francs. At 11 per cent inflation remained higher than France's closest competitors. The franc was under pressure within the EMS and measures had to be taken by the Banque de France to prop it up. Thus, during the winter of 1982–83 the economic choices which had been faced in June 1982 were again top of the policy agenda.

During the first two months of 1983 Mitterrand met on a regular basis with Riboud, Bérégovoy, Fabius and Chevènement all of whom repeated their call for France to withdraw from the EMS. At the same time, Delors and Mauroy, with the help of their closest advisers, drew up another, more substantial *plan de rigueur* in absolute secrecy.[13] The need for secrecy was due to the imminence of the municipal elections in March 1983. The municipals were the first national set of elections since the 1981 legislatives. The right expected to do well and it was feared by the government that any threat of an austerity programme would further demobilise the left's electorate and increase opposition gains. Thus, when the leader of the CFDT, Edmond Maire, announced after a meeting with the President on January 31st that a new austerity programme was being drawn up, it was immediately denied by Mauroy and the rest of the government.[14]

Candidates of the Union of the Left did badly in the municipal elections. On the first ballot the left lost 16 towns with more than 30,000 inhabitants. On the second ballot it lost 15 more. Thus, the opportunity to resolve the economic policy debate coincided with a weakening in Mauroy's position as Prime Minister because of the government's poor showing in the elections. Giesbert quotes Serge July's editorial in *Libération* on Monday March 14th, the morning following the second round of municipal election results. July at this time was very close to the President and is said by Giesbert to have articulated the President's private opinion:

> the President has decided . . . there will be a new Prime Minister and a new government whose job it will be to implement new policies.[15]

This point marks the beginning of the nine-day period which saw the debate over whether to remain in or pull out of the EMS and over whether Mauroy should remain as Prime Minister.

On Monday morning Mitterrand met Mauroy and proposed that he should form a new government which would oversee the withdrawal of the franc from the EMS. The Prime Minister refused, but the two agreed to meet later in the day to discuss the matter again.[16] In the meantime,

Mauroy met with Delors who reassured him that he was in agreement with the Prime Minister. Therefore, safe in the knowledge that he had at least one senior government member who supported his position, Mauroy repeated to the President during their evening meeting that he was unwilling to head a government which pulled out of the EMS. Although Mitterrand's analysis of the situation differed from the Prime Minister's, he agreed that Jean-Louis Bianco (who had replaced Bérégovoy as *Secrétaire général de l'Elysée* in June 1982) should leave immediately for Bonn where he would sound out the German government and the Bundesbank as to the possibility of a revaluation of the Mark. He was also sent to discover their reaction to the idea of France leaving the EMS. He reported back the next day that a revaluation was possible in return for a French devaluation and an austerity programme. This was the policy that Mauroy and Delors favoured.

The question of whether Mauroy should remain as Prime Minister was also the subject of much debate and manœuvering. Mauroy himself received contradictory advice as to whether he should stay on. Senior members of his *cabinet* argued that it would be better for his personal image if he was to leave, rather than stay on and be responsible for implementing a policy to which it was publicly known that he was hostile.[17] However, the Prime Minister's closest governmental and parliamentary colleagues, Jean Le Garrec, Roger Fajardie and Christian Pierret, all argued that he should remain. At the same time Mitterrand, then still intent on introducing '*l'autre politique*' and believing Mauroy to be hostile to it, offered the premiership to Delors in the afternoon of Tuesday March 15th on condition that he accept the withdrawal of the franc from the EMS.[18] Delors refused the offer, arguing that he could not accept responsibility for such a policy.

Although the question of who should be Prime Minister remained unanswered for several days, the question of which policy should be adopted was effectively resolved on Wednesday March 16th. During his traditional pre-Council of Ministers meeting with Mitterrand on that day, the Prime Minister announced that he had changed his mind and was willing to take responsibility for a withdrawal of the franc from the EMS. It is not clear whether by so doing Mauroy was playing for time in the belief that the President would change his mind and that he could remain as Prime Minister, or whether he had simply agreed to accept responsibility for a policy to which previously he had been opposed. Nevertheless, it appeared as if the partisans of '*l'autre politique*' had won the day.

However, Mitterrand in typical fashion was not to be hurried. He made no mention of which policy was going to be adopted during the subsequent Council of Ministers. Instead, at the end of the meeting, Mitterrand asked

Fabius to contact the Treasury division of the Finance Ministry and obtain information about the economic consequences of leaving the EMS.

The inspiration behind Mitterrand's decision to seek further clarification about the consequences of *'l'autre politique'* can be traced back to the previous day.[19] On Tuesday, Mauroy had met Delors and Jacques Attali at Matignon. Attali, the President's special adviser, was strongly in favour of remaining in the EMS. He argued that, in order to have their policy accepted, they needed to convince someone close to the President who was currently in favour of withdrawal to change his mind. It was agreed that Attali would suggest to the President that he should ask Fabius to contact the *directeur du Trésor*, Michel Camdessus. Delors knew that Camdessus was opposed to *'l'autre politique'* and that Fabius would be alarmed by the figures with which he would be presented.

The strategy devised by Mauroy, Delors and Attali worked. Camdessus argued that withdrawing from the EMS would necessitate a steep rise in interest rates, thus preventing the increase in investment which Fabius and others had envisaged. Defferre was presented with the same scenario from the governor of the Banque de France, Renaud de la Genière.[20] When they both presented their information to Mitterrand, the President decided that there was no alternative but to remain in the system. Favier and Martin-Roland quote Fabius as having said:

> I believe that I triggered off the President's decision.[21]

While Fabius is no doubt correct, the inspiration behind the President's decision can be traced back to Mauroy, Delors and Attali.

Following the President's decision Delors was charged with conducting negotiations with the Germans with regard to a readjustment of the parities within the EMS.[22] On Tuesday he had contacted the Germans informally on this issue. On Wednesday he contacted the German Finance Minister, Gerhard Stoltenberg. The latter came secretly to Paris the following day in order to negotiate with Delors in person. However, an agreement could not immediately be reached and discussions continued over the weekend in Brussels where Finance Ministers from all countries in the EMS were meeting. Only on Monday March 21st were terms agreed with which everyone was satisfied.

During the period from Wednesday 16th to Monday 21st, the notion of withdrawing from the EMS was used only as a bargaining tool (*un épouvantail*)[23] by Delors in order to scare the other countries into accepting a realignment of parities favourable to France. As July noted:

It is a fact that in his negotiations Delors used threats so as to relax the German positon. But nobody was ignorant of the fact that Delors's position was just the opposite, the most resolute opponent of the policy of breaking with Europe.[24]

Thus, whilst it may have appeared to outside observers as if France was still contemplating leaving the EMS, in fact, the debate had already been sealed. There was not to be a withdrawal. Instead, Delors was under orders from the President to negotiate a devaluation on the best possible terms for France. One of the strategies he used to achieve this aim was to act as if France would withdraw if the deal were not sufficiently attractive. However, the impact of this strategy was not great as Genscher has stated that he was never afraid that France would leave the system.[25]

It is noticeable that Mauroy played no part in these negotiations, although he did remain informed of proceedings by way of his brief, but regular contacts with Mitterrand and Delors. Indeed, for all of this period Mauroy felt that he was going to be dismissed as Prime Minister. Pfister has described this period of inactivity as '*insupportable*'.[26] Mauroy even went so far as to write a long resignation letter ready to give to the President on Tuesday March 22nd. At the same time his *directeur de cabinet*, Michel Delebarre, was hurriedly trying to rent a studio in Paris from which Mauroy would be able to conduct his post-prime ministerial affairs.

There were two main candidates to replace Mauroy. The first was Delors whom Mitterrand thought would accept the post now that the franc was staying in the EMS. It has been argued by Pfister and Bauchard that Delors himself thought that he was going to be appointed Prime Minister on Sunday March 20th when he suddenly rushed back from Brussels for a meeting with Mitterrand.[27] However, Giesbert argued that this was simply a ruse to up the ante and force the hand of the Germans.[28] This version is confirmed by Delors himself:

> It was a question my dramatising the affair for the benefit of our partners because an agreement hadn't yet been reached. So I threatened a clash. I didn't have it in mind that I wanted to be Prime Minister.[29]

When he returned from Brussels on Tuesday March 22nd Delors was in a strong position to gain the Premiership.

The second candidate was Pierre Bérégovoy, now the Minister for Social Affairs. He was one of the main proponents of '*l'autre politique*' and, even after it had been decided to remain in the EMS, he still felt that he might be appointed Prime Minister. On Thursday March 17th Mitterrand asked

Bérégovoy to draw up a government and the Minister took this request as a sign that his appointment as Prime Minister was imminent.[30]

The matter was finally settled in the afternoon of Tuesday March 22nd. Mitterrand lunched with Delors, Bérégovoy and Fabius. After lunch he offered Matignon to Delors who accepted on condition that he be allowed to remain as Finance Minister *à la* Raymond Barre in 1976. Mitterrand refused and passed over Bérégovoy in favour of retaining Mauroy. Thus, at the end of a nine-day period of waiting, Mauroy was charged with forming his third government and with presenting the new austerity programme to the country.

Political and Economic Motives for the 1983 Devaluation

The reasons behind the twin presidential decisions to stay in the EMS and to retain Mauroy were no less complicated than the motivations behind the public policy choices which were identified in previous chapters. This section will identify these motivations. It will be seen that, although familiar political constraints were apparent in the decision-making process, the decision to remain in the EMS was partly the result of pressures arising from the international political economy. Also, while the President was the undisputed decision maker for both issues, his decision was influenced by the actions of a not insubstantial number of other political actors. Before engaging upon an analysis of the President's decisions, it is necessary to explain precisely the two competing policy options and to identify their supporters.

The people who supported a withdrawal of the franc from the EMS were variously described to be in favour of a policy of '*neo-protectionism*'[31], '*national-protectionnisme*'[32] and '*gaullo-protectionnisme*'.[33] The supporters of this policy argued that withdrawing from the system and allowing the franc to float freely would not only bring about the necessary devaluation in its value, but would also avoid the need for a simultaneous austerity programme which the Germans insisted upon as the prerequisite of any realignment of EMS parities. Thus, France would be able to lower its interest rates and encourage industrial investment. At the same time as a withdrawal from the EMS, France would impose mandatory deposits on importers in order to reduce the balance of trade deficit. It would also raise national barriers to free trade within the limits laid down by the EC and GATT agreements. It was this latter proposal that was essentially protectionist in nature. Although the supporters of this view did propose an extension of the prices and wages freeze with exceptions for trades unionists, this strategy was essentially one of economic expansion and monetary independence.

This view was supported by a number of senior governmental figures and by some of the President's closest advisers. Amongst these were Ministers such as Pierre Bérégovoy, Jean-Pierre Chevènement, Gaston Defferre and Laurent Fabius. Two of the President's advisers on economic policy, Alain Boublil and Charles Salzmann, were also in favour of it along with several senior industrialists. These figures included Jean Riboud, Georges Plescoff and Jean Deflassieux, head of Crédit Lyonnais. It was also supported by some leading economists such as Jean Denizet, Pierre Uri and Serge-Christophe Kolm. In addition, senior party figures, such as Jean Poperen and Louis Mermaz, argued in favour of withdrawal, while the communists were also generally favourable.

This view was opposed by an equally firm set of ideas which was supported by an equally influential group of people. They argued that it was essential to remain in the EMS, but that a realignment of parities was necessary. The Mark was to be revalued by as much as possible and the franc was to be devalued by as little as possible. In order to combat the trade deficit and to lessen future pressures on the franc, an austerity programme similar to the one adopted in June 1982 had simultaneously to be engaged upon. However, in addition to another wages and prices freeze there would have to be an increase in social security contributions and an increase in income tax. These latter measures would serve to reduce the public's purchasing power.

In addition to these arguments, the people in favour of remaining in the EMS argued that a withdrawal would be disastrous for the country's economy. They argued that French protectionism would only lead to tit-for-tat measures against French exports from other countries. They also argued that their opponents underestimated the dependence of the French economy on the international market.[34] Moreover, they did not realise the precarious state of the country's financial reserves which meant that the Banque de France would only be able to support the franc for a short time after its flotation. After this time interest rates would have to rise and an even harsher dose of austerity would have to be undertaken. It was this message that Camdessus passed on to Fabius on Wednesday 16th March. As Fabius has noted:

> I left this meeting in the knowledge that if we were to leave the EMS, then the supposed advantages of this decision would only lead to greater budgetary rigour, because the franc would tumble on the markets.[35]

It was this argument which convinced Mitterrand to abandon '*l'autre politique*'.

Those people who wished the franc to remain in the EMS were small in number, but they occupied some particularly influential positions. As was clear from the preceding exposé, the two most important partisans of this view were Mauroy and Delors. They were supported by a group of senior presidential advisers which included Jean-Louis Bianco, Jacques Attali, Elisabeth Guigou, Christian Sautter and François-Xavier Stasse. They were in close contact with senior figures in Mauroy and Delors's *cabinets*. The head of both the Treasury Division at the Ministry of Finance and the governor of the Banque de France were also in favour. Favier and Martin-Roland note that certain heads of industry, such as François Dalle from L'Oréal, also supported this line. Therefore, whilst the partisans of this policy were less numerous than their opponents, they constituted a formidable political and intellectual bloc against '*l'autre politique*'.

For some of the supporters of both camps the motivation behind their stance was purely economic. Thus, Riboud, Plescoff, Uri and Denizet argued in favour of withdrawing because of the benefits that they thought would accrue to French industry from this policy. Conversely, Camdessus and de la Genière were opposed to this policy because of the financial and monetary problems that they believed it would cause. A purely economic motivation was also, in part, the reasoning behind Mauroy's attitude. For example, on Tuesday March 15th, two of Mauroy's advisers, Jean Peyrelevade and Henri Guillaume, were so convinced of the economic merits of staying in the EMS that they suggested to Mauroy that he should see a presentation about the alternative option from two of its proponents, Jean Deflassieux and Pierre Uri. As Mauroy's advisers had thought, the Prime Minister was left unconvinced by the cogency of their presentation.[36]

For most people, however, the motivations behind their support of a particular policy were primarily political. The two main political reasons present were determined by the different ideological conceptions of socialism that the protagonists held and by their personal ambitions.

Hall has identified three different conceptions of socialism which were in competition after the 1981 election.[37] He classifies these tendencies as 'a neo-Marxist enclave' surrounding Chevènement; '*la deuxième gauche*' around Rocard; and 'an eclectic group of social democrats' which included Mitterrand who stood in the middle. While the definition of the third of Hall's categories smacks of a catch-all group whose broad characterisation only serves to mask a more complex web of beliefs, the partisans of the first category are certainly identifiable during the March 1983 debate.

Chevènement's brand of socialism was state centred. He felt that only the state, not the market, could produce wealth which did not disadvantage some to the profit of others. Moreover, he felt that this wealth could only be produced behind restrictive trade barriers as far removed from the international economy as possible. He believed in national independence for practical and symbolic reasons. This was the gaullist component of his socialism. This conception of socialism was present during the March debate. As Chevènement has written:

No-one can force us to accept policies in the monetary or commercial sector where the rules of the game are biased and where they reduce further our room to manœuvre. No, France should not take on board this all pervading policy of monetarism.[38]

It is natural from this base that Chevènement should have supported a policy of withdrawal from the EMS, protectionism and reflation in one country.

Chevènement was supported by a group led by Poperen which included many communists whose reasoning was similar, but not exactly the same. They believed that any austerity plan would disproportionately hurt the working class. Such a policy was denounced as '*révisionnisme*'.[39] It was the task of a PS/PC government to defend the interests of this class and, therefore, they argued for '*l'autre politique*' as it seemed to be a way of avoiding this austerity.

In contrast to these two approaches, there was the conception of socialism favoured by Delors. He preached 'financial rectitude'.[40] This belief was the rationale behind his call for a pause in reforms in November 1981 and his support for the three devaluations up to and including the March 1983 example. For Delors, reforms which improved the social conditions of the less well off could only be embarked upon if the country had a firm financial base from which to operate. This meant low inflation and a strong currency. Only an austerity programme could bring about these conditions.

The 'eclectic' nature of the third group which Hall identified meant that its component parts did not necessarily favour either position. Thus, Bérégovoy and Mauroy who would both normally be classed in this group supported opposing policies. The fact that Mitterrand also belonged to this group would help to explain why he was able to change his mind and move from one policy to the other in a short space of time. In fact, several more specific reasons behind the President's decision will be examined below.

The other main political motivation behind the actions of some of the protagonists lies in their personal ambitions. It is apparent, for example, that Mauroy at first refused to accept the President's decision to conduct '*l'autre politique*' because he was sure, having consulted with Delors during the afternoon of Monday March 14th, that he would not be isolated within the government when arguing to remain in the EMS. Such a position would have been untenable and he would have been forced to resign, or capitulate leaving him in a weakened situation. It is also possible that he changed his mind on Wednesday March 16th and decided that he was willing to accept responsibility for leaving the EMS because several of his senior political advisers counselled him to act accordingly.

Personal ambitions were not absent from Bérégovoy's calculations. As the main proponent of '*l'autre politique*' he stood to gain most from its adoption. Even after the policy had been rejected, he still harboured his personal ambitions:

> This policy of rigour will fail. We will leave the EMS and I will be Prime Minister within six months.[41]

Although he emerged from this period with a more senior position in the governmental hierarchy, he was still as yet frustrated in his ambition to become Prime Minister.

By contrast, Delors's ambition to be Prime Minister would have been realised had he not demanded too much of Mitterrand on Tuesday 22nd March. Delors felt that he would only have sufficient political weight as Prime Minister to be able to combat Bérégovoy and Fabius, his personal rivals, if he controlled the Finance Ministry as well as Matignon. Mitterrand could not accept these terms as it would threaten his authority over the government. Therefore, the President rejected Delors's conditions.

Whatever the motivations of the various actors, the responsibility for deciding which policy option to take and who to appoint as Prime Minister belonged to no-one other than the President. He was the ultimate arbiter who was, in his own words, '*le premier responsable des affaires publiques*'.[42] Indeed, not only did the President take these decisions himself, but he was recognised by all concerned as the only person who had the authority to take them. In this sense, his responsibility was never challenged. His authority was seen most vividly with the Delors/Mauroy/Attali plan to change the President's mind. Although they targeted Fabius directly, they knew that by so doing they would reach the President.

The question then arises as to why these decisions should have been the sole responsibility of the President. With regard to the decision to remain in the EMS, the usual answer to this question is that since the mid-1960s the area of currency stability has always been part of the President's *domaine réservé* and that the March 1983 decision was merely a further example of this situation.[43] In the sense that Presidents have intervened personally in this area on several occasions, this schema may accurately reflect the policy process. However, it is unrewarding academically as it does not point to the reasons why Presidents intervene so. It leaves the original question unanswered.

In March 1983 there were several important reasons as to why the President was left personally to decide. The main reason was that the nine day period was a period of crisis. As was stated in the introduction to this chapter, crisis periods call for political leadership. The President as the ultimate political authority had to give such leadership. Moreover, the view that the President had no option but to assume responsibility for decision making is reinforced by the fact that Mauroy, the only other senior political figure who might have been able to arbitrate between the different options, was himself personally implicated with one of the policies. Therefore, he was in no position to take the final decision. The only person who was in such a position was the President. The fact that the decision lay in an area which was traditionally considered to be part of his reserved domain only reinforced the necessity for a presidential arbitration which was in fact determined by other reasons.

By contrast, the fact that the President was responsible for appointing the Prime Minister needs very little commentary. The President is constitutionally responsible for naming the Prime Minister. Therefore, necessarily the decision as to whom to appoint belonged to the President. This situation did not mean that Mitterrand did not consult with his colleagues. Indeed, all accounts of this period suggest that the President talked about the different prime ministerial options to a wide range of people. Nevertheless, the final decision belonged to Mitterrand.

Although attention was focused upon the President after the second round of the municipal elections, neither the decision to remain in the EMS, nor the decision as to whom should be Prime Minister was taken immediately. The first of these two questions was settled by Wednesday March 16th, after which time any threat of leaving the EMS was simply '*un épouvantail*' to scare the Germans into accepting a realignment of parities on terms favourable to the French. The second question was resolved after a period of nine days. The reasons behind the delay over both questions are twofold. Firstly, as Machin and Wright have argued, the presidency is an institution which is structurally weak. They state:

occasional indecisiveness is scarcely surprising in a President who is immersed in foreign, European, defence and a whole range of domestic issues, who has only a small personal staff, is confronted with multiple and cross-cutting pressures, and who receives advice from several quarters.[44]

During a time of crisis when the repercussions of policy decisions are great, the President, faced with the above structural constraints, is likely to take some time in reaching his decision. Secondly, the delay was partly due to Mitterrand's personal style of working. He liked to solicit advice simultaneously from several different quarters. He liked then to have that advice confirmed from other sources. He worked in this way during the March 1983 crisis. As Mitterrand himself has stated about the beginning of the crisis period:

> I didn't want to leave. The decision was difficult. My mind wasn't made up and I wanted to have enough arguments so has not to have to do it.[45]

Thus, Mitterrand's personal style counted for what journalists described as a period of hesitation and indecision by the President.

The President's final decision not to withdraw from the EMS was taken for a variety of economic and political reasons. The decision itself was taken after he was presented with Fabius's report on the economic consequences of leaving the EMS. These consequences themselves were the result of France's position in the international political economy. This situation has been described by Machin and Wright as 'the dictatorship of the conjunctural'.[46] Therefore, in this sense the decision was imposed upon France and upon Mitterrand from outside. According to Jospin, the President saw his decision in this way:

> He had the impression that he made an extremely difficult concession in the face of the reality which was imposed upon him by others, of having to give in before penalties inflicted on him from abroad. For him it was the end of a certain French way, innovative, socialist and proud of its own personality when compared with the ferociously egotistical liberals.[47]

Thus, policy making was not an essentially domestic affair, but involved international considerations and pressures as well.

The overriding political reason was Mitterrand's desire not to break with the EC. For Jospin this aspect represented the other main motivation behind Mitterrand's decision. He states:

> there were two essential components to his decision to stay in the EMS: the feeling that leaving the system would be a dramatic event without the guarantee of it being useful as a way of helping the balance of trade; the desire to conduct a grand policy towards Europe.[48]

Attali followed the same reasoning. For him the decision to stay in the EMS meant that: '*Tout en Europe, économiquement, politiquement, restait possible*'.[49]

A further reason lay in the political strengths of the people who argued for the different policies. Those people in favour of remaining in the EMS were led by Mauroy and Delors. They had considerable political weight. Although Mauroy finally agreed to accept responsibility for leaving the EMS if the President so decided, Delors refused. The President could ill afford to lose Delors from his government.

Moreover, the position of those in favour of '*l'autre politique*' was not strong. The most senior political figure to support it was Chevènement. However, he was never a *mitterrandiste* and his opinion had less importance for the President accordingly. In addition, his political weight had recently declined since secretly he had made it known before the municipal elections that he was going to resign from the government. Other Ministers who supported this policy, such as Bérégovoy and Fabius, did not have the political stature at that time to rival Mauroy or Delors.

Similarly, the communists, who might be thought to have been in a position to have played an important part in the President's decision, were also outside of the process. Although they were part of the governmental coalition, they did not have access to the President's inner circle. More importantly, they could not threaten to withdraw from the coalition at that time because they would have been seen by their supporters to be breaking with the Union of the Left. They wanted to avoid this situation. Marchais followed this line of reasoning:

> Why didn't we leave? Simply because all the men and women who voted for the left in 1981 wouldn't have understood us. By leaving at this point in time, we would have been held responsible for the rupture.[50]

Mitterrand was aware that the communists would accept either policy option and, thus, he was free from this constraint when taking his decision.

Whilst it has been argued that the President was responsible for staying in the EMS and for retaining Mauroy as Prime Minister, it is important to avoid the conclusion that he took these decisions alone. In fact, one of the striking aspects about the March 1983 crisis was the number of people who were instrumental in the decision-making process. In the first place, as was seen earlier, senior German officials played an important role. Their influence was particularly marked on Tuesday March 15th when Bianco went to Bonn to sound out representatives of the government and the Bundesbank as to the likelihood of the Mark being revalued in return for a devaluation of the franc. He returned with the belief that they would agree to such a policy, but only in return for a French austerity programme. As a result of this visit, Mitterrand was aware that the policy supported by Delors and Mauroy was feasible. By contrast, '*l'autre politique*' appeared to be a leap in the dark.

The President's decision was also greatly influenced by the work of the Mauroy/Delors/Attali axis. They were successful in having their policy adopted by the President because they were familiar with the exigencies of the policy process. They knew which channels to follow so as to influence the President. Thus, they suggested that Fabius should contact Camdessus and report back to Mitterrand. Moreover, they were well positioned to influence the President. Mauroy met Mitterrand at least once a day during the early period of the crisis. Delors also had individual meetings with the President. In addition, he sent Mitterrand numerous notes in which he outlined the dangers of withdrawing from the EMS. Finally, Attali, as the President's special adviser with a room adjacent to Mitterrand's main office, was particularly well placed to follow the debate and to act accordingly. Their proximity to the centre of decision making along with the political weight of Delors and Mauroy were instrumental in influencing the President's decision.

Colombani has argued that the influence of a third group of people was also important. He calls the people in this group 'technocrats'. He argues that a group of technocrats in the *cabinets* at the Elysée, Matignon and the Finance Ministry, then at the Rue de Rivoli, worked together to draw up a coherent austerity programme based on the franc remaining in the EMS and avoiding the problems that they saw with its withdrawal. He identifies these people as François-Xavier Stasse at the Elysée, Henri Guillaume and Pascal Lamy at Matignon and Philippe Lagayette at the Finance Ministry. According to Colombani:

> In fact, a veritable network was set up between the Elysée, Matignon and the rue de Rivoli . . . They played a vital role from June 1982 to

March 1983, that is to say, at the time when the key economic decisions were made.[51]

There is no doubt that this group of people played a very important role in the preparation of the final decision. They provided Delors and Mauroy with information useful to their case. Moreover, the position that Stasse held at the Elysée was also strategically important because he was in contact with the other presidential advisers, the majority of whom were also hostile to leaving the EMS.[52]

Nevertheless, it would be wrong to call this group of people technocrats. The word has little meaning in this case. If it refers to their common educational background, then Delors, Rocard and Chevènement should also be called technocrats. However, these people are clearly politicians. In fact, all of the people whom Colombani identifies were themselves political figures and not technocrats. They worked in the *cabinets* of the country's three most senior political figures. It is impossible to dissociate their action from the interests of the people they served and from the motivations that have already been identified. Thus, whilst they played an important role during the crisis period, they should not be treated as a separate influence on the President's decision.

Conclusion

The importance of this case study lies in its portrayal of the President as chief decision-maker. In the previous case studies the President has either been largely peripheral to the policy process, as in the case of *cohabitation*, or has been seen to intervene only intermittently, if decisively, at the end of a long preparatory process. On these other occasions, the Prime Minister has either been the main policy maker, or he has at least been the key figure in the arbitration process. The crisis surrounding the 1983 devaluation, however, led to an arbitration which was undisputedly presidential and of which, as a result, Giesbert has said that during this period, '*France n'a plus de chef du gouvernement*'.[53]

At the same time, however, in many respects the decision-making process examined in this chapter closely resembled the one which was encountered in the previous chapter. In both cases, decisions had to be made under crisis situations. Whilst in the previous chapter the situation was arguably more fluid, in this chapter the stakes were still very high and there was little room for compromise. It is not surprising, therefore, that there was evidence of the same sort of vacillation on the part of the

President on this occasion as there had been by the Prime Minister in the previous chapter.

That point aside, it might also be argued that this case study provides evidence to back up the second variant of the segmented decision-making model. That is to say, in March 1983 there was a policy crisis based on the problem of currency stability. In this sense, the devaluation crisis would seem to belong naturally to the extended version of the President's reserved domain. However, precisely because there were both important international and economic policy considerations at stake and because there was no available compromise policy, it was necessary for Mitterrand to assume the responsibility for policy leadership himself. That is to say, there are reasons which differentiate the circumstances of non-routine policy making from those of routine policy-making and which encourage the President to assume leadership functions in the former. Thus, not only might the segmented decision-making model be seen to depict accurately the policy process on this occasion, but reasons can be provided as to why this should be the case. This advance is important for the model which in the Chapter 2 was seen to have been purely descriptive.

7 The Limits to Prime Ministerial Influence

It was clear from the examination of the case studies that, in the ten-year period from 1981, the influence of the Prime Minister in the policy process was not constant. It was at its greatest during the period of *cohabitation*, whilst it was at its weakest during the crisis period concerning the decision over whether or not to remain in the EMS. In between these two extremes, there were examples of considerable prime ministerial influence, the 1982 broadcasting act, for example, and examples of marginal prime ministerial involvement, such as the 1985 budget.

In the final two chapters it is necessary to account for the reasons why the level of prime ministerial influence should have fluctuated. It will be argued that there are three ways in which it is possible to account for the variations in prime ministerial influence. Each of these three ways will be examined and the problems associated with them will be identified. It will be shown that none of them successfully manages to quantify prime ministerial influence.

As a result, a different way of approaching the nature of prime ministerial influence will be examined. This approach considers the concept of 'influence' as a relationship between two or more people or institutions. According to this approach, the influence of the Prime Minister can only be considered in relation to the influence of the other variables which operate in the political system. These variables may be categorised as belonging to three different sets of factors: systemic factors, conjunctural factors and momentary factors. The bulk of this chapter will be spent in analysing the nature of these factors. The final chapter will consider the nature of prime ministerial influence in the light of this analysis.

Methods of Quantifying Prime Ministerial Influence

The first way in which the Prime Minister's influence might be quantified is by charting the variations in the frequency of committees and councils throughout the Fifth Republic.[1] This approach deals with the Prime Minister's influence in relation to the President. Given that the Prime

Table 7.1   The incidence of interministerial committees during
the Fifth Republic[2]

President	Prime Minister	Year	Comités
de Gaulle	Debré	1961	118
	Pompidou	1966	145
Pompidou	Chaban-Delmas	1970	145
	Messmer	1973	74
Giscard	Chirac	1975	93
d'Estaing	Barre	1979	74
Mitterrand	Mauroy	1982	134
	Fabius	1985	24

Minister chairs committees, whereas the President chairs councils and assuming that whoever chairs these meetings controls their outcome, then by charting the variations in the frequency of these meetings over the years it might be possible to measure the relative influence of the Prime Minister and the President in the policy process.

When these calculations are made, the results show that, apart from a flurry at the beginning of the Mitterrand presidency, the number of interministerial committees per annum has generally decreased during the course of the last thirty years, suggesting a decline in prime ministerial influence (see Table 7.1). It might also be added that, since the departure of Debré in 1961, one type of prime ministerial meeting, the *Conseil de Cabinet*, has disappeared altogether.[3]

By contrast, the number of interministerial councils has varied from an average of 1.3 per month from 1969–72 under the premiership of Chaban-Delmas to 4 per month under Chirac's premiership from 1974–76. These figures suggest an increase in presidential influence. However, during the first two years of the Barre premiership, the average number of councils fell to 2 per month, suggesting a decline in presidential influence.[4]

In fact, this statistic illustrates how misleading it is to try to measure the influence of an institution in this way. Firstly, the inference that, for example, a decline in the number of councils is a sign that presidential influence has decreased is not necessarily correct. Paradoxically, such a decline might be the result of an increase in presidential influence, as Suleiman has shown in the case of Raymond Barre. Here, unlike the situation during Chirac's premiership, Giscard d'Estaing was confident that Barre knew what the President's wishes were and that he would abide by them. As a result, there was no need to hold councils for every bill, because the Prime Minister's loyalty and subservience to the President

Table 7.2   Number of people serving in prime ministerial
cabinets, 1958–88[5]

Prime Minister	Year	No. in cabinet
Debré	1959	18
Pomp.	1962	21
Couve	1968	20
C-D	1969	33
Messmer	1972	28
Chirac	1974	21
Barre	1976	29
Mauroy	1982	56
Fabius	1984	20
Chirac	1986	35
Rocard	1990	34

was in no doubt.[6] Secondly, as was evident from the case studies, the policy process also includes a great number of informal meetings which go unrecorded, such as the Elysée lunch to discuss the content of the 1989 broadcasting bill. However, these meetings often have a bearing on the final policy outcome. Therefore, the official figures, as presented above, do not take these informal meetings into account and, as such, may be misleading. Finally, this approach is limited because it only compares the Prime Minister's influence to that of the President. In fact, the Prime Minister's influence will be dependent on his relations with other people and institutions as well. This approach, therefore, is useful, but flawed.

Another way in which influence might be measured is by looking at the size of the administrative services which the different actors in the political system control. The person commanding the greatest number of services might be in a position to exert the greatest amount of influence on the policy process. One way in which services might be measured is by counting the number of people in a person's *cabinet* (see Table 7.2). On this basis, it would appear as if Mauroy was the most influential Prime Minister during the period under consideration. However, in fact, prime ministerial influence was at its height under Chirac. It would appear, therefore, as if this measurement of prime ministerial influence is also misleading.

Another way of measuring an institution's services would be to add up the whole range of administrative resources that it possessed. If these calculations are made, then the Prime Minister is shown to be the most influential institution in the country followed by different Ministries, such as Education, Finance and the Interior, with the presidency being one of the weakest institutions in the system. These results seem to be counterintuitive.

Even aside from these results, this approach is less than perfect. Firstly, as was noted in Chapter 1, from the beginning of the Fifth Republic, the President has been able to colonise the services of both the Prime Minister and different Ministries. For much of the Fifth Republic, the *cabinet* of, for example, the Prime Minister has been busy carrying out the President's legislative programme, as laid down by presidential candidates in their election manifestos.[7] Therefore, it is misleading simply to calculate the number of people which each institution directly controls, because by so doing the indirect control which Presidents have had over the political system is not taken into account. Secondly, over the years Presidents have borrowed administrative resources from other areas.[8] The President often has the help of advisers who are 'on loan' from government Ministries. These advisers are not counted amongst the President's official entourage and so, once again, the brute figures mask a more complex reality. The problems associated with this approach mean that it is generally unsuitable as a method of measuring the influence that different institutions possess in the policy process.

A third measure of prime ministerial influence might be taken as the incidence of times when the Prime Minister's viewpoint is adopted as the final policy outcome. This approach has the advantage that it assumes that the policy process is a bargaining game and that the Prime Minister is only one actor amongst many. Moreover, it accounts for the possibility that there can be fluctuations in the level of prime ministerial influence over time. At times, the Prime Minister's views will be adopted more frequently than at others. On such occasions, it might be concluded that there was prime ministerial government. Conversely, if the President's viewpoint were consistently to be adopted, then it might be said that there was presidential government.

However, in its attempt to quantify prime ministerial influence, this approach poses as many problems as the ones previously considered. As can be seen from the case studies, it was sometimes difficult to identify the Prime Minister's viewpoint on a particular matter. Most governmental deliberations were secret and only rumours of what policy the Prime Minister favoured for each bill managed to escape. Similarly, on certain occasions the Prime Minister did not even articulate a particular viewpoint. This silence may be an indication that he thought the matter to be unworthy of his attention, or it may be, as in the case of the fiscal component of the 1990 budget, that he feared defeat and, therefore, refused to commit himself. Moreover, Prime Ministers may deliberately cede on some issues in order to win on others. Once again, it must be concluded that there are great difficulties associated with measuring prime ministerial influence in this way.

Influence as a Relationship between Individuals and Institutions

As a result of the problems associated with the three approaches discussed above, it is necessary to examine the nature of prime ministerial influence in a different way. It must be appreciated that influence is not a concept which easily lends itself to quantification. George Jones's statement about power could easily apply to the concept of influence as well. He states:

> it is impossible to measure the power of prime ministers by weighing their possession of different amounts of different resources. The power of the prime minister is affected by other actors the prime minister is dealing with; so it is fruitless to seek to calculate precisely how much resources each prime minister has, let alone to compare the amount held by one prime minister with that of another.[9]

The attempt to quantify prime ministerial influence is fruitless, as it treats the different actors in the policy process as being independent the one from the other. The concept of influence can only be appreciated as the interaction of two or more people. As Jones again states:

> Since power involves a relationship between at least two actors, the power of each is elastic, capable of expansion and contraction, depending on each side of the equation and the circumstances in which they operate. A resource is not a solid object that can be picked up. It has to be seen in relation to what others have.[10]

As was seen in the case studies, prime ministerial influence is not simply dependent on the relationship between the Prime Minister and another actor, but on his relationship with a multitude of different people: the President, Ministers, party representatives, members of interest groups and people from foreign governments and institutions.

Therefore, whilst this study is concerned with the nature of prime ministerial influence, it is impossible to consider the Prime Minister in isolation. The influence of the institution needs must be placed in the context of the entire system. This point is tacitly acknowledged by

Peter Hall in the development of his argument about the organisational factors which have determined the course of French economic policy since 1945. In his early papers on this subject, he argued that there were three organisational factors which were important in the determination of economic policy: the organisation of labour, the organisation of capital and the organisation of the state, by which he meant the legislative, executive and judicial branches of government.[11] However, in the final version of his argument, he adds two other organisational features to his list, namely, the position of the country in the international economic system and the organisation of the domestic political system.[12] The latter is a catch-all clause which includes the electoral system, party system and so on. Hall is no doubt right to argue that economic policy-making since 1945 was determined by a vast range of factors. In a similar vein, it will be argued here that the influence of the Prime Minister in the policy process can only be considered in relation to the influence of the totality of elements in the domestic and international political and economic system.

Therefore, the only way to consider the Prime Minister's influence in the policy process is to identify the other elements with which the head of government has to interact. The extent of the Prime Minister's influence will depend upon his relationship with these other elements. As the relationship between them changes, so the influence of the Prime Minister will change, sometimes increasing, sometimes decreasing. In fact, the Prime Minister's influence in the policy process is dependent upon his relationship with three different sets of elements: systemic factors; conjunctural factors; and momentary factors. Each of these three sets of factors will be considered in turn.

Systemic Factors

Prime ministerial influence is limited by a set of systemic factors. The general boundaries within which the Prime Minister can influence the outcome of the policy process are determined by the relations that he enjoys with these factors. As his relationship with them varies, so his influence will vary. Indeed, over time, these variations may be considerable. However, in normal circumstances, his relations with them will vary only slowly and incrementally. Only crises and ruptures of the existing order will change these systemic factors quickly. In the absence of such violent changes, these factors are, therefore, of a quasi-permanent nature. In the ten-year period from 1981 there were no terminal crises. Therefore, the Prime Minister's relations with them fluctuated only mildly and his influence with regard to them remained largely constant during this period.

In France, there are three types of systemic factors. First, the position of the domestic state in relation to the international economic and political order. Second, the configuration of the domestic state itself. Third, the internal configuration of the executive branch of government. Each of these three types of factors will now be considered in turn.

The Prime Minister's influence is first of all limited by the position of the French state in the international political and economic system. The way that this system is organised imposes limitations on the domestic policy preparation process. The impact of these limitations was seen particularly clearly at the time of the crisis surrounding the decision to devalue the franc in March 1983.

As Cerny states, France is an 'intermediate economy' when compared with other national economic systems.[13] That is to say, in terms of the types of goods it produces and exchanges with other countries, there is a structural gap between France and other more advanced national economies, whilst the country has a structural advance over other less developed economies. The result of France's position in the world economic order means that, on occasions, it can only adopt the policy it desires with difficulty, if at all, because of the consequences that this policy would have on the country's internal economic situation. As Cerny states:

> In reacting to the policy problems embedded in the 'intermediate economy''s structural position, national policy makers have a range of responses with which to work. Each one of these responses has potential benefits for the national economy, but each can also have severe disadvantages in the context of the world economy.[14]

These disadvantages were the source of the devaluation crisis in March 1983. The country's economic problems were caused by its position in the world order, but withdrawing from the EMS would only have aggravated these problems, precisely because of the structural position of France in this order. The realisation of what the consequences would be of leaving the EMS accounted for Fabius's 'road to Damascus' conversion from '*l'autre politique*' and his subsequent advice to Mitterrand to stay in the EMS.

However, it should not be concluded that France could not have pulled out of the EMS in March 1983. The decision to stay in the system was not pre-determined and the reasons behind this decision were essentially political. Nevertheless, withdrawal would have entailed severe economic consequences which would have had to have been addressed at a future date. As Cerny again notes:

> Countries in a weak structural trade position have less room to manœuvre. Policy makers are continually having to navigate between policy combinations which, in particular conjunctural conditions, may prove not only to be ineffective and internally incompatible, but also to be counterproductive and to involve significant opportunity costs.[15]

The opportunity costs of withdrawing from the EMS in March 1983 were so great that, although it would technically have been possible to leave, in practice, the economic arguments in favour of remaining in the system were overwhelming.

The other international systemic factor which was identified in the case studies was the EC. It was present both as a political and as an economic constraint. Its political importance was great during the 1983 devaluation crisis and its economic importance was noticeable during the preparation of the three budgets which were examined, especially with regard to their fiscal component.

The EC is a good example of how these systemic factors can vary in the extent to which they limit the policy process of the domestic state. Clearly, before 1958, the EC was absent from domestic policy calculations. Since the signing of the Treaty of Rome, its influence has grown, particularly after the ratification of the Single European Act in 1987. Moreover, its influence is likely to increase further with the development of political and economic union.

Indeed, the influence of the EC grew during the period under consideration. Its increasing role was seen in the case studies. For example, the EC had little impact on budgetary politics in 1984, except for agricultural policy. However, by 1990, there were several important fiscal reforms the inspiration for which can be traced back to the EC and the government's desire to prepare itself for the Single European Market. Thus, for example, VAT rates were reduced, company taxation was reduced and there were changes to savings policy. It would be wrong to conclude that the only motivation behind these changes was the EC, again political reasons were important too. However, it is important to realise that, as the influence of the EC grew, so the room for manœuvre for domestic policy-makers diminished. Over time, the relation between the EC and the domestic decision-makers, including the

Prime Minister, is gradually changing and the influence of the latter is decreasing.

It can be seen, therefore, that the Prime Minister's influence is constrained by international systemic factors, but it is also constrained by the configuration of the domestic state. The French state exhibits two main characteristics. First, the central state dominates all local state, or government institutions. Second, within the central state, the executive branch of government under the Fifth Republic has dominated the legislative and judicial branches. These characteristics will be considered in turn.

As was shown in the Chapter 2, the central state in France is highly developed. Hayward has described this situation as, 'the monolithic character of the political and administrative state apparatus'.[16] The absence of any constitutional provision for federalism means that there are few limits to the central state's law-making domain. There is no territorial separation of powers. In this sense, the local governmental authorities do not act as a check on the central institutions. The capacity of the Prime Minister and of other decision makers at the centre to prepare policy is not officially limited by sub-central units. Thus, the potential for governmental and prime ministerial influence is present. This point can best be illustrated by comparing the unitary state in France with the constitutional federalism which exists in Germany. In the latter case, the prerogatives of the *Länder* immediately act as a limit on the capacity of the Federal Chancellor to influence the policy process. The same situation is not present in France.

Therefore, at no time during the case studies was the local state structure an impediment to the central state's capacity for action. When local interests were important, for example, over the question of whether or not to permit advertising on local radio in the 1982 broadcasting act, the local representatives were acting *qua* pressure group and used the appropriate channels to lobby the government. They were not acting as a legal-constitutional block to the central institutions. This is not to say that the local dimension is bound to remain weak. Indeed, Mazey has argued that its influence is gradually increasing.[17] Nevertheless, from the evidence of the previous case studies, it had little impact on the policy process and was not a constraint on prime ministerial influence.

Within the institutions of the central state, the executive branch of government was dominant. In comparison with the legislative and judicial branches, its control over the policy process was great. With regard to the executive's relation to the legislature, Frears has noted:

The constitutional and procedural constraints can be summarised thus: complete executive supremacy in the legislative process, severely limited opportunities for general debates criticising the government, virtually no opportunities for scrutinising executive acts and making the executive give an account of them.[18]

Frears goes on to add that there is little procedural opportunity for the opposition to scrutinise the government. It might also be added that there is little opportunity for the majority to do so either. Indeed, when Parliament did influence the policy process, for example, the 1986 broadcasting act, or the 1990 budget, it was due to conjunctural reasons, such as party politics, as described below. Most of the Prime Minister's administrative resources which were geared towards Parliament were designed to overcome these conjunctural problems. For example, Guy Carcassonne's role as Rocard's parliamentary adviser was oriented towards combatting conjunctural problems, rather than towards combatting problems created by the constitutional and procedural influence of Parliament.

Nevertheless, Parliament was not impotent. As a national platform for debate, it had the capacity to embarrass the government. Moreover, as was seen by the obstructive tactics of the Senate during the passage of the 1986 broadcasting bill, it had the ability to delay and even influence legislation. On this occasion, the Prime Minister personally was called upon to arbitrate between the Senate majority and the Culture Minister, François Léotard. Inter-party rivalries were the cause of the problems, but these problems were only able to develop, because of the procedural capacity of the Senate to delay government legislation. However, this example is very much the exception that proves the rule. In the rest of the case studies, Parliament *per se* was only a minor constraint on prime ministerial influence.

In certain respects, the judicial branch acted as a much stronger constraint on the executive than did the legislature. In terms of the policy preparation process, two institutions of the judicial branch need to be considered: the Council of State and the Constitutional Council. Of these two bodies, the Council of State was the least influential.

The Council of State was called upon to scrutinise all bills and to consider their conformity with the Constitution. However, it only had the power to advise the government as to whether a bill, or part of it, was unconstitutional. The government had no obligation to abide by its recommendations. Whilst governments did not like to ignore the advice of the Council of State, as could be seen in the case of the 1982 broadcasting act, they did so if they felt that the political situation demanded it. For example, while some of the Council of State's recommendations were taken on board by Léotard in the preparation of the 1986 broadcasting act, others were not. Indeed, the fact that these recommendations were presented to the government in secret meant that it was easier for them to be ignored as there would be no public debate of the government's decision. While leaks did occur, they were not frequent. Thus, the Council of State played the role of an early warning system for the government, rather than acting as a major constraint.

By contrast, the Constitutional Council was a potentially serious limit to the executive's control of the policy process. The government had to abide by its rulings. Thus, for all six case studies which ended with the passage of a law, the Council was called upon to give a judgement as to their constitutionality. On all six occasions, the Council found some aspect of the bill to be unacceptable. Indeed, its ruling on the 1986 broadcasting act struck down such an important part of the bill that it necessitated the passage of a further small piece of legislation after the adoption of the main text.

Indeed, over the years, the Council's influence has increased markedly. In 1971, it issued its first negative ruling against the government; in 1982, its rulings on the socialists' nationalisation programme struck down an important part of the government's legislation and the Council was seen to be a major check on executive power. The change in the Council's role and the increase in its influence has had a marked effect upon the government's legislative capacity.

The Council's influence was doubly important because of the pre-parliamentary exercise in autolimitation to which governments increasingly committed themselves. As Stone notes:

> Governments today routinely draft and accept amendments to their legislation so as to avoid negative rulings.[19]

This practice of autolimitation was conceded by several senior governmental figures during interviews with the author. Its impact on the 1986 and 1989 broadcasting bills was particularly important. Indeed, autolimitation became increasingly important with the growth in the Council's body of case law. The rulings which governments have to take into account have grown rapidly.

Whilst the Council's role has become more important over the years, its influence should not be overestimated. As Stone notes, there were limits to the extent to which governments engage in autolimitation:

there are certain boundaries beyond which governments are unwilling to go in the self-limitation process. These lines are fixed politically, not constitutionally, accounting perhaps for the poor success rate of self-limitation.[20]

Moreover, the traditional limitations to the Council's influence need to be reiterated: its members are political appointees; it has no power to determine for itself which bills it wishes to examine; and it cannot make retrospective judgements. Thus, whilst the Council was a constraint upon the executive and the Prime Minister, its influence was curtailed by political and constitutional factors.

The third set of systemic factors which need to be examined concern the *rapport de force* within the executive itself. Here, the Prime Minister's influence has to be set against that of the President, Ministers and the bureaucracy. However, it must immediately be noted that in this section the emphasis is upon the constitutional and administrative resources that these institutions possess, rather than their political resources. The former resources vary only incrementally and, thus, belong in the category of systemic factors. The latter may change quickly and violently and, thus, belong in the category of conjunctural factors.

The influence of the Prime Minister is usually set against that of the President. Yet, as was shown in the opening chapter, the President's constitutional and administrative resources were meagre. As Foyer and Lardeyret noted:

> The President's position of power over the Prime Minister is not set out in the Constitution . . .   The de facto predominance of the President has a political and not a juridical base.[21]

Indeed, as was stated above, if constitutional and administrative resources were to be the yardstick by which influence was measured, then the Prime Minister would be the most powerful institution in the country, followed by sundry Ministers and with the President trailing far behind. However, the Prime Minister clearly did not occupy such a position. Therefore, we can conclude that the relative influence of the different parts of the executive was not based upon systemic factors, but on conjunctural and momentary factors.

It should not be concluded, however, that constitutional and administrative resources were not unimportant to the influence of different actors in the policy process. The case studies showed that on occasions they were highly significant. For example, the constitutional situation defined the boundaries of presidential action during *cohabitation*. Similarly, the poor administrative resources possessed by the Culture Ministry in 1986, as compared to the Finance Ministry, meant that Léotard had to forego the control over the preparation of certain parts of the 1986 broadcasting bill. Nevertheless, conjuctural factors were a much better pointer to the relations between the Prime Minister, President and Ministers.

As for the permanent administration, there was no evidence from the case studies to support the first variant of the bureaucratic politics model, as outlined in Chapter 2. That is to say, the permanent administration did not act as a power bloc. Indeed, the notion that policy was being directed by a technocratic élite was shown to be analytically flawed during the devaluation crisis. Although *cabinet* members and members of the permanent administration wished to remain in the EMS, they were not directing policy and the motivation behind their action was as much political as economic. Indeed, it was shown that these people could not properly be classed as technocrats. Elsewhere there was no evidence of a power bloc co-ordinating policy.

By contrast, there was some evidence to support the second variant. The influence of individual parts of the permanent administration was clearly visible on certain occasions. For example, it was seen in the role of the SJTI in 1982 and 1989; in the influence of the Budget Division of the Finance Ministry during the preparation of all three budgets; and in the role of the Treasury Division during the devaluation crisis. In fact, there were clear demonstrations of departmentalism. Conflicts within the administration were drawn along departmental lines. Each department had its own interests which its administration tried to defend. Ministers were an important part of the administration's strategy to pursue its self-interest. The administration needed the support of Ministers to add political weight to their case, while Ministers needed to press the case of their own departments to prove their competence. Such interministerial conflicts were most clearly seen during the budgetary spending arbitrations, although they were also present in the preparation of the broadcasting acts between the Finance Ministry, Culture and Communications Ministries and the Telecommunications Ministry.

However, it should not be concluded from this evidence that there was bureaucratic government. The political components of the executive possess important elements of control over the administration. Firstly, the Prime Minister, President and Ministers have a considerable power of patronage. Secondly, in contrast to technocratic theory, the *cabinet* system serves to reinforce the position of the political components of the executive by providing them with a loyal team of policy advisers.

Thirdly, the Prime Minister and President have to arbitrate between the demands of the conflicting Ministries. It does not necessarily follow from this point that they are neutral in the arbitration process. For example, it was seen that they promoted their own preferred policy options on issues such as the composition of the regulatory authorities for broadcasting. It does mean, however, that there is the opportunity for decision making above the ministerial level. The permanent administration is poorly placed to control decision making at this level. Organisations which were well placed to influence policy at this level, for example, the GSG, showed no signs of having made an impact on the content of policy. Therefore, while the permanent administration possessed the resources to challenge the influence of the Prime Minister, President and Ministers in the policy process, it did not have the capacity to dominate them. The political component of the executive was faced with a important constraint, but not an insurmountable one.

Therefore, it can be seen that there are a number of systemic factors which affected the Prime Minister's influence on the policy process. Some of these factors limited the Prime Minister's influence, for example, the position of France in the world economic and political system and the strength of the permanent administration. Other factors increased his capacity to intervene in the policy process, for example, the strength of the central state and the executive branch of government and the high level of his administrative resources. In general, the extent to which these factors limited the Prime Minister's capacity for action varied over time, but only slowly.

It must also be noted, however, that these systemic factors were not free from the impact of the conjunctural factors to be examined below. While they can be analysed separately, they were not independent and isolated. Indeed, this conclusion is consistent with the notion of the influence being a relationship between two or more people or organisations. Given that the Prime Minister's influence can only be considered in relation to the influence of the totality of factors which operate in the political system, it would be surprising if there were to be no interaction between systemic and conjunctural factors.

Conjunctural Factors

The second set of elements upon which the Prime Minister's influence depended was comprised of conjunctural factors.[22] Whilst the general limits to prime ministerial influence were determined by his relationship

Table 7.3   Support for the President in the National Assembly, 1958–91

President	Majority	Majority opposed	Relative majority
de Gaulle	1962–69		1958–62
Pompidou	1969–74		
Giscard d'Estaing	1974–81		
Mitterrand	1981–86	1986–88	1988–

with the set of systemic factors, these conjunctural factors delineated more specifically his impact upon the policy process. They were subject to much more rapid variations than the systemic factors. Therefore, they account for why the Prime Minister's influence fluctuated so greatly during the ten year period since 1981. Whereas, during this period, the impact of systemic factors varied only incrementally, the impact of conjunctural factors varied considerably. There are four components to this set of factors: electoral politics, party politics, personality and public opinion. Each component will be considered in turn.

The first component of the set of conjunctural factors is the outcome of presidential and legislative elections. The results of these two sets of elections were the major conjunctural factors which determined whether there was to be presidential government or prime ministerial government.

The results of these elections were so important because of the semi-presidential nature of the Fifth Republic after the 1962 constitutional reform. In semi-presidential systems, these two sets of elections are both, to a greater or lesser extent, determining elections. Under the semi-presidential system, there can be two general outcomes following these elections: the President can belong to the same party, or parties which make up the parliamentary majority; or the President can belong to an opposing party, or set of parties than that of the parliamentary majority. The existence of these two possible outcomes leads to a system which Frèches has described as possessing '*une plasticité républicaine*'.[23]

This 'plasticity' is general to semi-presidential régimes. The Irish case has provided a good recent example of the change from a coincidence of presidential and parliamentary majorities to the presence of two opposing majorities, following the election of Mary Robinson as President. However, France is unique amongst semi-presidential régimes in that the coincidence of these two majorities, or their disjunction, was the main determinant on policy making.

In this way, the results of both presidential and parliamentary elections and the subsequent coincidence or disjunction of presidential and parliamentary majorities were the key conjunctural determinants of prime ministerial influence. To date, the most usual situation has been the coincidence of majorities, or as Servent has put it: *'la conformité des majorités'*.[24] Only the 1986–88 period saw opposing majorities, although the President was only backed by a relative majority in Parliament after the 1988 legislative elections (see Table 7.3). One reason for the relative absence of opposing majorities is that the system was designed to encourage a coincidence of majorities. The President had the power to dissolve Parliament and this weapon has been used on several occasions, notably in 1981 and 1988, so as to ensure that a friendly parliamentary majority was elected by way of a presidential coat-tails effect.

In both 1981 and 1988, Mitterrand was elected on the basis of a particular policy programme, the 110 Propositions and the *Lettre à tous les Français* respectively. The parliamentary majority was composed of people who campaigned in support of that programme. Therefore, the President was able to appoint a Prime Minister who ensured that the programme, or as much as the President thought fit, was then legislated. In this situation, the Prime Minister was aware that he owed his appointment to the President. He was also aware that he was responsible to a Parliament which was loyal to the President and not to him. It is natural in such a situation that political leadership should belong to the President and not the Prime Minister. In the sense that during these times the President was the source of most policy initiatives and that he asserted the *de facto* right to intervene in the decision-making process when he so desired, then there can be said to have been presidential government.

The 1981–84 period was an example of this situation and was reflected in the case studies which were examined. The 1982 broadcasting act, in particular, saw the President intervening personally on major policy decisions, whilst various members of his entourage oversaw the detailed preparation of the bill. In this case political leadership did not belong to the Prime Minister, but to the President. As Feigenbaum has stated:

> During the 'normal' situation of a President with a friendly majority in the National Assembly, decision making has been hierarchical.[25]

However, this situation did not mean that the Prime Minister and his advisers were politically impotent, but rather that they were clearly subordinate to the President. In this sense, prime ministerial influence was not necessarily negligible, but it was less than presidential influence.

The case of a disjunction of presidential and parliamentary majorities occurred during *cohabitation*. Under *cohabitation*, the parliamentary majority was loyal to the Prime Minister and hostile to the President. On this occasion, the Prime Minister assumed the responsibility for policy leadership. The Prime Minister was personally identified with a legislative programme derived from the election platform upon which the RPR/UDF coalition had campaigned and won the legislative elections. The Prime Minister, therefore, enjoyed the loyalty of the parliamentary majority as he executed the coalition's legislative programme. The President, by contrast, was only able to fulfil his meagre constitutional functions. The Prime Minister was able to supplant policy leadership from the President because his popular mandate, albeit indirect, was newer than the President's. As Colombani and Lhomeau noted, the Prime Minister benefited from:

[a] legitimacy derived from his position as head of the governmental majority elected on the 16th March. A fresher legitimacy than that of the President.[26]

This theoretical argument backed up the practical situation of prime ministerial dominance.

Under *cohabitation*, therefore, the Prime Minister controlled public policy. As Wright has stated:

Cohabitation was to demonstrate that a government with a friendly majority in parliament could displace the President as the centre of domestic decision making.[27]

The Prime Minister's newfound influence was seen in the case studies. It was Chirac who decided which parts of the electoral platform to legislate. For example, he took the decision to delay the preparation of the telecommunications law. It was also the Prime Minister who took the most important policy decisions, such as the number of television companies to privatise. Similarly, even though Chirac delegated much of the responsibility for drawing up the 1987 budget to Balladur, this situation was a sign of strength not weakness. Balladur was a loyal lieutenant who could be trusted to draw up policy in a manner consistent with the Prime Minister's preferences.

It is apparent, therefore, that the main conjunctural factor upon which prime ministerial influence depended was the results of presidential and legislative elections. This observation, whilst fundamental, is not sufficient in order properly to explain all of the variations in prime ministerial influence. The main problem is that election results do not account for the variations in prime ministerial and presidential influence between elections. For example, there were major differences in prime ministerial influence during the Mauroy and Fabius premierships, despite the fact that they both served under the same President with the same parliamentary majority. The same observation would also be true when there was a disjunction of majorities, although the unique example of *cohabitation* means that this can only be posited as a hypothesis and cannot be proved.

Variations of influence within electoral periods can partly be ascribed to changes in the second conjunctural factor under which the Prime Minister operated, namely, party politics. It must be appreciated that party politics affected the Prime Minister's influence in their widest sense. To this end, consideration needs to be made of inter-party relations, intra-party relations and party organisations.

The main impact of inter-party relations upon prime ministerial influence was seen when there were coalition governments. During the period covered by the case studies there were two radically different types of coalitions which were witnessed. Both of these types of coalition had a different impact upon the policy process. The first type was a two party coalition (PS/PCF) with one dominant party (PS). This coalition survived from 1981 until 1984. The second type was a two party coalition (RPR/UDF) with both partners having equal weight. This situation occurred under *cohabitation*.

In the first scenario, the effect of the minor coalition partner on overall government policy-making was minimal. In the specific Ministries which were headed by PCF representatives, there was naturally a much greater role for the junior party. However, the overall impact of the PCF on policy making was small. It could be seen, for example, that the PCF was not formally involved in the preparation of the 1982 broadcasting act. The only input came informally from Ralite at the request of Lang and had no discernible impact on the wording of the bill. Moreover, no concerted attempt was made by the government to prevent the communists from abstaining on the vote in the National Assembly. Indeed, more attempt was made to woo the RPR in the Senate. Similarly, apart from several minor concessions on expenditure for the PCF Ministers, the influence of the communists on the preparation of the 1985 budget was also meagre. It might be concluded, therefore, that the influence of the Prime Minister in the policy process was hardly affected by the nature of the governmental coalition from 1981–84.

By contrast, the impact of the 1986–88 coalition upon decision making was great. During *cohabitation*, the fact that Chirac headed a coalition of two equal parties did have an impact upon his influence in the policy process. In order to keep the coalition together so as to pass laws through Parliament, Chirac had to negotiate with and on occasions make concessions to his coalition partner. Indeed, the impact of inter-party politics on the policy process was so great that it was called '*la deuxième cohabitation*' by Léotard. As Servent has noted:

> To the first cohabitation between the President and the Prime Minister might be added a second between the components of the parliamentary majority each backing different presidential candidates (Chirac, Barre, Léotard).[28]

The preparation of the 1986 broadcasting act was a good example of this situation. Léotard, aided and abetted by Giscard d'Estaing, tried to use his position to draw up what could be considered to be a Republican Party law. As a result, he naturally came up against fierce opposition from the RPR, particularly in the Senate. The fact, however, that Chirac felt that he had to arbitrate in Léotard's favour on several key occasions showed that the Prime Minister was not simply able to carry out the wishes of his own party, but that he was constrained by the exigencies of the parliamentary coalition. These same exigencies could be seen at work during the preparation of the 1987 budget, particularly with regard to the fiscal component. The *barristes* made their opposition to the government's original plans very plain and, as the price for the budget's smooth passage through Parliament, Balladur had to concede several costly amendments. Thus, whilst the UDF, or certain components of it, could not dictate its terms to the Prime Minister and the RPR, nevertheless, it still had an impact which Chirac could not ignore in the arbitration process.

The two other parliamentary situations in which the government found itself also had repercussions upon prime ministerial influence. In the first of these situations, that of a single party government with a parliamentary majority, the Prime Minister had little to worry about with regard to inter-party relations. However, in the second case, that of a minority government, the Prime Minister had to take the wishes of other parliamentary parties very seriously into account. The second situation was the one under which Rocard had to operate during the preparation of the 1989 broadcasting act and the 1990 budget. The minority situation in which he found himself had a demonstrable effect upon the Prime Minister's influence in the policy process.

The minority situation obliged the Prime Minister to bargain with the UDC and the PCF on every bill that was presented to Parliament.[29] This bargaining took place both before and during the parliamentary stage and was usually conducted informally. The need to win the support, or abstention, of either the UDC or the PCF meant that concessions had to be made which altered the nature of the bill, as it had already been agreed in the interministerial arbitration meetings. Changes were made which would not otherwise have been made. In this sense, the minority situation had an effect upon the role of the Prime Minister. The effect of this bargaining could be most clearly seen in the preparation of the 1989 broadcasting act. Here, some not insubstantial alterations were made to the bill as a result of the Prime Minister's desire to win the support of the UDC.

The influence of the UDC and the PCF after 1988 was important, but not unlimited. Rocard used Article 49–3 to pass both the 1989 broadcasting bill and the 1990 budget, so as to avoid having to accept amendments which were totally unpalatable. Indeed, the UDC set its demands so high over the former bill because it was worried about the effects that supporting the government would have on its inter-party relations with the RPR and the UDF. Thus, the evidence available shows the importance of inter-party relations on government policy. With regard to the Prime Minister in a minority situation, however, while his room for manœuvre was limited, he still retained a certain space in which to operate.

Intra-party politics were also important as a conjunctural factor upon the Prime Minister. Whilst the nature of intra-party disputes is often seized upon and exaggerated by the press, they did have an impact upon the outcome of public policy and, hence, the influence of the Prime Minister in the policy process. As Gaffney has noted:

> All changes in the balance of power within the party have, therefore, potentially far-reaching consequences.[30]

Largely due to the break up of the Mitterrand *courant*, the internal party problems within the PS increased noticeably after 1988. The exchanges between the *fabiusiens* and the *jospinistes* during the preparation of the 1990 budget provide evidence of the increasing tensions within the party. Rocard's strategy at this time was to appear to take neither side, so as to enhance his position as arbitrator. Whilst this strategy was designed to improve Rocard's long-term chances as a future *présidentiable*, it also meant that he was sometimes not able to pursue the policies which he favoured. In particular, he had to acquiesce to certain decisions on the fiscal side of the 1990 budget to which previously he had been hostile.

The importance of intra-party politics meant that the position of the Prime Minister within the party affected his influence on the policy process. Intuitively, the stronger the Prime Minister's position within the party, the greater his capacity is for influencing policy. In this respect, the contrast between, for example, Chirac and Rocard was great. Chirac was the founder of the RPR and its undisputed leader in 1986. As such, all other RPR Ministers were loyal and subordinate to him. Rocard, by contrast, has always been rather a maverick figure within the PS. As Cole noted about Rocard's position in the post-1988 period:

> He is distrusted not only by the new PS leadership under the control of Mauroy, but also by a majority of anti-Rocardian PS deputies.[31]

In fact, the position of all three socialist Prime Ministers during the period in question was one of subordination to the President. Mitterrand's authority was derived not only from his election, but also from his position of co-founder and 'historic' leader of the PS. Mitterrand's position of authority limited the potential influence of both Mauroy, Fabius and Rocard. As Lemaire stated about Mitterrand's first two Prime Ministers:

> Mitterrand placed the party on probation by ensuring the dominance of his own faction. It is for this reason, amongst others, that he appointed Mauroy as Prime Minister because, from Matignon, he could never claim to be leading the party. Similarly, Laurent Fabius had no real support within the party; therefore, François Mitterrand could remain the supreme arbiter . . . [32]

Thus, the Prime Minister's position within the party after 1981 was particularly important with regard to the President.

With regard to Ministers, the impact of intra-party politics upon the Prime Minister's influence was less important. At the time of their premierships, neither Mauroy, nor Fabius, nor Rocard enjoyed a position of strength within the socialist party. Mauroy had still not been forgiven by the *mitterrandistes* for having committed the crime of *lèse-majesté* at the 1979 Metz party congress. In 1984, Fabius was too young to have been able to build up a personal power base within the party. Similarly, in 1988, Rocard was still considered to be an outsider and inherently untrustworthy by much of the PS. As a result, it can be argued that the influence of all three socialist Prime Ministers after 1981 was not derived from their position within the party. Indeed, it might also be argued that that their weakness within the PS was a disadvantage in the bargaining process with regard to Ministers and, in particular, with regard to the President.

A further element of this conjunctural factor upon the Prime Minister's influence was that of the party *qua* individual actor. For example, after 1981 the party leadership of the PS was consistently associated with policy preparation, usually through a series of informal policy meetings at Matignon or the Elysée.[33] Whilst it was difficult to dissociate the independent influence of party leaders from the interests of their constituent parts, such as factions and the parliamentary party group, the party could be said to have had an influence.[34]

Party organisation should also be considered as an influencing factor. In general, parties which follow their leaders have less impact upon the policy process than parties which delegate their leaders. The PS should certainly be classed in the former category. After 1981, it was frequently referred to as a *godillot* party 'totally subordinated to presidential directives'.[35] It might be argued that the Fifth Republic's institutional structure tends to create parties which follow their leaders (*présidentiables*). As such, the impact of the mass membership of the party after 1981 was barely discernible. Only at the élite level, as noted above, did the party have any influence.

In most of the aspects considered above, party politics acted as a constraint on the Prime Minister's influence. His relationship to his own party and to opposing parties both inside and outside of the governing coalition was an important determinant of his role in the policy process. Indeed, Jones has argued that, of all the factors which impinge upon the head of government's influence in West European political systems, party politics is the most important. He states:

> The relationship between prime ministers and parties is the most important of all linkages for most prime ministers . . . Party is the critical resource and constraint: the key to the power of both the prime minister and the other actors and institutions.[36]

Certainly, it was clear that the factors identified above were central to an explanation of the Prime Minister's influence and, equally importantly, to an explanation of why that influence changed over time.

A further conjunctural factor which determined the level of prime ministerial influence was that of personality. In this case, the variations in his influence were due at least in part to the interaction between the personality of the different Prime Ministers and those of the other senior office holders. An immediate proviso must be made, however. It would be wrong to argue that personality was the main determinant of the Prime Minister's influence. Individuals always operated within systems which possessed certain structural characteristics. These structures, as outlined

Table 7.4   Barber's classification of presidential styles

	Active	Passive
Positive	Active-Positive	Passive-Positive
Negative	Active-Negative	Passive-Negative

above, set the limits to the influence of a particular institution. Here, it is argued that within those limits the personality of the different protagonists was important. Greenstein has suggested a set of circumstances within which personality can influence political behaviour.[37] It is under such circumstances that personality was a determinant of prime ministerial influence.

It is important to give some content to the notion of 'personality' as it is being used here. What is not implied are characteristics presented in anecdotal accounts of politicians' behaviour, such as, for example, Chirac's reputation for having a short temper. Even if he were to have a short temper, it would not be the basis for an analytical account of his influence in the policy process. Personality studies approach the notion of psychological characteristics more analytically. These characteristics are one of the factors which may determine a person's influence in the policy process. Lasswell, for example, introduced the concept of the 'psychopathology' of leaders.[38] He argued that the reaction of leaders to particular events was due to the individual's childhood experiences, for example. Similarly, Iremonger's study of British Prime Ministers concluded that the driving force in their political careers could be traced back to their being deprived of the love of their parents in childhood.[39] Thus, the impact of personality may depend on such psychological characteristics.

One way in which it might be possible to operationalise such characteristics is by identifying the policy styles of different Prime Ministers. A previous attempt at such an exercise can be found in Barber's classic study of the American presidency and the presidential character.[40] He proposed two baselines for the study of the presidential character, namely, activity-passivity, meaning the degree of energy which a person invests in the presidency and, secondly, the positive-negative affect towards this activity, meaning how a person feels about what s/he does in office. These two baselines combine to form four configurations, which may be applied to individual Presidents (see Table 7.4). For Barber, these character configurations are equivalent to personality and consist in the interplay of character itself, world view and style. He provides examples

Table 7.5   *Barber's typology as applied to French Prime Ministers,*
1981–91

	Active	Passive
Positive	Mauroy '81–'83 Rocard	Fabius
Negative	Chirac	Mauroy '83–84

of US Presidents who conformed to the above configurations. Kennedy
is said to be active-positve, Taft passive-positive, Hoover active-negative
and Coolidge passive-negative. If a similar exercise is undertaken for the
French Prime Minister, then the following classifications might be the
result (see Table 7.5). Despite Rocard's unwillingness to intervene on
certain issues after 1988, he should be classified as an active-positive
Prime Minister alongside Mauroy in the first two years of his premiership.
Rocard's desire to bring an end to the New Caledonian crisis and to pass
laws such as the *Contribution Sociale Généralisée* would seem to justify
this classification. Similarly, Mauroy's contribution to the advertising
on local radio debate and his intervention in the preparation of the
1982 broadcasting bill would indicate that he be placed in the same
category. However, after the 1983 devaluation and during the period of
controversy over the Savary education bill, it would be more appropriate
to place Mauroy in the passive-negative category. The fact that he failed
to complete the arbitrations on the spending component of the 1985 budget
might be taken as evidence to justify this classification. By contrast, Fabius
would seem to be better suited to the passive-positive category. He had
little doubt about the worth of his own actions, but his premiership did not
see many major reforms taking place. Conversely, Chirac was undoubtedly
an active Prime Minister. However, his reaction to certain events, notably
the Devaquet crisis, was muted and worthy of a negative classification.
Whilst these classifications are open to some debate, they do give an idea
of how the personality of the Prime Minister can affect his role in the policy
process.

In addition to prime ministerial styles, other personality based factors were of demonstrable importance. For example, both Greenstein
and Machin have argued that skill plays an important role in the
policy process.[41] This factor could be demonstrated, for example, in
intragovernmental negotiations, in the timing of political issues and in the
oratorical, or televisual capacity which an individual possessed. Similarly,
the absence of such skill was a factor. Individuals may possess such skills
innately, or, more likely, they will learn them during the early years of their

political formation. People who come to top positions after much ministerial experience often deal better with the rigours of office than those who are young and relatively inexperienced. For example, Rose has noted:

> Mitterrand's leanings stem from his several decades of experience as Minister and deputy.[42]

Certainly, Mitterrand's experience was a decisive factor in his handling of the 1983 devaluation crisis. One aspect of this factor will be whether the individual has had a background in local politics, or administration. Rose again notes:

> Prime Ministers who come to office by way of the National Assembly or local politics, like Chaban-Delmas and Mauroy, have other priorities than a Prime Minister who began as a technocrat, such as Raymond Barre.[43]

It was clear that Fabius's background as an *inspecteur des finances* and as a former Budget Minister meant that he was better placed to intervene in the budgetary decision-making process than Mauroy before him.

Presidential and prime ministerial relations were also particularly affected by the ambitions of the two protagonists. As Servent has put it, the Prime Minister is on *'l'avant-dernière marche du pouvoir'*.[44] He is, or is at least seen to be, the main contender for the President's title. Some Prime Ministers use their time in office to prepare the way for a future presidential campaign. This was true for Rocard from 1988–91. His desire to avoid making enemies in the run up to the next presidential election was one of the motivations behind his refusal to take sides in the disputes between Bérégovoy and Chevènement over the defence budget in 1989. However, ambitious Prime Ministers are usually faced with Presidents who are reluctant to give up their office to anyone except their favourite dauphin. In such a situation, the President and Prime Minister naturally clash. Thus, for example, Rocard and Mitterrand never had each other's trust during the former's premiership.

The personal relations that the Prime Minister enjoyed with the President and other Ministers were also important. Some Prime Ministers have enjoyed close personal relations with the President before coming to office, others have been sworn enemies (see Table 7.6). Fabius was a loyal presidential acolyte before his appointment as Prime Minister, Mauroy largely became one on being appointed. On the other hand, Chirac and Rocard were long-term presidential rivals. Thus, personal likes

Table 7.6   Typology of presidential/prime ministerial relations, 1958–92

President	PM: subordinate	PM: rival	PM: opponent
de Gaulle	Debré Pompidou Couve de Murville		
Pompidou	Messmer	Chaban-Delmas	
Giscard	Barre	Chirac	
Mitterrand	Mauroy Fabius	Rocard	Chirac

and dislikes as well as ambitions are likely to influence the nature of the relations between the two institutions.

Similarly, the relations between the President and Ministers, or between individual Ministers had an affect on the Prime Minister's role. For example, successive socialist Prime Ministers were limited by Lang's relations with Mitterrand, which often allowed the Culture Minister to succeed in interministerial arbitrations. In addition, Chirac's position was made more difficult in 1986 because of the animosity between Monory and Devaquet.

The final conjunctural factor which needs to be considered is the role played by the public. The influence of the public manifested itself in two different ways. First, through the action of pressure groups and, second, through public opinion in general. Although the two ways are related and the analysis of them will overlap, it is useful to consider them separately.

There is a temptation to place the role of pressure groups in the category of systemic factors. The debates which have raged over recent years as to whether France can be considered to have neo-corporatist, meso-corporatist, or pluralist modes of interest group organisation would seem to be predicated upon a relatively stable framework of group/government interaction. Similarly, sociological studies, which suggest that the French are a nation of individualists who do not like joining voluntary associations, suggest that this characteristic is a permanent feature of French political life, not a conjunctural one.

In fact, pressure group activity is best considered alongside the other conjunctural factors. The case studies showed that their influence was not constant. It varied from one study to the next. The main reason for the variations in their influence was that they were not associated with parties and there were few fixed channels of intermediation with the government. That is to say, for example, that parties were not dependent upon them for finance and that there were few official policy-making committees upon which they were represented. Thus, their capacity for influencing policy was structurally weak. Instead, their influence was dependent upon, for example, the level of public sympathy for their cause and the immediate economic situation.

On the occasions when the situation operated in favour of the pressure groups, then the Prime Minister's influence was constrained. A particularly clear example of this situation was the Devaquet crisis in 1986. The UNEF-ID was not structurally strong, nor did it occupy a position of strategic importance in the productive process liable to increase its bargaining position relative to that of the government. Instead, the movement used the means at its disposal, such as demonstrations and television appearances, so as to build up a body of public opinion in favour of its position, sufficient to force Chirac to withdraw the bill in question. Indeed, the Devaquet crisis was a good example of the interaction of the influence of pressure groups and public opinion. The student protest movement was powerful because it went beyond the lobbying practices of UNEF-ID to incorporate a wider social movement that was much more threatening to the government.

Pressure group influence was also seen during various other case studies. For example, the lobbying surrounding the introduction or otherwise of advertising on local radio in the 1982 broadcasting law. In 1982, the anti-advertising lobby succeeded because it had a powerful ally in Mauroy who, at that time, had considerable authority within the executive. On this occasion, therefore, pressure group lobbying helped the Prime Minister's cause, rather than hindering it as in 1986. Thus, pressure group activity may be either a constraint or a resource for the Prime Minister.

Similarly, as Jones has argued, public opinion may act as a constraint on the Prime Minister's influence, or a resource which increases it.[45] He goes on to argue that the most important public are the voters, because election results depend upon their preferences. Rocard recognised the importance of public opinion for his position as Prime Minister when he incorporated a professional pollster, Gérard Grunberg, in his *cabinet* for the first time. One of the tasks of the pollster, whether s/he is institutionalised in the *cabinet* or not, was to alert the Prime Minister to potentially unfavourable movements of public opinion as the result of a bill being passed. Therefore, the Prime Minister tried to anticipate public opinion. On occasions, such as Savary education bill in 1984 or the Devaquet crisis in 1986, the polls were signally unsuccessful in their capacity as an early warning device and the Prime Minister was faced with a massive movement of discontent.

It can be seen, therefore, that conjunctural factors were an important determinant of the Prime Minister's influence. There is a fundamental difference, however, between this set of factors and the set of systemic factors. In the latter set, some of these factors limited the Prime Minister's influence, while others increased it. By contrast, each element of the set of conjunctural factors may be either a limit or a resource for the Prime Minister. For example, pressure groups may help the Prime Minister's cause, or hinder it. Similarly, one Prime Minister may have a powerful position in the party which increases his overall level of influence, while another Prime Minister may be a minor party figure.

Moreover, even though there may be a slow change in the importance of systemic factors over time, they do set the general boundaries within which the Prime Minister may act. In this case, variations are usually only incremental. By contrast, the Prime Minister's relationship with the set of conjunctural factors is open to quick and violent fluctuations. For example, election results have an overnight effect. Similarly, a change of Prime Minister introduces someone to the office who may have a very different character to the person who is being replaced.

It is precisely because of this situation that the Prime Minister's influence cannot be quantified. Each Prime Minister found himself in a unique position which was itself inherently unstable. The Prime Minister's influence varied according to the slow changes in systemic factors and to the rapid fluctuations in conjunctural factors. However, the movement of these factors was not necessarily consistent the one with the other. For example, Chirac was in a stronger position than Fabius in terms of his position of leadership over his own party and because of the fact that the President was largely disempowered. However, at the same time his position was weaker than that of Fabius in that he faced a difficult electoral coalition which enjoyed only a fragile parliamentary majority. Thus, their relative influences are difficult to assess. We can only point to the factors upon which that influence was dependent.

Momentary Factors

The third set of factors which determined the level of prime ministerial influence are of a momentary nature. The impact of the elements in this set of factors was abrupt and immediate. They did not have any medium or long-term effects on the extent of prime ministerial influence, but their short-term, or momentary, impact on the outcome of public policy were occasionally great indeed. Thus, they cannot be ignored.

Unlike the two previous sets of factors which were identified, the elements in this set cannot be listed definitively. All that it is possible to do is to give examples of them, such as were present in the case studies. These examples will give a pointer as to the elements that need to be included in this set of factors, even if, by their very nature, a full list is impossible to provide.

The first momentary factor to be considered concerns the relation of the bill in question to past and forthcoming bills. For example, during the parliamentary stage of the 1989 broadcasting bill, the leader of the UDC, Méhaignerie, was reluctant to do a deal with the government because his party had just facilitated the passage of the 1989 budget. Méhaignerie was aware that, if he had allowed his group to vote for or abstain on the broadcasting bill, then it would have appeared to his RPR/UDF allies as if his group were not an independent parliamentary group, but one which supported the socialists. In the run up to the 1989 municipal elections, Méhaignerie had to avoid giving this impression as it would have weakened his bargaining position with the RPR/UDF in the negotiations over the preparation of coalition lists for March elections.

Therefore, whilst conjunctural party factors cannot be dissociated from this example, the content of the 1989 broadcasting law was in part determined by the UDC's decision a few days previously to vote for the 1989 budget. This example illustrates how momentary factors affected the outcome of policy. If the vote on the broadcasting bill had taken place before the vote on the budget, then the content of the final law may have been different.

A related example concerns the Prime Minister's role in the intergovernmental arbitration process. The Prime Minister could not consistently arbitrate in favour of one Minister, or against another. If he were to do so, then he would risk the charge of favouritism, on the one hand, or the Minister's resignation, on the other. This point is particularly important when it is realised that the Prime Minister may have to chair a number of *committees* in a short space of time. As one of Rocard's advisers noted, it is difficult not to acquiesce to a particular Minister's demands if, a few hours previously, he has been defeated on an important issue in the arbitration process of another bill.[46] Thus, it is impossible to consider preparation of any bill in isolation. Its contents may be in part determined by the debate which surrounds other bills being prepared at the same time.

A further example was witnessed most vividly during the course of the Devaquet crisis. The most acute moments of the Devaquet crisis were experienced after and because of the death of Malik Oussekine. The government had little or no control over the circumstances of his death, but the fact that it occurred created a wave of public sympathy for the students that forced Chirac to withdraw the bill. Thus, the impact of this exogenous, momentary factor was crucial to the outcome of the policy process.

As with the case of conjunctural factors previously, the impact of momentary factors can be a limit or a resource for the Prime Minister. In the case of Oussekine's tragic death, the Prime Minister was forced to withdraw a bill which, until that point, he had shown no signs of wanting to withdraw. In the case of the 1989 broadcasting bill, however, the Prime Minister was able to return to the text as it had been agreed in the pre-parliamentary arbitration process. Amendments originally inserted to accommodate the UDC group were withdrawn.

The incidence of momentary factors is highly unpredictable. In this sense, the set of momentary factors differs from the two previous sets of factors examined, which were to a large extent predictable. In no way could the death of Oussekine have been either predicted or prevented. Once it occurred, the government had to react and the odds were not stacked in its favour. Similarly, the consequences deriving from the parliamentary vote prior to the one in question, or to the previous prime ministerial arbitration on the content of the bills which follows, are equally unpredictable. It is simply *'le hasard du calendrier'*. Whether the result is favourable or unfavourable to the Prime Minister is contingent upon the prevailing circumstances, but his influence is in part determined by them.

Conclusion

Approaching the nature of prime ministerial influence in this way proves to be much more satisfying than any attempt to try and quantify the level of his influence. This approach provides a rounder picture of policy outcomes. It shows that they result from a complex process of interaction between a series of different actors and institutions. The result of this interaction is conflict, negotiations and bargaining. While the Prime Minister has several strategic structural advantages in this interaction process, such as his own constitutional powers and the powers of the executive over the legislature, his short-term influence ultimately depends upon the conjunctural factors with which he is faced at any one time.

However, it is also important to see how the three sets of factors identified above relate to each other. They do not operate independently the one from the other. Thus, systemic factors affect the nature of conjunctural and momentary factors. For example, the party system will in part be determined by the constitutional framework within which the system operates.[47] Similarly, conjunctural factors will have an effect on the functioning of systemic factors. For example, the President's influence over the core executive is determined to a large part by election results and the state of the party system. The system is never static. There is always interaction between its different components. Thus, the level of influence of the various protagonists is constantly changing.

It is also important to realise that what has been presented is a general picture of the nature of an institution's influence over the policy process. In the present case, attention has been focused on the Prime Minister. However, a study of the President's influence on the policy process would have to identify his relationship with all of the factors identified above. If such a study were undertaken, it might be found that the President's position was stronger than the Prime Minister's in relation to some of the elements identified above. However, it would also have to be concluded in a similar vein that his influence was not fixed and that the main set of variables which affected it were conjunctural factors.

8 The Capacity for Systemic Dynamism

In the light of the conclusions reached in the previous chapter, it is now necessary to reconsider the different models of core executive operations which were identified in Chapter 2. By virtue of the evidence gleaned from the case studies, it will be shown that none of these models accurately accounted for the nature of core executive operations and for the role of the Prime Minister, in particular, throughout the whole of the 1981–91 period. Rather than constructing an alternative all-embracing model, it will be argued that it is best to appreciate that the system is dynamic in that it can move from one model to another in a relatively short space of time.

It will then be argued that this capacity for systemic dynamism is due to changes in the impact of the different elements of the three types of factors which were identified in the previous chapter. On the whole, changes in the impact of systemic factors were slow to take effect and determined the influence of the executive branch of government as a whole. Conversely, changes in the impact of conjunctural and momentary factors often had a rapid effect and, especially in the case of the former, usually determined the relations between the different elements within the core executive itself.

Finally, when accounting for the dynamic capacity of the system, it will be shown that there are several reasons as to why the impact of these factors upon the system should change. In this way the dynamic capacity of the system is realised and is not simply latent. In fact, over the 1981–91 period, it will be argued that the impact of these factors changed, so as to produce periods of both relatively strong and weak presidential government, as well as a form of prime ministerial government and that, at times, the impact of Ministers and of bureaucrats was far from negligible. It is necessary to begin, however, by returning to the different models of core executive operations as they were identified in the opening chapter.

Models of Core Executive Operations Revisited

In the opening chapter six different models of core executive operations in France were identified. These models were: presidential government;

segmented decision-making; executive co-operation; prime ministerial government; ministerial government; and bureaucratic co-ordination. The role of the Prime Minister was shown to vary with each different model. In this chapter, the models are evaluated in the light of the evidence provided by the case studies, so as to show whether any of them can account for the nature of core executive operations throughout the 1981–91 period. In fact, as will be shown, no single model successfully captured core executive operations for all of this period, but each model accurately could be said to have depicted certain elements of those operations during that time. The strengths and weaknesses of the different models will now briefly be examined.

The 1982 and 1989 broadcasting acts were examples of presidential government. That is to say, the President was personally responsible for making major policy decisions. For the 1982 broadcasting act, the President and his advisers oversaw the preparation of the bill and Mitterrand himself arbitrated on a number of key policy matters. The same was true for the 1989 broadcasting law when, in addition to the situation in 1982, the President himself, through the *Lettre à tous les Français*, was also the inspiration behind the creation of the CSA. Nevertheless, it would be incorrect to conclude from this evidence that there was presidential government throughout the 1981–91 period. It was certainly absent, for example, during *cohabitation*, whilst the preparation of the 1985 and 1990 budgets saw the President only playing a relatively minor role.

These variations in presidential influence lead to the conclusion that it is necessary to distinguish between periods of relatively strong presidential government and limited presidential government. In the former situation, the President and his advisers intervened frequently in the policy process, with most major policy decisions and many minor policy decisions being taken either directly by the President in formal or informal councils, or by his advisers in interministerial committee meetings. In the latter situation, the President and his advisers intervened less frequently and fewer policy decisions emanated directly or indirectly from the Elysée. The preparation of the 1982 broadcasting act was an example of the former situation, whereas the preparation of the 1989 broadcasting act was an example of the latter.

The case studies also appeared to identify various elements of the segmented decision-making model. As was outlined in the opening chapter, this model states that the President is solely responsible for taking key decisions in the areas of foreign and defence policy, EC policy and decisions relating to currency stability. The debate surrounding the devaluation of the franc in 1983 provided the clearest example of this model in practice. The decision to remain in the EMS and to devalue the franc was taken by Mitterrand personally. The Prime Minister's role was merely secondary. The President's involvement in the preparation of the 1990 defence budget provided another example of this model. The defence budget of that year was of great importance as its preparation coincided with the important defence decisions which had to be taken relating to the *loi de programmation militaire*. As a result, the key budgetary decisions were taken by the President during a *conseil de défense* at the Elysée, when the strategic choices concerning the *loi de programmation* were also made. The greater role played by the Prime Minister in the preparation of all other aspects of the 1990 budget showed that the President's influence was only confined to certain sectors and that he did not dominate the policy process as a whole.

However, despite the above evidence in support of this model, it still fails to capture the intricacies of the policy process as revealed in the case studies. In the first place, the 1987 defence budget was prepared by the government alone without anything but the formal involvement of the presidency. Similarly, the 1987 *loi de programmation militaire* was agreed between the President and the Prime Minister. As such, the segmented decision-making model was not seen to operate during *cohabitation*. Secondly, even outside of *cohabitation*, this model may be called into question. For example, the role played by the Finance Minister, Defence Minister and Prime Minister in the preparation of the 1990 defence budget should not be underestimated. The President was obliged to fix the level of defence spending cuts, so as to keep the support of these other actors. Whilst Mitterrand made the final decision, it represented a compromise which appeased all interested parties. In this sense, defence policy (and, it might be argued, the other policy areas in this model as well) was not an area of decision making reserved for the President's attention alone. Rather, decisions in this area were the result of a complex process of interaction between several different actors. Thirdly, in areas outside of the President's supposed reserved policy domain, the Prime Minister was not free to legislate as he saw fit. The influence of other Ministers, for example, limited his actions. Moreover, the President was also able to intervene when he so desired. For example, Mitterrand's call in 1989 for more low-cost housing to be built meant that the level of spending allocated to the Housing Minister had to be increased.

Thus, whilst the President may have been personally responsible for taking the major policy decisions regarding currency stability and defence policy, when he did so he was not free from the influence of other key political actors. Conversely, in other policy areas where, according to the original model, the Prime Minister's role was critical, the President was not absent from decision making and his influence was still great. Thus, the analytical coherence of this model can be called into question. The division of responsibilities which it posits does not stand up to close scrutiny. Indeed, it might be noted that the notion of the reserved domain was first conceived of in 1959 not as an analysis of how the Fifth Republic functioned, but as an attempt to discourage recalcitrant gaullist deputies from pursuing the policy of *Algérie française* to which de Gaulle was then opposed.[1] Nevertheless, it is clear that the President's influence in defence and foreign policy matters particularly was consistently great. Therefore, whilst the model itself is open to question, it is still necessary to account for the President's authority in these two areas.

The key elements of the executive co-operation model also appeared to be present in the case studies. One noticeable feature of the decision-making process was the close relationship between the *cabinets* of both the President and Prime Minister. Representatives of both teams attended interministerial committee meetings and there were often substantial informal contacts between members of both *cabinets*. Similarly, several of the Prime Minister's services, such as the GSG and the SJTI for the broadcasting acts worked in close contact with the Elysée. Their role was important in both the co-ordination of policy and its preparation. Moreover, the President regularly met alone with each of the different Prime Ministers during the period under examination. On these occasions policy matters were discussed.

However, there are certain weaknesses to the model as well. Firstly, it does not apply to the period of *cohabitation.* At that time, co-operation between the two parts of the executive was minimal. The only regular contacts were between Bianco at the Elysée and Ulrich at Matignon. Secondly, there is an inherent problem with the model itself, because it assumes that, when there is co-operation, then neither institution is dominant. This assumption is false. Even when the President's influence was at its greatest, during the March 1983 devaluation crisis, for example, there was still co-operation between the Prime Minister and his advisers and the President and his team. There were daily contacts throughout the crisis period, but the President still took the decisions to stay in the EMS and to retain Mauroy as Prime Minister.

In fact, like the segmented decision-making model, the executive co-operation model seems analytically weak. There will always have to be co-operation between the President and Prime Minister in order for the system to function effectively. Similarly, there will always have to be co-operation between the Prime Minister and Ministers and, apart from the period of *cohabitation*, between the President and Ministers. The rigours of government necessitate the relaying of information between institutions, so as to prepare decisions and then to implement them. In this way, there will always have to be contacts and, in this sense, co-operation between the different components of the executive. However, simply because there is co-operation of this sort does not mean that one institution, usually the President or the Prime Minister, is not able to dominate the decision-making process. Thus, this model tells us little about the nature of the relations between the different elements of the core executive, even if it does underline the fact that they will have to communicate with each other in order for the system to operate effectively.

In contrast to the previous model, the prime ministerial government model was clearly identifiable, if only during the period of *cohabitation*. During this time, the Prime Minister was responsible for taking the major policy decisions of the government, such as the decision to withdraw the Devaquet bill, the decision to privatise only one television channel and the choice of TF1 as the channel which would be privatised.

A problem with this model is that, because *cohabitation* only occurred for a single brief two-year period, it is impossible to distinguish between possible variations of this model. As with the case of presidential government, it is possible that there might be occasions when there is relatively strong prime ministerial government and other occasions when there is weak prime ministerial government. However, because of the absence of any similar situations with which the second Chirac premiership could be compared, it is impossible to say whether the 1986–88 period was an example of strong or limited prime ministerial government. Nevertheless, it is possible to state that the Prime Minister's power during this period was not unlimited. Notably, Ministers were given considerable leeway by Chirac to run their own departmental affairs and, admittedly outside of the scope of the case studies, the President's influence over defence and EC policy in particular was not negligible. Despite these examples, *cohabitation* did provide some form of prime ministerial government for the first time during the whole of the history of the Fifth Republic to date.

By contrast, at no period between 1981–91 was ministerial government unequivocally identifiable. However, during this time Ministers were not simply subordinate to the wishes of the President and/or the Prime Minister. Indeed, it would have been surprising if this were to have been the case. Ministers are senior political figures who would be likely to resign, rather than accept such subordination. Instead, Ministers were largely responsible for the laws which were drawn up in their particular spheres of influence. For example, for all three broadcasting laws, Fillioud, Léotard and Tasca played a major role in determining the content of the legislation. However, also on all three occasions, both the Prime Minister and especially the President were also involved in the decision-making process.

In fact, it might be argued that ministerial government was most prevalent during *cohabitation*. As was stated above, at this time there was undoubtedly a form of prime ministerial government at work, however, the influence of individual Ministers was also at its greatest. For example, Chirac's delegation of responsibility for budgetary and financial affairs to Balladur meant that the role of the Finance Minister and, indeed, the Budget Minister was greater than it had been in previous years. Similarly, the 1986 broadcasting law was drawn up largely by Léotard and his *cabinet*. Also, the responsibility for managing the Devaquet crisis was devolved first upon the eponymous Minister himself and then upon Monory. Thus, individual ministerial influence was great. However, it was also observed that Chirac did arbitrate in the most important of the budgetary disputes, as was the case for the key decisions of the broadcasting act. Similarly, it was his decision to withdraw the Devaquet bill once the crisis had become unmanageable. In this sense, there was still prime ministerial government during this period, even if elements of ministerial government were also present.

Finally, as was noted in the previous chapter, it might be argued that the bureaucratic co-ordination model was also identifiable. For example, it could be seen in the preparation of the 1982 broadcasting act when the SJTI tried to sell its own policy preferences to the government. Similarly, in the course of the 1989 broadcasting act, the SJTI was also actively trying to impose its own policy agenda. It could also be seen with the involvement of the *Direction du Budget* in the preparation of all three budgets studied. However, it must be noted that its influence was greater during the period of economic stagnation in the mid-1980s than it was in the late 1980s during the period of economic growth. The evidence suggests, therefore, that bureaucrats did play a major role in policy preparation.

However, it must be emphasised that the claim made by the model that politicians were disempowered and that the policy process was effectively controlled by top civil servants was not seen to be correct. In all of the examples cited above, the major and, indeed, many of the minor policy decisions were taken by politicians free from the influence of bureaucrats. Thus, whilst the permanent administration on occasions had its own policy preferences which it tried to have adopted, the evidence does not suggest that it had the means to succeed.

An Alternative Approach to the Study of Core Executive Operations

Whilst all six of the original models of core executive operations contained certain descriptive truths about the policy process, none of them fully captured the complexity of that process and none of them accurately portrayed the true nature of core executive operations and the respective influences of the President, Prime Minister, Ministers and bureaucrats for the whole of the 1981–91 period.

As a result of these observations, the study of prime ministerial influence may approached in three different ways. The first of these approaches is to construct an all-embracing model of the central government decision-making process which captures the positive aspects of the above theories, whilst dispensing with their negative aspects. This approach, whilst tempting, is ultimately unrewarding. Even if it were possible to construct such a model, it is likely that it would suffer from the same basic problem as the ones presented above. Namely, it might account for any one part of the 1981–91 period, but it is unlikely that it could account for all of the period. As Ardant has noted:

> There is not just one type of Prime Minister in the Fifth Republic, a single reference model. There are various types of Prime Ministers . . . [2]

The variations in the relative influences of the different components of the core executive were so great during the 1981–91 period, that to try to capture all of them in a single model would be a unproductive exercise.

The second approach is the one which Wright has championed. He has avoided the temptation of constructing a global model by tempering his presentation of presidential government with the frequent addition of provisos. Consequently, his argument is rendered more flexible. For example, at one point he states:

> *With the exception of the nomination of Jacques Chirac in March 1986 (when the president had no alternative to appoint),* all prime ministers have owed their office to the president.[3]

Similarly, a few pages later he states that the President:

> . . . is the general spokesman of the government and its principal peda-gogue (*again, the exception of the 1986–88 period must be noted*).[4]

These provisos occur regularly during the course of his book.

There is no doubt that the provisos are necessary. As such, this approach is a great advance upon the desire to construct a global theory. The argument is more flexible as it is able to account simultaneously for two of the models presented above. However, as presented above, the argument here is still limited. It needs to be extended even further so as to account for the scenarios of ministerial and bureaucratic government and so as to allow for an appreciation of the differences between strong and limited presidential and prime ministerial government.

In fact, a third approach is favoured here. This approach emphasises the dynamic quality of core executive operations. We argue that the régime can move from one model of core executive operations to another in a relatively short period of time. That is to say, it is possible to move successively from a system of, for example, relatively strong presidentialism to one of limited presidentialism. Similarly, it possible for the system to move from the latter to strong or limited prime ministerial government. Indeed, should the necessary conditions arise (however unlikely that may be), the system could move from any of the above systems to ministerial government, or bureaucratic co-ordination. The argument, here, is that the move from one model of core executive operations to another is the result of exogenous changes in the nature of the three types of factors (institutional, conjunctural and momentary) which were examined in the previous chapter.

In the study of core executive operations, the capacity for systemic dynamism has been under appreciated. One reason for this is that much of the work on core executive operations has been carried out on the British system of government. However, one of the features of the British system is its systemic stability. For long periods of time the system has operated under a two party system with stable, single party, majority governments. This situation has led to what Dunleavy and Rhodes have described as: 'the static quality of traditional controversies'.[5]

Moreover, the capacity for systemic dynamism has also been overlooked in the French case, because the configuration of the three types of constraints which prevail upon core executive operations has, under the Fifth Republic, generally favoured the exercise of presidential government. As a result, the dynamics of the system have not been obviously apparent. In fact, the dynamic potential of the régime was only fully realised with the advent of *cohabitation* in 1986. Certainly, the possibility of victory in the 1978 legislative elections by the Union of the Left had raised the issue of *cohabitation* previously. However, only when the situation actually occurred was its impact properly appreciated. The 1986–88 period put into relief the hitherto latent dynamic capacity of the system. As a result, it is necessary to consider not simply a single model of core executive operations as being sufficient to describe the workings of the political system, but rather to appreciate that the system can move from one model to another in a short space of time.

Systemic Dynamism

The move from one model to another is induced by changes in the nature of the three types of factors identified in the previous chapter. These factors were shown to limit the actions and influence of the different components of the core executive. However, changes in these factors do not affect core executive operations equally. The nature of systemic factors, because of their quasi-permanent characteristics, usually vary only gradually over a long period of time. Thus, for example, the impact of the EC has evolved slowly, although since 1986 this evolution has been more rapid. Similarly, the jurisprudence of the Constitutional Council has increased only incrementally. On occasions, however, the impact of changes in systemic factors may happen quickly. The move from the Fourth to the Fifth Republic being a prime example of this situation.

It must be stressed, however, that changes in systemic factors usually only limit or expand the potential of the core executive as a whole. For example, the increase in the influence of the Constitutional Council has not altered the nature of the relations between the different elements of the core executive itself. Rather, it changed the relations *in toto* between the judicial and executive branches of government. Similarly, the position of France in the world economic and political system limits the actions of the President, Prime Minister and Ministers equally. Nevertheless, on occasions, variations in the nature of institutional constraints may alter the relative influence of the individual components of the core executive. For example, it was seen that, during the course of the 1985 budget, the international economic constraints with which France was faced due to the world recession increased the role of the permanent administration in the policy process over the other political elements of the core executive.

Therefore, it is important to appreciate that prime ministerial influence is affected in two ways by the impact of systemic factors. First, they determine the boundaries within which the core executive (and the Prime Minister as part of the core executive) may operate. Second, they may alter the relations between the different elements of the core executive.

In contrast to systemic factors, changes in the nature of conjunctural factors may occur very rapidly. Indeed, from 1981–91 it was variations in this set of factors which served to alter most frequently core executive operations and which led to the move from one model to another. So, for example, the results of presidential and legislative elections had an overnight impact on the system. The clearest example of this situation was in 1986 with the move from limited presidentialism to prime ministerial government, following the March legislative elections. Whilst not all elections produced great variations in core executive operations, during the 1981–91 period they were critical on three occasions, namely, 1981, 1986 and 1988.

Similarly, the Prime Minister's relationship to party matters may also vary rapidly. For example, inter-party relations may become more or less restrictive after elections. This situation was seen with the uneasy RPR/UDF parliamentary majority in 1986, or with the minority situation in 1988, when compared with the stable, single-party PS government from 1984–86. Similarly, the impact of the intra-party situation on the Prime Minister's influence may change over time and from one Prime Minister to the next. For example, the internecine struggles within the PS grew worse as the decade passed, while Chirac's position of hegemony over the RPR contrasted greatly with Rocard's weak position within the PS.

As was noted in the previous chapter, changes in the impact of conjunctural factors are not necessarily all one-way. That is to say, Chirac enjoyed a greater control over his party than had been the case under Fabius and the PS, whereas Chirac was also faced with managing difficult coalition problems which his predecessor had been spared. Thus, changes may effectively cancel each other out. However, the dynamic capacity of the system is still apparent.

By contrast with the impact of conjunctural factors, momentary factors are rarely of sufficient importance to induce a shift in the nature of core executive relations from one model to another. That is not to say that they are unimportant. Indeed, as was shown in the last chapter, their impact on policy decisions may be great. However, by their nature they are rarely system changing. Even so, Malik Oussekine's death did weaken Chirac's position as Prime Minister. He was not only forced to withdraw the Devaquet bill, but he also called a pause in the government's legislative programme and he was then faced with a debilitating series of public sector strikes partly inspired by the success of the students. Moreover, it was at the time of the Devaquet crisis that his standing in the opinion polls started to plummet, affecting his presidential ambitions. So, whilst Oussekine's death was not the only reason for the above sequence of events, it did have an impact on Chirac's influence and it shows the importance that momentary factors can have. Nevertheless, it should be reiterated that such factors are unlikely to be system changing.

Systemic Dynamism and Models of Core Executive Operations

It is apparent, therefore, that variations in the nature of systemic, conjunctural and momentary factors provide the dynamic for the transition from one set of core executive operations to the next. Indeed, the capacity for systemic dynamism means that, in so far as the models are themselves correctly formulated and analytically coherent, there is no reason why any model should not apply if the necessary conditions are met, even if in normal times the system favours the exercise of presidential government. However, the requirement that the models be correctly formulated and analytically coherent is of great importance. It is for this reason that the models of both segmented decision-making and executive co-operation are most problematic. As regards the former, it was argued that the strict division of responsibility between the President and Prime Minister did not seem to hold good. The Prime Minister and Ministers were not absent from the decision-making process in the President's sector, whilst the President and Ministers were not absent from the process in the Prime Minister's domain. Thus, the model appears to be flawed. Nevertheless, it is clear that successive Presidents have indeed enjoyed a great hold over defence and especially foreign policy matters and that their attention has been turned more towards these questions, rather than towards other domestic policy matters. There are good constitutional and practical reasons for this situation. The former refer to the President's constitutional prerogatives as they are set out in Articles 5, 15 and 52. The latter refer, for example, to the benefits which the President can derive from media coverage of state visits abroad.

Therefore, instead of persevering with an analytically flawed model, it is better to integrate its positive aspects into the other, more analytically sound models. As a result, it might be argued that, even under limited presidential government, the head of state will retain a substantial influence over foreign and defence policy. Indeed, the President might enjoy some influence in these areas under both strong and limited prime ministerial government. The 1986–88 period showed that the President retained a certain (but still reduced) influence in both of these areas, whereas he had no impact on domestic policy-making at all.

As regards the model of executive co-operation, it was shown to be no less flawed analytically. The model was not able to account for variations

Table 8.1   Typology of executive leadership, 1981–91

Strong presidential government	Limited presidential government	Prime ministerial government
1981–84	**1984–86**	**1986–88**
1981 broadcasting act	1985 budget	1986 Devaquet crisis
1983 devaluation	**1988–91**	1986 broadcasting act
(c.f. Mitterrand's views	1989 broadcasting act	1987 budget
on the 1985 budget)	1990 budget	

in the influence of the President and Prime Minister. Moreover, it did not consider the impact of Ministers or the bureaucracy on the outcome of policy. In these two respects, the model was deficient. Nevertheless, it was also shown that, even under periods of strong presidentialism, there was co-operation between the President and Prime Minister. Once again, this positive aspect should be integrated into the other models. It may be argued, therefore, that the models of relatively strong and limited presidentialism and that of limited prime ministerial government do not preclude co-operation between the two elements of the executive. Indeed, even under a period of relatively strong prime ministerial government, the Prime Minister would need the President's co-operation for a variety of administrative and constitutional matters.

Thus, there remains four models of core executive operations, the first two of which each have two variations. These models are: presidential government, with relatively strong and limited variations; prime ministerial government, again with relatively strong and limited variations; ministerial government; and bureaucratic government. According to the evidence derived from the previous chapters, the 1981–91 period produced examples of both relatively strong and limited presidentialism. There was also a form of prime ministerial government, although the absence of other examples of this type of government means that it is difficult to state whether the Prime Minister's influence was strong or limited (see Table 8.1). In addition, it was also concluded from the case studies that Ministers and bureaucrats both had a certain influence in the policy-making process during this period, even if the full set of requirements was not met for the models of ministerial government or bureaucratic co-ordination to be in operation. Nevertheless, it is still necessary to take account of their role in the policy process as well (see Table 8.2). For each example it is only possible to indicate crudely the extent of the influence of each actor. Nevertheless, Tables 8.1 and 8.2 give an impression of the variations in influence that the different participants in the policy process underwent during the period in question.

Table 8.2   Participation in the policy-making process, 1981–91

	President	PM	Ministers	Bureaucrats
Broadcasting				
1981	strong	strong	strong	strong
1986	absent	strong	strong	absent
1989	strong	strong	strong	strong
Budget				
1985	strong	weak	weak	strong
1987	absent	strong	strong	weak
1990	weak	weak	strong	weak
Devaquet	absent	strong	strong	absent
Devaluation	strong	weak	weak	weak

Even though the dynamism of the system has been demonstrated and various of the different models of government were seen to operate between 1981 and 1991, it must be recognised that the Fifth Republic is more likely to produce a form of presidential government than any other type. The system encourages presidentialism. For example, presidential elections are often, even if not always, the critical elections which determine how the system will operate. The elections of 1981 and 1988 provide examples of their importance. On these two occasions, the legislative elections were largely presidential coat-tail elections which broadly mirrored the result of the previous presidential election. Similarly, parties organise their structures around presidential elections. Party leaders become *présidentiables* and party activity is centralised around these figures, rather than in favour of rank-and-file militants. Moreover, in addition to the normal advantages which a head of state enjoys in any country, such as media attention, patronage and the role as a world statesman, a French President inherits the mantle of de Gaulle who was able to impose his *de facto* presidentialist reading of the Constitution on the *de jure* prime ministerial reading. Mitterrand simply followed in the footsteps of the tradition of presidentialism which had been created by his predecessors. Finally, it might also be noted that both the public and the political class have tended to assume that presidential government is the norm. Opinion polls have suggested that the President is the chief policy maker in the country.[6] At the same time, even the most senior politicians defer to the President's authority. For example, one of the reasons why Chirac did not press his right to intervene more in defence and foreign policy-making during *cohabitation* was that he did not wish to denude the office to which he aspired of all the powers which it had acquired since 1958.

It is precisely because the system favours a form presidential government that, as was noted above, the capacity for systemic dynamism has been under-appreciated. However, it must be realised that, even if there is a demonstrated tendency in favour of presidential government, the President is not always able to be the dominant political force. On occasions, the conjunction of factors may be unfavourable to him, as happened, for example, under *cohabitation*. Indeed, it is precisely because these factors are always present that the first variant of presidentialism has been classed as 'relatively strong presidential government'. This terminology has been used so as to discourage the temptation to believe that Presidents can ever be all-powerful. They will always face certain constraints and, thus, their power is always less than absolute. Thus, whilst the combination of factors may facilitate presidentialism, it is necessary to appreciate the dynamism of the system, so as to be able to account for the move to alternative types of core executive operations when the occasion arises.

Accounting for Systemic Dynamism

From the above analysis, it is apparent that the dynamic potential of the system is great. The question remains, however, as to why these factors themselves should change. It has been assumed that they do change and, indeed, these changes and their effects have been identified. However, it is necessary to explain why the nature of the factors should vary in the first place. After all, in some countries, notably under totalitarian régimes, the political system can remain frozen for many years with power consistently being exercised by one person and his successors. In France, however, the system has not remained frozen and there have been great variations in the nature of the factors. It is necessary to account for these variations. In essence, there are four reasons as to why these factors may change. They are: the electoral cycle; exogenous international factors; institutional uncertainty; and time. Each of these reasons will be considered in turn.

The electoral cycle is the first major reason as to why there are variations in the nature of the factors which affect the system. It was shown in the previous chapter that the most important conjunctural factor which determined core executive operations was that of elections, both presidential and legislative. The fact that these elections were not synchronised, because of the seven year presidential term and the five year legislative term, meant that there was a constant potential for change in the system. In fact, the lack of synchronisation between presidential and legislative election produces a (complicated) electoral cycle which repeats

Table 8.3   Theoretical cycle of presidential and legislative elections

P	1988		1995		2002			2009		2016		2023
L	1988	1993		1998		2003	2008		2013		2018	2023
Y	5	2	3	4	1	5	1	4	3	2	5	

P = presidential elections   L = legislative elections
Y = years between elections

itself every 35 years.[7] Assuming an initial coincidence of presidential and
parliamentary elections, as in 1988, the cycle in theory is as follows (see
Table 8.3). In fact, the neat 35-year cycle has not as yet come anywhere
near to being repeated during the course of Fifth Republic. The President's
right to dissolve the National Assembly and unforeseen events, such as de
Gaulle's resignation in 1969 and Pompidou's death in 1974, have led to
the following cycle during the Fifth Republic (see Table 8.4).

As can be seen, the theoretical cycle (5, 2, 3, 4, 1, 5, 1, 4, 3, 2, 5)
differs markedly from the actual cycle (4, 3, 2, 1, 1, 4, 1, 4, 3, 5, 2).
Nevertheless, in each case, the potential for change is apparent in both
theory and practice. As a result, there is ample opportunity for there to
be a disjunction of presidential and parliamentary majorities, allowing a
period of *cohabitation* to occur and the system to move from one set of
core executive operations to another.

In addition, there are two other factors associated with the electoral cycle
which could provoke the move from one set of core executive operations
to another. Firstly, even if elections to the National Assembly were to
be held immediately following a presidential election, then there would
still be no guarantee that a presidential majority would be returned to
the legislature. As was noted above, the nature of the régime means that
it is highly likely that such a majority would be returned as a result of
the presidential coat-tails effect. However, the extent of the coat-tails
effect can vary greatly. In 1981, following Mitterrand's narrow victory
in the presidential elections, the socialists obtained an absolute majority
in the legislative elections. In 1988, despite the fact that Mitterrand easily
defeated Chirac in the presidential elections, the socialists only managed to

*Table 8.4   Actual cycle of presidential and legislative elections,
1958–91*

P	1958		1965			1969		1974		1981		1988
L	1958	1962		1967	1968		1973		1978	1981	1986	1988
Y	4	3	2	1	1	4	1	4	3	5	2	

obtain a relative majority in the legislative elections which ensued. It is far from inconceivable that a future President may immediately have to embark upon a period of cohabitation following a set of presidential and legislative elections. Such is the personalisation of politics in a presidential system in the age of the photo-opportunity and the sound bite that an individual may be sufficiently popular so as to be elected President only to find that his/her party is sufficiently unpopular that it fails to win the legislative majority necessary for the President's mandate to be carried out.

Secondly, there is sufficient evidence from events in the Fifth Republic to date to suggest that even the threat of a disjunction of presidential and legislative majorities is enough to provoke a shift in the nature of core executive operations. For example, in the run up to the 1986 legislative elections and following Fabius's appointment as Prime Minister, Mitterrand took the decision to withdraw from any intervention in the details of domestic policy-making. The effects of this decision can be seen in a letter from Fabius:

> In the first period of my time in office, certain Ministers had the habit of trying to 'call upon' the Elysée to overturn certain decisions taken at Matignon: they soon learned that the President had taken the decision to trust his Prime Minister. Therefore, the temptation to do so stopped.[8]

This decision effectively marked the transition from the period of relatively strong presidential government to that of limited presidential government. It might also be noted that, after 1978, Giscard took a similar decision in order to distance himself from the unpopular policies of his government, so as to increase his chances of re-election in 1981. In both cases, the transition occurred during the electoral cycle in anticipation of the results of the next elections.[9] Once again, the system changing importance of the electoral cycle is apparent.

The second reason as to why the nature of the constraints which affect the system may change is due the impact of exogenous international factors. It was shown in the previous chapter that one of the main components of the set of systemic factors was the position of France in the international economic and political system. The global influence of the Prime Minister and, indeed, of any of the other domestic actors was limited by the position that France occupied in the international system.

As a result of this situation, events which occur in other countries will affect the impact of this factor upon the decision-making process in France. Thus, the actions of the oil producing countries in the early 1970s brought about the first oil price shock which greatly affected the

French economy and limited the Prime Minister's and the government's room for manœuvre in the policy-making process. Similar consequences for the domestic decision-making process could be derived from the impact of budgetary and financial policies of the United States or Germany, from war in the Gulf, or from decisions emanating from the European Court of Justice, for example.

The third reason concerns Ashford's notion of institutional uncertainty.[10] Ashford argues that, when compared with other western democratic systems, France has only a low level of institutional stability. That is to say, beliefs about the use of collective authority are not widely shared; there is little alternation of parties in power; the roles of the executive and legislature are poorly defined; and the checks on the use of collective authority by political and administrative actors are not clearly established.[11] The reasons for this situation can be found in the country's historical and political development, which did not foster the growth of institutionalised political and social behaviour. The result is that the system faces constant uncertainty about the basic tenets of what is and what is not acceptable behaviour for both political and social actors. As Ashford notes, 'uncertainty is critically important in the French policy process because institutions are poorly defined'.[12]

In fact, Ashford's argument *per se* seems particularly applicable to the early years of the Fifth Republic. Over the past two decades, the system has seen the development and implantation in the public psyche of most of the requirements which Ashford states are necessary for there to be institutional stability. In this respect, the 1981 and 1986 alternations in power play a major role, as does Mitterrand's refusal to abuse his power as President.

Nevertheless, Ashford's argument is still of relevance. Its strength is that it emphasises the impact of social behaviour on the policy process. That is to say, the importance of shared societal values, popular mores, sociological norms and cultural traditions. These elements are difficult to identify with great precision. They are also fluid. Beliefs are not necessarily the same from one generation to the next, for example. As a result, an element of uncertainty is introduced into the policy process. Political actors are only vaguely aware of the nature and importance of these factors. As a result, their judgement in the policy process when confronted with issues of society is often flawed.

The clearest example of this phenomenon in the case studies came with the Devaquet crisis. The government was refighting the battles of 1968 when, in fact, the social system had changed immeasurably in the meantime. The government's inability to comprehend the rationale behind the student movement was as great a factor in the outcome of the crisis as the death of Malik Oussekine. In this instance, the element of uncertainty served to alter the nature of the constraints operating upon prime ministerial influence and Chirac was left with no option but to withdraw the offending bill.

A fourth reason concerns the impact of time upon the factors identified above. Time is particularly critical in its influence upon the impact of personalities on the policy process. It was shown that, although structural factors are of primary importance, questions of personality may have an impact upon the decision-making process. By definition, however, the impact of personalities is linked to individual people and people are subject to the march of time. For example, the individual impact of de Gaulle upon the post-1958 policy process was great indeed. However, with the passage of time, his impact upon the system has become less salient. He has become a figure whose place is largely confined to studies of the early years of the Fifth Republic. Even though the leaders of the RPR still pledge their allegiance to his memory, the policies and rhetoric of the party are far removed from those of their mentor. The same will undoubtedly be true of Mitterrand in a few years time. Thus, given that the policy process is affected by aspects of personality, then the passage of time will ensure a turnover of political personnel and a constant fluctuation in the impact of particular personalities upon the political system.

In all, these findings have two important implications for the study of prime ministerial influence and core executive operations both in France and elsewhere. First, it is important to appreciate that Prime Ministers cannot be studied in isolation. Because of the diverse nature of the factors which determine their influence, the study of prime ministerial influence must also involve the study of the different elements which go to make up those constraints. Thus, it is necessary to study in depth, for example, the electoral process, parties and the party system, presidential and ministerial resources and bureaucratic politics. The study of the Prime Minister is not a separate discipline, but one which is integrated with the whole gamut of disciplines of contemporary political studies.

Second, it is also important to realise that the conclusions reached in the above study are not applicable simply to France alone. The study of prime ministerial influence and of core executives in any country can be approached in the manner described above. Each country which is studied will yield different results. The Prime Minister's relationship with the different types of factors and their individual components will differ from one country to another. However, the same approach is valid for each individual system. Indeed, this approach represents the best way to tackle the study of Prime Ministers and all of the different aspects of their activity. Thus, whilst the present study has focused upon France, it is hoped that it has provided the starting point for the comparative study of heads of government.

Appendix: List of Interviewees

1981-91

- Mawoy
- Fabius
- Chirac
- Rocard

Prime Minister
Laurent Fabius (written reply to questions)
Raymond Barre

1982 broadcasting act
M-A. Laumonier, adviser to the Prime Minister
P. Moinot, president of the special commission
A. Simon, adviser to the Communications Minister
M. Berthod, adviser to the Communications Minister
M. Bodin, adviser to the Telecommunications Minister
F. Beck, adviser to the Culture Minister
D. Sapaut, head of the SID
B. Cousin x 3, head of the SJTI

1986 broadcasting act
F. Léotard, Culture and Communications Minister
G. Longuet, Telecommunications Minister
M. Ulrich, adviser to the Prime Minister
J. Frèches, adviser to the Prime Minister
M. Boutinard-Rouelle, adviser to the Prime Minister
X. Goyou-Beauchamps, adviser to the Culture Minister
M. Boyon, adviser to the Culture Minister
J-P. Fourcade, senator
M. Péricard, deputy
M-A. Feffer, head of the SJTI

1989 broadcasting act
B. Chetaille, adviser to the President
S. Hubac, adviser to the Prime Minister
B. Delcros x 2, adviser to the Communications Minister
B. Schreiner, deputy
J. Barrot (written reply), deputy
T. Leroy, head of the SJTI
J. Desandre and G. Bourgougnou, permanent administrators to the National
    Assembly's Finance Commission

1985 budget
H. Emmanuelli, Budget Minister
J-D. Comolli, adviser to the Prime Minister, Laurent Fabius
G. Beauffret, adviser to the Prime Minister, Laurent Fabius
J. Choussat, *directeur du Budget*

1987 budget
E. Rodocanachi x 2, adviser to the Prime Minister
G. Rameix, adviser to the Prime Minister
J. Friedman, adviser to the Finance Minister
J-M. Fabre, adviser to the Finance Minister
C. Blanchard-Dignac, adviser to the Finance Minister
P. Suet, adviser to the Finance Minister
D. Bouton, adviser to the Budget Minister
P-M. Duhamel, adviser to the Budget Minister
J-F. Hébert, budgetary adviser to the Culture Minister
M. Goulard, budgetary adviser to the Telecommunications Minister
B. Durieux, deputy
E. Alphandery, deputy
X. Roques, permanent administrator to the National Assembly's
     Finance Commission

1990 budget
I. Bouillot, adviser to the President
G. Carcassonne, adviser to the Prime Minister
B. Chevauchez, adviser to the Prime Minister
P. Wahl, adviser to the Prime Minister
M. Valls, adviser to the Prime Minister
O. Mallet, adviser to the Finance Minister
S. Romaret, budgetary adviser to the Defence Minister
D. Strauss-Kahn, President of the National Assembly's Finance
     Commission
R. Douyère, deputy
M. Wiedermann-Goiran, adviser to Strauss-Kahn

Crisis politics
J. Toubon, head of the RPR parliamentary group
D. Vitry, adviser to the Higher Education Minister
M. Rosenblatt, former president of UNEF-ID
J-C. Cambadelis, deputy and former president of UNEF-ID
P. Darriulat x 2, president of UNEF-ID
I. Thomas x 2, student leader

A. Bauer, student leader
B. Pignerol, adviser to J. Dray

Notes

Chapter 1

1. F. Wilson, 1987, p. 4. The following paragraphs on methodology are based on the three categories that Wilson identifies.
2. Ibid., p. 5.
3. The term 'core executive' was first used in an article by P. Dunleavy and R. A. W. Rhodes, 1990. In its French context, it may be taken to include the presidency, the premiership, ministries, executive committees, executive administrative services (including the secret services) and sundry advisers and officials who report to or are employed by the government.
4. See, for example, P. Servent, 1989, F-O. Giesbert, 1990 and R. Schneider, 1992.
5. The three main examples here are A. Claisse, 1972; J. Massot, 1979; and S. Rials, 1985.
6. The exception is P. Ardant, 1991.
7. See P. Dunleavy and R. A. W. Rhodes, 1990, pp. 4–5.
8. See M. Duverger, 1976.
9. O. Duhamel, 1991, p. 73.
10. Except where indicated all translations are by the author. All translations of the Constitution are taken from D. Pickles, 1960, p. 203.
11. P. Ardant, 1991, p. 110.
12. See the article by Bertrand Le Gendre, 'L'écurie Rocard au petit trot', in *Le Monde*, 30 November 1990.
13. This point is discussed in more detail in R. Elgie and H. Machin, 1991, pp. 67–68.
14. This table is adapted from R. Elgie and H. Machin, 1991, p. 69.
15. See the figures in R. Py, 1985, pp. 115–21.
16. For a fuller account of the GSG and the Prime Minister's *cabinet* see R. Elgie, 1992.
17. These figures are taken from J. Fournier, 1987, p. 143.
18. R. Elgie and H. Machin, 1991, p. 70.
19. S. Rials, 1985, p. 106.
20. R. Py, 1985, p. 44.
21. P. Bauby, 1984, p. 30.
22. Figures are taken from J. Fournier, 1987, p. 212. There are no figures for the Couve de Murville premiership, because he did not serve for a complete year. As a result, precise figures are difficult to extract from the existing data.
23. J. Fournier, 1987, p. 212.

Chapter 2

1. P. Dunleavy and R. A. W. Rhodes, 1990, p. 4.
2. Ibid.
3. This definition is adapted from P. Dunleavy and R. A. W. Rhodes, 1990, p. 5.
4. O. Duhamel, 'The Fifth Republic under François Mitterrand', in G. Ross, S. Hoffman and S. Malzacher, 1987, p. 14.
5. H. Machin, 'Political Leadership', in P. Hall, J. Hayward and H. Machin, 1990, p. 104.
6. A. Duhamel, 1982, p. 173.
7. A. Duhamel, 1980, p. 23.
8. E. Suleiman, 'Presidential Government in France', in E. Suleiman and R. Rose, 1980, pp. 103–4.
9. A. Duhamel, 1980, p. 23.
10. Ibid., p. 195.
11. O. Duhamel, 'President and Prime Minister', in P. Godt, 1989, p. 10.
12. E. Suleiman, 'Presidential Government in France', in E. Suleiman and R. Rose, 1980, p. 111.
13. H. Machin, 'Political Leadership', in P. Hall, J. Hayward and H. Machin, 1990, p. 99.
14. P. Williams and M. Harrison, 1971, p. 173.
15. Y. Galland, 'Monarchie absolue', in *Le Monde*, 19 September 1990.
16. D. Maus (b), 1985, p. 24.
17. P. Williams and M. Harrison, 1971, p. 179.
18. D. Maus (a), 1985, p. 81.
19. D. Maus (b), 1985, p. 24.
20. S. Cohen, 1986, p. 20.
21. R. Hadas-Lebel, 'La République fonctionne', in *Le Monde*, 19 September 1990.
22. Ibid.
23. V. Wright, 1989, p. 55.
24. J. Massot, 1988, p. 33.
25. P. Gaborit and J-P. Mounier, in W. Plowden, 1987, pp. 100–101.
26. E. Burin des Roziers, in Institut Charles de Gaulle and AFSP, 1990, p. 87.
27. O. Duhamel, 'President and Prime Minister', in P. Godt, 1989, p. 3.
28. P. Servent, 1989.
29. O. Duhamel, 'The Fifth Republic under François Mitterrand', in G. Ross, S. Hoffman and S. Malzacher, 1987, pp. 144–5.
30. Ordinances are enabling bills by which Parliament, in a single vote, allows the Prime Minister to legislate across a range of issues without any subsequent parliamentary deliberation.
31. See, for example, J. Larché, *Le Monde*, 29 March 1986, O. Duhamel, *Le Monde*, 12 April 1986, Y. Gaudemet, *Le Monde*, 18 April 1986, and J. Robert, *Le Monde*, 18 April 1986.

32. R. Elgie, 1992.
33. See the account of the New Caledonian crisis in *L'Express*, 11 May 1990, pp. 90–100.
34. P. Dunleavy, 'Government at the Centre', in P. Dunleavy, A. Gamble and G. Peele, 1990, p. 106.
35. J. Rigaud, 1986, p. 13.
36. V. Wright, 1989, p. 88.
37. D. Hanley, A. P. Kerr and N. H. Waites, 1979, p. 113.
38. S. Mesnier, 1990, p. 498.
39. P. Dunleavy and R. A. W. Rhodes, 1990, p. 12.
40. J. Fournier, 1987.
41. V. Wright, 1990, p. 115.
42. H. Machin and V. Wright, 1985, pp. 11–12.
43. J. Frèches, 1989, p. 124.
44. P. Birnbaum, 1977.
45. A. Peyrefitte, 1976.

Chapter 3

1. For a brief history of French broadcasting prior to 1981 see R. Kuhn, 1983.
2. From the minutes of the interministerial reunion of 18 June 1981, chaired by Mauroy's *directeur de cabinet*, Robert Lion.
3. Note dated 6 October 1981.
4. M. Cotta, 1986, and C. Estier and V. Neiertz, 1987.
5. Interview with the author.
6. Press conference of 7 August 1981.
7. Interview with the author.
8. Such were the reasons given in a note to the President dated 2 November 1981.
9. Member of Lang's *cabinet*.
10. Internal memorandum dated 28 October 1981.
11. Interview with the author.
12. Interview with the author.
13. M. Cotta, 1986, p. 82.
14. Interview with the author.
15. See Chapter 7.
16. Note dated 2 November 1981.
17. F. O. Giesbert, 1990, p. 269. This account was verified during interviews with the author.
18. See J. Frèches, 1989, p. 39. M. de Villiers declined to be interviewed stating that he played no part in the preparation of the bill.
19. Interview with the author.
20. Interview with the author.
21. Confirmed by several people interviewed.

22. M. Cotta, 1986, p. 197.
23. Interview with the author.
24. Admitted in various interviews with the author.
25. See J. Frèches, 1989, p. 165.
26. Interview with the author.
27. See J. Frèches, 1989, p. 167.
28. Interview with the author.
29. Retold in J. Frèches, 1989, p. 169.
30. Interview with the author.
31. J. Frèches, 1989, p. 37.
32. Interview with the author.
33. Interview with the author.
34. Interview with the author.
35. Interview with the author.
36. Confirmed in an interview with the author.
37. Interview with the author.
38. On the *méthode Rocard*, see the article by R. Elgie, 1991.
39. Interview with the author.
40. Confirmed in an interview with the author.
41. See a résumé of the report in *Le Monde*, 15 August 1988.
42. Interview with the author.
43. Interview with the author.
44. *Le Monde*, 7 December 1988.
45. Letter received from J. Barrot, 11 May 1990.
46. See B. Delcros and F. Névoltry, 1989, p. 6.
47. These positions were outlined in inter views with the author.
48. Interview with the author.
49. Interview with the author.
50. Interview with the author.
51. Interview with the author.
52. *Le Nouvel observateur*, 30 September– 6 October 1988.
53. Letter from J. Barrot, 11 May 1990.

Chapter 4

1. M. Prada in his contribution to a conference published by the Institut Français des Sciences Administratives, 1988, p. 31.
2. The most complete account of the budgetary preparation procedure, even if it is a little outdated now, is G. Lord, 1973.
3. See L. Schweizer, 1983–4, p. 81.
4. M. Prada, 1989–90, p. 47.
5. See M. Prada, 1989–90, p. 51, for the composition of these meetings.
6. For a detailed account of the parliamentary process, see J-P. Bonhoure, 1985.
7. It should be noted that throughout the following year, year n, there

may be adjustments to the Finance act, notably, almost every year a mini-budget is passed, *La Loi des Finances rectificative*. The importance of these on-year adjustments may be substantial, however, the present study will confine itself to the preparation of the budget in the year $n-1$.

8.　Refer, for example, to A. Fontaneau and P-A. Muet, 1985.
9.　Interview with the author.
10.　Interview with the author.
11.　Interview with the author.
12.　Interview with the author.
13.　Interview with the author.
14.　Interview with the author.
15.　Interview with the author.
16.　*Libération*, 5-6 May 1984.
17.　Interview with the author.
18.　See P. Bauchard, 1986, p. 263.
19.　Interview with the author.
20.　A telling, if tongue-in-cheek in an interview with the author.
21.　Interview with the author.
22.　Interview with the author.
23.　Interview with the author.
24.　Interview with the author.
25.　Confirmed in an interview with the author.
26.　Interviews with the author.
27.　Interview with the author.
28.　Interview with the author.
29.　Interview with the author.
30.　Interview with the author.
31.　Interview with the author.
32.　Interview with the author.
33.　Interview with the author.
34.　Interview with the author.
35.　Interview with the author.
36.　Interview with the author.
37.　Interview with the author.
38.　Interview with the author.
39.　Interview with the author.
40.　One adviser, in an interview with the author, said that Léotard considered everything to be a priority.
41.　Interview with the author.
42.　Interview with the author.
43.　Interview with the author.
44.　Interview with the author.
45.　The change in procedure over the two years was described in an interview with the author.
46.　Interview with the author.

47. See the report in *Le Monde*, 21 October 1989, which was confirmed in an interview with the author.
48. These categories are outlined in *Profession politique*, 24 April 1989.
49. Lang's strategy was confirmed in an interview with the author.
50. This information comes from an interview with the author.
51. See *Le Monde*, 3 September 1989.
52. Interview with the author.
53. This weakness was admitted without the slightest trace of acrimony in an interview by the author with a prime ministerial adviser.
54. This agreement was recounted in an interview with the author.
55. This aspect was emphasised in an interview with the author.
56. In an interview with the author, a government adviser argued adamantly that this secrecy was necessary, otherwise consumers would have anticipated the decrease and reduced spending until it came into effect.
57. Interview with the author.
58. Announced in the *Le Nouvel observateur*, 12–18 October 1989, and confirmed in an interview with the author.
59. Interview with the author.
60. *Libération*, 18 October 1989.

Chapter 5

1. P. Dunleavy and B. O' Leary, 1988, p. 59.
2. M. Dobry, 1986.
3. Taken from his article in *Politix*, no. 1, winter 1988, p. 38.
4. A. Devaquet, 1988, p. 56.
5. Ibid.
6. See ibid., p. 159 and confirmed in an interview with the author.
7. UNEF-ID was by far the largest of the student organisations and was at the vanguard of the movement.
8. Asserted in the article by M. Dobry in P. Favre, 1990.
9. See the poll in *Le Quotidien de Paris* on December 8th which showed the high level of public support for the students.
10. The Senate produced what was generally considered to be a relatively faithful account of what happened, although it stopped short of criticising the government as a whole, or Chirac in particular. The report from the National Assembly, however, was highly criticised for its insistence on the role of the trotskyists, for its vilification of the media and for admonishing the government only slightly.
11. This meeting is described in A. Devaquet, 1988, pp. 228–9 and was confirmed in an interview with the author.
12. P. Boggio and A. Rollat, 1988, p. 285.
13. Ibid.
14. The three factions were the trotskyist LEAS group, *Questions*

Socialistes and the largely socialist, majority coalition faction. The machinations within the student movement cannot properly be understood without an examination of the struggle between the three main factions within UNEF-ID. For the best account of the relationship between these factions, see C. Chambraud in *Politix*, op. cit.

15. In *SOS-Génération*, 1987, p. 91, Julien Dray notes that contact had been established with Méhaignerie, while in an interview with the author, this contact was confirmed and it was stated that another senior centrist, Simone Weil, was aware of the situation.

16. *Libération*, 1 December 1986.

17. This charge was made against the student movement by the Senate's special commission. It was also confirmed in an interview with the author that one of Devaquet's main aims at this time was to counter this misinformation.

18. Interview with the author.

19. Quoted in F-O. Giesbert, 1987, p. 422.

20. Chirac's responsibility for this decision was confirmed by E. Balladur, 1989, p. 126.

21. A. Devaquet, 1988, p. 249.

22. Interview with the author.

23. This claim is made in F-O. Giesbert, 1987, p. 422.

24. This point is made by Giesbert and also by Boggio and Rollat, 1988, p. 288.

25. A. Devaquet, 1988, pp. 247–8.

26. Interview with the author.

27. A. Devaquet, 1988, p. 254.

28. Devaquet asserted this point in his book and it was confirmed in an interview with the author.

29. Interview with the author.

30. Interview with the author.

31. A. Devaquet, 1988, p. 256.

32. See Monory's testimony to the National Assembly's special commission.

33. The title of an article in *Libération*, 3 December 1986, was 'l'extrême gauche tente un OPA sur le mouvement étudiant'.

34. Recounted in D. Assouline and S. Zappi, 1987, p. 13.

35. Interviews with the author.

36. Interview with the author.

37. See M. Dobry in P. Favre, ed., 1990, p. 378.

38. Accounts of this meeting appear in Giesbert, 1987, Boggio and Rollat, 1988, and *Le Monde*, 10 December 1986.

39. Recounted in Giesbert, 1987, pp. 425–6.

40. Interview with the author.

41. Interview with the author.

42. N. Prévost, 1989, p. 48.

43. See, for example, the opinion poll in *Le Matin*, 4 December 1986.

44. Interview with the author.

Chapter 6

1. P. Dunleavy and B. O'Leary, 1988, p. 59.
2. Ibid.
3. Ibid.
4. P. Favier and M. Martin-Roland, 1991, p. 484.
5. F-O. Giesbert, 1990, p. 170.
6. There are various accounts of economic policy-making after 1981. See, for example, P. Bauchard, 1986, or P. Hall, 1986.
7. T. Pfister, 1985, p. 246.
8. This version of events is to be found in P. Bauchard, 1986, p. 52.
9. P. Bauchard, 1986, p. 89.
10. D. Cameron, *The Ambiguous Record of French Socialism*, unpublished paper given to the American Political Science Association, 1988.
11. Here, accounts differ as to the timing of the decision to devalue. Jacques Attali in an interview with *Globe*, no. 57, May 1991, p. 53, argues that the decision to devalue was taken three weeks before the Versailles summit. Favier and Martin-Roland quote Mitterrand as saying that the issue was decided during the summit when the American attitude became clear.
12. See Favier and Martin-Roland, 1991, pp. 426–7.
13. G. Milesi, 1985, p. 206.
14. In fact, Estier says that he was told by Mitterrand that the President and Maire had not discussed economic policy, but that Maire had unilaterally used this occasion to damage the government with a false accusation. C. Estier and V. Neiertz, 1987, p. 157.
15. Quoted in F-O. Giesbert, 1990, p. 169.
16. Both Favier and Martin-Roland, 1991, p. 466, and Pfister, 1985, p. 257, give detailed accounts of the events of the next few days.
17. Pfister, 1985, p. 262.
18. See Giesbert, 1990, p. 176, and Favier and Martin-Roland, 1991, p. 469.
19. See Favier and Martin-Roland, 1991, p. 469.
20. A. Boublil, 1990, p. 90.
21. Favier and Martin-Roland, 1991, p. 471.
22. F-O. Giesbert, 1990, p. 179.
23. S. July, 1986, p. 95.
24. Ibid.
25. Favier and Martin-Roland, 1991, p. 474.
26. T. Pfister, 1985, p. 271.
27. Pfister, 1985, p. 269, and Bauchard, 1986, p. 147.
28. Giesbert, 1990, p. 180.
29. Favier and Martin-Roland, 1991, pp. 476–7.

30. Ibid., p. 473.
31. P. Hall , 1986, p. 201.
32. F-O. Giesbert, writing in *Le Nouvel observateur*, 4 March 1983, p. 23.
33. The same author in *Le Nouvel observateur*, 11 April 1983, p. 23.
34. This view is argued in H. Machin and V. Wright, 1985, p. 4.
35. Favier and Martin-Roland, 1991, p. 471.
36. Ibid., p. 469.
37. P. Hall, 1986, p. 193.
38. Quoted in Favier and Martin-Roland, 1991, p. 490.
39. Poperen quoted in *Le Nouvel observateur*, 4 March 1983, p. 23.
40. Machin and Wright, 1985, p. 24.
41. As said to Attali and quoted in Favier and Martin-Roland, 1991, p. 482.
42. Ibid.
43. V. Wright, 1989, p. 59.
44. Machin and Wright, 1985, p. 16.
45. Quoted in Favier and Martin-Roland, 1991, p. 462.
46. Machin and Wright, 1985, p. 2.
47. Quoted in Favier and Martin-Roland, 1991, p. 488.
48. Ibid.
49. Interview with Attali in *Globe*, op. cit., p. 54.
50. Quoted in Favier and Martin-Roland, 1991, p. 490.
51. J-M. Colombani, 1985, p. 38.
52. See the account in Bauchard, 1986, p. 143.
53. F-O. Giesbert, 1990, p. 177.

Chapter 7

1. See, for example, J. Massot in M. Duverger, 1986, p. 295.
2. Figures for committees are taken from J. Fournier, 1987, p. 212.
3. It should be noted that interministerial councils are chaired by the President, but that *Conseils de Cabinet* were chaired by the Prime Minister. It should also be noted that meetings of the *Conseil de Cabinet* were reintroduced for a short time under the premiership of Jacques Chirac in 1986.
4. Figures are taken from J. Massot, 1979, p. 164.
5. The figures from 1958–76 are taken from M. Long, 1981 , p. 57. The figures for 1981–86 are taken from J. Fournier, 1987, p. 143. The 1988 figures are calculated from the *Journal officiel*.
6. E. Suleiman in R. Rose and E. Suleiman, 1980, p. 116.
7. See, for example, R. Elgie, 1992, pp. 113–15.
8. An example of this point would be the President's effective control of the SGCI as described by C. Luquesne in *Projet*, juillet–août, 1987, pp. 41–54.
9. G. Jones, 1991, p. 163.

10. Ibid.
11. See, for example, his chapter in S. Bornstein, D. Held and J. Krieger, 1983, p. 24.
12. P. Hall, 1986, p. 232.
13. P. Cerny, 'State Capitalism in France and Britain', in P. Cerny and M. Schain, 1985, p. 213.
14. Ibid., p. 214.
15. Ibid., p. 215.
16. J. Hayward, 1983, p. 12.
17. S. Mazey, 'Power Outside Paris', in P. Hall, J. Hayward and H. Machin, 1990, pp. 152–67.
18. J. Frears, 1990, p. 33.
19. A. Stone, 1989, p. 17.
20. Ibid., pp. 24–5.
21. J. Foyer and G. Lardeyret, 1991.
22. The term 'conjunctural' is taken from H. Machin and V. Wright, 1985, for example, p. 8.
23. J. Frèches, 1989, p. 63.
24. P. Servent, 1989, p. 244.
25. H. Feigenbaum, 1990, p. 275.
26. J-M. Colombani and J-Y. Lhomeau, 1986, p. 190.
27. V. Wright, 1989, p. 73.
28. P. Servent, 1989, p. 239.
29. For a more complete analysis of Rocard's minority government, see R. Elgie and M. Maor, 1992.
30. J. Gaffney, 1988, p. 49.
31. A. Cole, 1989, p. 17.
32. G. Lemaire, 1983, p. 88.
33. For a list of such meetings refer to J-Y. Lhomeau, in *Le Monde*, 26 October 1983.
34. A fuller account of the influence of the PS after 1981 can be found in R. Elgie and S. Griggs, 1991.
35. A. Cole, 1989, p. 19.
36. G. Jones, 1991, pp. 174 and 177.
37. F. Greenstein, 1967, pp. 629–41.
38. H. D. Lasswell, 1960.
39. L. Iremonger, 1970.
40. James D. Barber, 1977.
41. F. Greenstein, 1967, p. 635 and H. Machin, 'Political Leadership', in P. Hall, J. Hayward and H. Machin, 1990, p. 108.
42. R. Rose, 1987, p. 22.
43. Ibid.
44. P. Servent, 1989, p. 260.
45. G. Jones, 1991, p. 169.
46. Interview with the author.
47. See the article by H. Machin, 1989, pp. 59–81.

Chapter 8

1. This point was made by François Goguel at a conference chaired by Maurice Duverger and entitled, 'A propos de son livre Echec au Roi', 18 February 1978, and published under the same name, Paris, ASFP, 1978, p. 13.
2. P. Ardant, 1991, p. 48.
3. V. Wright, 1989, p. 28.
4. Ibid., p. 33. The emphasis is mine.
5. P. Dunleavy and R. A. W. Rhodes, 1990, p. 24.
6. Figures in M. Duverger, 1987, p. 212.
7. The two tables which follow are taken from O. Duhamel, 1991, pp. 135–36.
8. Letter to the author from Laurent Fabius.
9. Although Giscard did face a set of legislative elections in 1978, the ruling coalition was victorious. Thus, Giscard's decision to intervene less in the policy-making process was more akin to Mitterrand's decision in 1984, rather than the situation after 1986.
10. D. Ashford, 1982.
11. Ibid., pp. 11–12.
12. Ibid., p. 300.

Bibliography

Ardant, P. *Le Premier Ministre en France*, Paris: Montchrestien, 1991.

Ashford, D. *Policy and Politics in France: Living with Uncertainty*, Philadelphia: Temple University Press, 1982.

Assouline, D. and Zappi, S. *Notre Printemps en Hiver*, Paris: La Découverte, 1987.

Balladur, E. *Passion et Longueur du Temps*, Paris: Fayard, 1989.

Barber, James D. *The Presidential Character: Predicting Performance in the White House*, Englewood Cliffs, NJ: Prentice-Hall, 1977.

Bauby, P. *Le cabinet du Premier ministre depuis l'alternance au pouvoir de 1981*, Paris: AFSP, 1984.

Bauchard, P. *La Guerre des Deux Roses*, Paris: Grasset, 1986.

Birnbaum, P. *Les Sommets de l'Etat*, Paris: Seuil, 1977.

Blondel, J. and Müller-Rommel, F. eds, *Cabinets in Western Europe*, London: Macmillan, 1988.

Boggio, P. and Rollat, A. *Ce Terrible M. Pasqua*, Paris: Olivier Orban, 1988.

Bonhoure, J-P. Particularités de la Discussion Budgétaire. Paper given to a conference entitled *L'Assemblée Nationale Aujourd'hui*, Paris: AFSP, 21–22 November 1985.

Bornstein, S., Held D. and Krieger, J. eds, *The State in Capitalist Europe*, London: Allen & Unwin, 1983.

Boublil, A. *Le Soulèvement du Sérail*, Paris: Albin Michel, 1990.

Cerny P. and Schain, M. eds, *Socialism, the State and Public Policy in France*, London: Frances Pinter, 1985.

Chenot, B. Le ministre, chef d'un administration, in *Pouvoirs*, no. 36, 1986.

Claisse, A. *Le Premier ministre de la Ve République*, Paris: LGDJ, 1972.

Cohen, S. *La Monarchie nucléaire*, Paris: Hachette, 1986.

Cole, A. The French Socialist Party in Transition, in *Modern and Contemporary France*, no. 37, April 1989.

Colombani, J-M. *Portrait du Président*, Paris: Gallimard, 1985.

Colombani, J-M. and Lhomeau, J-Y. *Le Mariage Blanc*, Paris: Grasset, 1986.

Cotta, M. *Les Miroirs de Jupiter*, Paris: Fayard, 1986.

Delcros, B. and Névoltry, F. *Le Conseil Supérieur de l'Audiovisuel*, Paris: Editions Victoires, 1989.

Devaquet, A. *L'Amibe et l'Etudiant*, Paris: Odile Jacob, 1988.

Dobry, M. *Sociologie des Crises Politiques*, Paris: Presses de la FNSP, 1986.

Dray, J. *SOS-Génération*, Paris: Ramsay, 1987.

Duhamel, A. *La République giscardienne*, Paris: Grasset, 1980.

Duhamel, A. *La République de M. Mitterrand*, Paris: Grasset, 1982.
Duhamel, O. *Le pouvoir politique en France*, Paris: PUF, 1991.
Dunleavy, P., Gamble, A. and Peele, G. eds, *Developments in British Politics 3*, London: Macmillan, 1990.
Dunleavy, P. and O'Leary, B. *Theories of the State*, London: Macmillan, 1988.
Dunleavy, P. and Rhodes, R. A. W. Core Executive Studies in Britain, in *Public Administration*, vol. 68, Spring 1990.
Duverger, M. *La Monarchie Républicaine*, Paris: Laffont, 1974.
Duverger, M. *Echec au Roi*, Paris: Albin Michel, 1976.
Duverger, M. ed., *Les Régimes Semi-présidentiels*, Paris: PUF, 1986.
Duverger, M. *La Cohabitation des Français*, Paris: PUF, 1987.
Elgie, R. La méthode Rocard existe-t-elle?, in *Modern and Contemporary France*, no. 44, January 1991.
Elgie, R. The Prime Minister's Office in France: A Changing Role in a Semi-Presidential System, in *Governance*, vol. 5, no. 1, January 1992.
Elgie, R. and Griggs, S. A quoi sert le PS? The Influence of the Parti socialiste on public policy since 1981, in *Modern and Contemporary France*, no. 47, October 1991.
Elgie, R. and Machin, H. France: The Limits to Prime-ministerial Government in a Semi-presidential System, in *West European Politics*, vol. 14, no. 2, 1991.
Elgie, R. and Maor, M. Accounting for the Survival of Minority Governments: An Examination of the French Case (1988–91), in *West European Politics*, vol. 15, no. 4, October 1992.
Estier, C. and Neiertz, V. *Véridique histoire d'un septennat peu ordinaire*, Paris: Grasset, 1987.
Favier, P. and Martin-Roland, M. *La Décennie Mitterrand: 1, Les Ruptures*, Paris: Seuil, 1991.
Favre, P. ed., *La Manifestation*, Paris: Presses de la FNSP, 1990.
Feigenbaum, H. Recent Evolution of the French Executive, in *Governance*, vol. 3, no. 3, July 1990.
Fontaneau, A. and Muet, P-A. eds, *La Gauche Face à la Crise*, Paris: FNSP, 1985.
Fournier, J. *Le Travail gouvernemental*, Paris: Dalloz et Presses de la FNSP, 1987.
Foyer, J. and Lardeyret, G. Dérive institutionnelle, in *Le Monde*, 18 April 1991.
Frears, J. The French Parliament: Loyal Workhorse, Poor Watchdog, in *West European Politics*, vol. 13, no. 3, 1990.
Frèches, J. *Voyage au centre du pouvoir*, Paris: Odile Jacob, 1989.
Gaffney, J. French Socialism and the Fifth Republic, in *West European Politics*, vol. 12, no. 3, July 1988.
Giesbert, F-O. *Jacques Chirac*, Paris: Seuil, 1987.
Giesbert, F-O. *Le Président*, Paris: Seuil, 1990.
Godt, P. ed., *Policy Making in France*, London: Pinter, 1989.

Greenstein, F. The impact of personality on politics: an attempt to clear away underbrush, *American Political Science Review*, vol. 61, no. 3, Sept. 1967.

Hall, P. *Governing the Economy*, Cambridge, Polity Press, 1986.

Hall, P., Hayward J. and Machin, H. eds, *Developments in French Politics*, London: Macmillan, 1990.

Hanley, D., Kerr A. and Waites, N. *Contemporary France: Politics and Society since 1945*, London: RKP, 1979.

Hayward, J. *Governing France: the One and Indivisible Republic*, London: Weidenfeld & Nicolson, 1983.

Institut Charles de Gaulle and AFSP, *De Gaulle et ses Premiers ministres*, Paris: Plon, 1990.

Institut Français des Sciences Administratives, *Le Budget de l'Etat*, Paris, 1988.

Iremonger, L. *The Fiery Chariot: a study of British Prime Ministers and the search for love*, London: Secker & Warburg, 1970.

Jones, G. West European Prime Ministers in Perspective, in *West European Politics*, vol. 14, no. 2, April 1991.

July, S. *Les Années Mitterrand. Histoire baroque d'une normalisation inachevée*, Paris: Grasset, 1986.

Kuhn, R. Broadcasting and Politics in France, in *Parliamentary Affairs*, vol. 36, 1983.

Lasswell, H. *Psychopathology and Politics*, New York: Viking press, 1960.

Lemaire, G. *Le PS face au pouvoir*, Paris: Cahiers du CERAT, 1983.

Lord, G. *The French Budgetary Process*, Berkeley: University of California Press, 1973.

Machin, H. Stages and Dynamics in the Evolution of the French Party System, in *West European Politics*, vol. 12, no. 4, Oct. 1989.

Machin, H. and Wright, V. eds, *Economic Policy and Policy Making under the Mitterrand Presidency*, London: Pinter, 1985.

Massot, J. *Le Chef du Gouvernement en France*, Paris: La Documentation Française, 1979.

Massot, J. *L'Arbitre et le Capitaine: la responsabilité présidentielle*, Paris: Flammarion, 1987.

Massot, J. La pratique présidentielle sous la Ve République, in *Regards sur l'Actualité*, no. 139, mars 1988.

Maus, D. (a) *Les grands textes de la pratique institutionnelle de la Ve République*, Paris: La Documentation Française, no. 4786, 1985.

Maus, D. (b) La Constitution jugée par sa pratique. Paper presented to a conference entitled *La Constitution de la Ve République* and published in Paris by the AFSP, 1985.

Mesnier, S. Le rôle du Quai d'Orsay de mai 1986 à mai 1988, in *La Revue Administrative*, 1990.

Milesi, G. *Jacques Delors*, Paris: Belfond, 1985.

Peyrefitte, A. *Le Mal français*, Paris: Plon, 1976.

Pfister, T. *La Vie Quotidienne à Matignon au Temps de L'Union de la*

Gauche, Paris: Hachette, 1985.

Pickles, D. *The Fifth French Republic*, Avonmouth: Western Printing Services Ltd., 1960.

Plowden, W. ed., *Advising the Rulers*, Oxford: Blackwell, 1987.

Prada, M. *Le Budget*, Paris: FNSP, service de polycopie, 1989–90.

Prévost, N. *La Mort indigne de Malik Oussekine*, Paris: Barrault, 1989.

Py, R. *Le Secrétariat général du gouvernement*, Paris: La Documentation Francaise, 1985.

Quermonne, J-L. Un gouvernement présidentiel ou un gouvernement partisan, in *Pouvoirs*, no. 20, 1982.

Rigaud, J. Pouvoir et non-pouvoir du ministre, in *Pouvoirs*, no. 36, 1986.

Rose, R. Présidents et Premiers ministres, éléments de comparaison, in *Pouvoirs*, no. 41, 1987.

Ross, G., Hoffman S. and Malzacher, S. eds, *The Mitterrand Experiment*, Cambridge: Polity Press, 1987.

Rials, S. *Le Premier ministre*, Paris: PUF, 1985.

Schneider, R. *La Haine Tranquille*, Paris: Seuil, 1992.

Schweizer, L. *Le Budget*, Paris: FNSP, service de polycopie, 1983–84.

Servent, P. *Oedipe à Matignon*, Paris: Balland, 1989.

Seurin, J-L. *La Présidence en France et aux Etats-Unis*, Paris: Economica, 1986.

Stone, A. In the Shadow of the Constitutional Council: the 'Juridicisation' of the Legislative process in France, in *West European Politics*, vol. 12, no. 2, April 1989. E.

Suleiman, E. and Rose, R. eds, *Presidents and Prime Ministers*, Washington DC: AEI, 1980.

Williams, P. and Harrison, M. *Politics and Society in de Gaulle's Republic*, London: Longman, 1971.

Wilson, F. *Interest Group Politics in France*, Cambridge: Cambridge University Press, 1987.

Wright, V. *The Government and Politics of France*, London: Unwin Hyman, 1989.

Index